Security and Suspicion

THE ETHNOGRAPHY OF POLITICAL VIOLENCE

Cynthia Keppley Mahmood, Series Editor

A complete list of books in the series is available from the publisher.

Security and Suspicion

An Ethnography of Everyday Life in Israel

Juliana Ochs

PENN

UNIVERSITY OF PENNSYLVANIA PRESS

PHILADELPHIA · OXFORD

Published by
University of Pennsylvania Press
Philadelphia, Pennsylvania 19104–4112
www.upenn.edu/pennpress

Printed in the United States of America on acid-free paper
10 9 8 7 6 5 4 3 2 1

Library of Congress Cataloging-in-Publication Data
Ochs, Juliana.
    Security and suspicion : an ethnography of everyday life in Israel / Juliana Ochs.
        p. cm. — (The ethnography of political violence)
    Includes bibliographical references and index.
    ISBN 978-0-8122-4291-1 (hardcover : alk. paper)
    1. Terrorism—Israel—Psychological aspects. 2. Survival skills—Israel—Psychological
aspects. 3. Terrorism—Israel—Prevention. 4. Arab-Israeli conflict—Influence. I. Title.
HV6433.I75O24   2010
363.32095694—dc22   2010017607

for Yaacob Dweck

Contents

Author's Note

In transliterations from the Hebrew, I use h for "hay," ḥ for "het," and ts for "tsadi." I use k for kaf, kh for khaf, and q for kuf. I use (ʿa) for "ayin" and (ʾa) for "alef" when necessary to separate consonants in the middle of a word. Prefixes are separated from the word with a hyphen. In cases where a conventional spelling differs from these guidelines, I follow the standard convention. In Arabic, I rely on conventional spelling. All quotations from individuals are my translation from the Hebrew, except when quoted by the media or when otherwise noted. The names and identifying details of individuals I interviewed and cite in this book have been changed.

Introduction: The Practice of Everyday Security

It was early February 2004, and Israeli Prime Minister Ariel Sharon had recently announced plans to remove all Israeli settlers from Gaza. The Israeli Defense Forces (IDF) launched armored raids in the Gaza Strip, killing numerous Hamas militants. A Palestinian police officer from Bethlehem killed eight Israelis in a suicide bombing of a Jerusalem bus, for which al-Aqsa Martyrs' Brigades claimed responsibility. Israelis and Palestinians were in the midst of a war for territory, sovereignty, and security fought through air strikes and gunfire, Qassam rockets and suicide bombs, curfews and land seizures. But in Holon, an industrial city outside Tel Aviv, in the home of Vered Malka, the war assumed a more intimate form.

The marriage of Vered's niece Ronit in Jerusalem was only a week away, and Vered was dreading the trip. Vered, who immigrated to Israel from Egypt in 1956 and settled in Holon soon after, lived in a small attached house in close proximity to her nine siblings. All were terrified of this journey to Jerusalem, a drive of under an hour. It was not the navigation itself that made Vered uneasy, for she was a taxi driver who spent her days driving the streets of Tel Aviv and Jaffa. "What do you mean, why am I afraid? From the terrorists, from the rocks they throw, from the hijacking, from it all. I never felt good in Jerusalem." To Vered and her family, Jerusalem had been off limits since the start of the second intifada in 2000. Jerusalem, to them, was a place of violence and danger, a place of bombings and precarious borders, and a place of Palestinians. Vered's young granddaughters had never been to Israel's capital, but Vered and her siblings were committed to attending the celebration and decided to put aside their fears, or at least to find a way around them. "I can't not go," Vered said. On the Friday afternoon of the wedding, wearing dresses and suits, energized but focused, the siblings and their spouses piled into four cars and drove from Holon to Jerusalem convoy-style, one car in front of the other, straight to Beit Shmuel, an event space overlooking the Old City of Jerusalem. "We went there and we returned, all together."

Security for Vered was not about constructing walls or exchanging hostages, but rather about relying on familiarity to generate a sense of control and protection. Driving in procession kept Vered's family members off and at a remove from buses, a common target of Palestinian suicide bombings and, even beyond that, surrounded each individual car with a familial buffer. The resultant protection was mobile and transient, shifting through space and time as they drove. Surrounded by familiar vehicles, the family found a way to travel to Jerusalem not only with minimized risk but also without perceiving the presence of Palestinians or feeling present in the city. At their weekly family Saturday lunches, the fears Vered and her siblings articulated in anticipation of this trip were enveloped in politicized discourses of threat and separation, and yet a simple family cavalcade enabled them to attain a sense of safety. In Vered's quest for security, the violence and fear of the Israeli-Palestinian conflict became inextricably bound with the routines and relationships of daily life.

If Israel exists in "a permanent state of emergency,"[1] security has become a medium of this unending crisis. Security was a central motif of the second intifada. It was not just that Israel's defense budget, approximately $10 billion in 2004, was the twelfth highest in the world, or that, in 2002, Israel's nongovernmental security services market was estimated at $700 million, with over 100,000 workers employed throughout the country (Lagerquist 2002: 1).[2] Even beyond this immense industry, security dominated Israelis' rhetorical framings and daily experiences. The government and media spoke of security measures, security lapses, security zones, and security threats. Military activities were often carried out in the name of Israeli security, from the construction of the separation wall (often called the "security fence") to the assassination of Palestinian leaders. "Only security will lead to peace," as Sharon put it.[3] In daily life, Israeli Jews described their neighborhoods as desirable or deficient "from the perspective of security," and malls became places with "good security" (or bad security) even more than they were places to shop. Israelis called the conflict itself "the security situation" (*ha-matsav ha-bithoni*), a naming that avoided direct reference to Palestinians while depicting the conflict as, above all, an effort to protect Israeli citizens from Palestinians.

The origin of the Israeli-Palestinian conflict lies in a very tangible clash: the claim by Jews and Palestinians in the late nineteenth and early twentieth centuries to the same piece of land. Concrete as the core conflict may be, its intensification and expansion came as the result of the more elusive but no less forceful factors of ideology, identity, and emotion. The intersection of these tangible and intangible aspects of the conflict is at the heart of national security's complexity. Security is a set of military strategies and political beliefs, but it is also a guiding force for daily experience. In one of the most conflict-ridden regions in modern history, in the clash between Israeli statehood and Palestinian desires for self-determination, between Israeli territorial expansion and Palestinian nationalism, security has become a part of Israeli culture. Security is a national discourse and partisan rallying cry that also assumes social, material, and aesthetic forms in daily life. It is the substance of conflict that manifests itself in everyday gestures, feelings, and intimate relationships.

For centuries, the legitimacy of the modern state has been built on its ability to protect its citizens.[4] Security has long rationalized state power and justified its monopoly over lawful violence. With the advent of security studies after the Cold War, scholars have studied national security as a state and military strategy; they have shown how diplomacy can isolate threats, how civil defense can facilitate national resilience, and how states can marshal economic power to compel international cooperation.[5] Recent fears of terrorism and the protrusion of national security on a global scale, however, draw our attention to the specifically social effects and underlying cultural character of national security.[6] That is, to the ways history can isolate threats, collective memory can facilitate national resilience, and states can marshal social capital to propel fear.

This book addresses the ways national security delineates individual experience as much as it demarcates sovereignty. Traditional political anthropology has tended to depict holistic political systems and organized political institutions, but this book sees security as a politics that is often intangible and fleeting, inconsistent and intimate, taking form in impressions and senses. Likewise, "security" does not refer in this book, as it often does, to state policies of preserving the integrity of the nation-state or to a formal political-military institution of defense. Here, security consists of everyday, routine, and sometimes unconscious engagements (Certeau 1988) with national ideologies of threat and defense. I use the term everyday security to describe the practices of self-protection that become the substance of people's lives and the discourses of danger and threat that, in contexts of conflict, delineate people's days. Like anthropological notions of everyday violence (Das et al. 2000, Scheper-Hughes and Bourgois 2004), everyday security is a cultural practice and a communal experience that crafts social life and is also an intimate experience that shapes individual subjectivity. Intimacy, involving feelings and practices of closeness and reciprocity, is a crucial domain for the everyday experience of security. If intimacy, as Lauren Berlant (2000) shows, builds public worlds and creates public spaces, then even when national security took the form of intimate signs and gestures, it laid claim to a collective and activated state power.

Observing national security through an anthropological lens, this book weaves together three distinct but interrelated arguments regarding the proliferation of state security in daily life. First, I argue that national discourses of security are reproduced at the level of bodily practice. Based on an ethnographic study of the daily life of Israeli Jews between 2003 and 2005, this book shows how discourses of security permeate individual sensibilities and habits and shape people's encounters with the state. Government rhetoric on danger, threat, and separation is not simply internalized but generated in visceral, emotive ways. Security takes shape at the intersection of government technologies and everyday sensibilities, of political rationalities and embodied behavior. The cyclical, self-perpetuating nature of security has been a recent theoretical concern to social and political theorists (Bauman 2007) and a longtime source of international military and diplomatic conflict. By describing the ways people embody state discourses of danger and effect senses of threat in their daily lives, I offer one way to understand why fear propagates a willingness to engage in violence in the name of security and why security becomes more likely only to provide senses of comfort than to proscribe violence.

The second argument of this book concerns the ways people see their fear and their desires for security as beyond politics, and thus become ignorant of the structural logics of exclusion that discourses of fear and security serve to reproduce. Israelis' avoidance of Palestinians and reliance on the country's military-industrial complex of security were often portrayed as strategies of coping with intense anxiety and fear. The seeming innocuousness of citizens' craving comfort and desiring bodily safety and the seemingly instinctive virtue of protecting family enabled Israeli Jews, including both those critical of the Israeli occupation and those who supported continued Israeli settlement, to think of themselves as participating in something private and impervious to politics. However, in this context of conflict, desires for comfort and well-being were often nationalism and exclusion in another form. The security that materialized in everyday habits and desires tended to extend, rather than oppose, sovereignty and violence. Everyday ways of talking about danger and threat, together with routines of circumnavigating feared spaces, cultivated the discursive and spatial invisibility of Palestinians to

Israelis. People's desires for security and their engagement with the artifacts and procedures of national security legitimized state security and helped produce and sustain the idea of the nation. Security, in this way, gained momentum and sway even as it produced a pervasive sense of vulnerability. It proliferated the very fears and suspicions it claimed to obviate. Security may stand as the core principle of state activity, but as Israeli fear rationalized fortification and separation and as anxiety perpetuated anticipations of danger, security transcended its position as a state domain, swelling larger than the state to generate and sustain sovereignty.

The third claim of this book is that fantasies about threat and protection were a crucial mode through which Israelis embodied security. Fantasies of security are different from illusions or delusions of threat and different from imaginaries of violence. They are also different from the "psychology of fear" that deals with emotional and cognitive responses to public fear-arousing messages, ranging from heightened anxiety to complacency. Fantasy, according to Yael Navaro-Yashin, describes the elements of the political that survive discursive deconstruction, criticism, and skepticism because of "unconscious psychic attachments" to state power (2002: 4). Fantasy is not opposed to reality but what sits at its very core (Aretxaga 2003: 402). Through fantasy, Israelis embodied national security even through practices that questioned, mocked, or ignored official registers. When I speak of fantasies of security, and likewise when I talk about imaginaries of danger or threat, this is not to disregard the very real danger that Palestinian aggression posed to Israel and the very real fears that Israelis held. Rather, I refer to the attachments that people develop to their anxieties and to state presentations of violence. Fantasy was a rubric through which people absorbed and resisted national discourses, and through which they personalized the effects of those discourses.

I carried out the fieldwork on which this book is based during a particularly severe period of violence during the second intifada, also called the al-Aqsa intifada. *Intifada* means "shaking off" in Arabic and is often translated as "uprising."[7] The concerns that undergirded this uprising had been present throughout decades of hostility, attack, confiscation, and occupation. At least since the founding of the State of Israel in 1948, Jewish nationalism and territorial control stood at odds with Palestinian desires for self-determination and national liberation. Since 1967, the status and future of the occupied territories and East Jerusalem, the question of a Palestinian state, the future of Palestinian refugees, and the fate of Jewish settlements in the occupied territories have fueled diplomatic dispute and military aggression. While Israel persistently supported Jewish settlement in Palestinian territory and restricted Palestinian life and livelihood, Palestinians did not recognize the right of the State of Israel to exist as a Jewish state. The Palestinian revolt that broke out in September 2000 was thus less inexplicable or abrupt than the media reported, a shift more in scale than in kind.

Once symbolically instigated by Sharon's visit to the Temple Mount on September 28, 2000, the uprising escalated into an armed military conflict. The militarization on both sides far surpassed that of the first intifada. Palestinian society now had a political structure in place, with a parliament and an armed security apparatus, and political solidarity was fortified both by a religious framework and by the growing power of media.[8] Unlike earlier forms of Palestinian resistance, this time the militant wing of Fatah had a substantial supply of small arms to fire on Israeli troops and Qassam rockets (named after the military wing of Hamas) to fire into Israeli residential areas. Militant groups including Hamas, Palestinian Islamic Jihad, and al-Aqsa Martyrs' Brigades waged a high-intensity campaign against Israel, in which stone-throwing youth were joined by combatants, who referred to themselves as "revolutionaries, martyrs, nationalists, or freedom fighters" to underscore their right to self-determination (Hage 2003: 72).[9] Palestinian combatants carried out a record number of suicide bombings against Israeli civilian targets in public spaces such as city buses and cafés.

In March 2002, in the largest military operation in the West Bank since 1967, Israel launched Operation Defensive Shield (Mivtsa Homat Magen), seeking to dismantle the infrastructure of the Palestinian Authority. With the stated aim of catching Palestinian militants, confiscating their weapons, and destroying weapons facilities, the IDF attacked Palestinian Authority installations, carried out assassinations of political and religious leaders, and imposed a series of collective punishments on the Palestinian civilian population. Sharon directed the IDF to avoid harming the civilian population (Sharon 2002), but, in reality, Israel targeted Palestinian militants and civilians alike by demolishing homes, destroying local infrastructure, and paralyzing movement and economic production.

Scholars of international relations often speak of the second intifada as "a low-intensity conflict,"[10] a euphemistic term that called attention to Israel's use of intelligence information to carry out assassinations of Palestinian leaders while obscuring the deadly nature of Israeli hostility (Pappe 2006). The popularity of the term in Israeli military discourse and the desire on behalf of Israeli political leaders to depict the conflict as "low-intensity" reflects the country's particular efforts in this period to veil and normalize violence. The government worked to keep IDF operations, including the Shin Bet's interrogation of Palestinians (categorized as torture by Israeli human rights groups), largely invisible to the public (B'Tselem 2007).

Despite claims of restraint and normalization, violence reverberated. When I began my fieldwork in Jerusalem in the summer of 2003, Yasser Arafat, chairman of the Palestinian Liberation Organization (PLO) and leader of Fatah, had just appointed Mahmoud Abbas as Palestinian prime minister; the U.S. government had begun to promote a "road-map" for Israeli peace and a Palestinian state; and Hamas and Islamic Jihad had recently declared a *hudna*, a temporary armistice on attacks against Israel. Violence decreased but only for forty-five days. In August, Israel's Special Police Unit killed four Palestinians and the Hamas leader Abdullah Qawasmeh during a gun and tank raid on Askar. Hamas responded with two suicide bombings, including one of a Jerusalem bus that killed over twenty Israelis, and Fatah with a third. The IDF captured or killed the plotters of the Jerusalem suicide bombings; enforced strict curfews in Nablus, Jenin, and Tulkarem; and demolished dozens of Palestinian shops. With each act, Israeli and Palestinian politicians sanctioned their own violence by presenting it as reprisal, such that every military action was rendered a reciprocal reaction. Sharon, Arafat, and the subsequent Palestinian prime minister Ahmed Qurei acted as if the threat of violence would accelerate diplomatic negotiations and dissuade opposing hostility, but this posture only exacerbated the conflict. The *hudna* soon ended.

During the second intifada, talk of terror and terrorist threat ricocheted around the world, their political force and emotional substance gaining momentum as governments unified against a shared and supposedly shadowy enemy. The events of September 11, 2001 and the subsequent U.S.-led invasion of Iraq, caused Israeli and American discourses of terror and counterterrorism to mingle and reinforce each other. A widespread demonization of and intense xenophobia toward Arabs seemed to give international sanction to long-standing Israeli fears. Still, terror was spoken of in Israel with specific connotations. In Hebrew, the English loanword *terror* referred broadly to violence against civilians but specifically connoted Palestinian militancy. In the words of Israel's Home Front Command (Pikud ha-Oref), founded as a unit of the IDF in February 1992 following the Gulf War and responsible for civilian defense, terror "casts a threat and spreads fear in a calculated manner through the helpless civilian population." Always ethnically inflected, the discourse of terror depicted Palestinian military actions as illegitimate, unpredictable, and lacking a motive beyond terrorizing (Hajjar 2005: 42). It generally did so, however, without explicit reference to Palestinians, whom Israelis visualized but whose agency was concealed by generic terms like "terror" and "suicide bombings." Like the terms terrorism and terror, reference to *terror* functioned simultaneously to describe and delegitimize violence committed by non-state political bodies. When I use the term terror in this book, I refer to the Israeli discourse of *terror* rather than to any specific political acts it might designate.

The term *pigu'a* (pl. *pigu'im*) described terrorist attacks in general, but it came during this period to refer almost exclusively to Palestinian suicide bombings. (Similarly, while *pigu'a yeri* literally means a shooting, the term came to connote almost exclusively a Palestinian shooting.) Israelis saw suicide bombings (*pigu'a hit'abdut*) as the most emblematic form of Palestinian terror. Influenced by politicians and IDF spokespeople, Israeli Jews saw Palestinian suicide bombers as lacking strategy and system, as aiming to destroy Israel's modernity and openness, as incoherent and invasive. "The confrontation with terror wrought by suicide strikers is like the fight against viruses," said one reserve colonel (Barzilai 2004). If most Palestinians saw the second intifada as a renewed effort to resist Israeli occupation, Israeli Jews tended to see the intifada foremost as a military campaign against suicide bombings.

Whether Palestinian bombings triggered Israelis' feelings of vulnerability or vice versa, Israeli society quickly became increasingly conservative in its views toward Palestinians and toward national security. Sharon, already the chairman of the center-right Likud Party, was easily elected prime minister in 2001 by promising greater force against Palestinians and greater security for Israelis. Political views once considered hawkish became centrist and, by the 2003 election, despite the deteriorating economic situation and increasing violence, voters strongly supported Sharon's reelection. In this climate, post-Zionist debates about Israel's democratic character, about its dispossession of the Palestinians, or about citizenship rather than religion as the determinant of rights, debates that had thrived in academic and popular arenas in the 1990s, lost their context as well as their conditions for possibility. Post-Zionism had entered a "deep freeze," as a headline in *Ha'aretz* declared in April 2004 (Shehori 2004). "Palestinian terrorism is pushing us back into the Zionist womb," journalist Tom Segev stated. There were certainly Israelis who described themselves as post-Zionists. As one woman in her mid-thirties who lived outside Jerusalem put it, "Post-Zionism is about our right to live here without any religious reasons and without a real narrative, a Zionist narrative, without any context. Just that we live here and this is our normal life, and we don't need to find reasons or to justify ourselves." Yet this woman and indeed nearly all the Israeli Jews I interviewed for this book considered themselves to be Zionists—even those who also called themselves post-Zionists, even those who were applying for European citizenship should the situation become untenable for them in Israel. Zionism was a multivalent concept, but its comfortable use during the second intifada reflected a greater concern for Jewish nationalism than for Israeli democracy.

Fear, specifically "fear of terror" (*paḥad mi-terror*), was spoken about as a social force that propelled government action and shaped everyday behavior. People spoke about living in constant fear, and newspapers reported on the large percentages of Israelis who were afraid they would be harmed in a suicide bombing. Israelis were deeply afraid for their own lives and for the existence of the State of Israel. As much as people looked toward the state for protection, they also disparaged their government for its inability to protect its citizens. To the right of the political spectrum, there was a need for greater state presence. To the left, the state was focused on goals other than protection of its citizens. Both the right and the left expressed a sense of abandonment by the state. As one young mother said to me: "What do I need a state for? They need to create order for me and for my family. If the government can't protect us, then the state is not functioning." The media griped that there was no umbrella institution to collect data on and respond to terrorism and that more money was going to security guards than to developing substantive protective technologies. As the director of the Shin Bet stated in 2003, "We have to say honestly, the defense establishment and, within it, the General Security Service have not provided the people of Israel the protective 'suit' they deserve" (O'Sullivan 2003).

The discourse of *terror* may have expressed profound fear, but the designation of something as *terror* was also a political tactic that delegitimized suicide bombings as a mode of political struggle by decoupling this form of resistance from a larger Palestinian nationalist effort. Israeli discourses of terror cloaked military operations in a veil of necessity and depicted state violence as a routine military response. Joseba Zulaika and William Douglass described a similar phenomenon in one of the first ethnographic studies to appraise representations of modern terrorism: "Once something that is called 'terrorism'—no matter how loosely it is defined—becomes established in the public mind, 'counterterrorism' is seemingly the only prudent course of action" (1996: ix).[11] In Israel, state officials presented the IDF killing of Palestinian militants as "reprisals" and the closure of Palestinian towns as "operational activities." Government rhetoric classified air strikes against Palestinian houses, restrictions of Palestinian movement through checkpoints, and the erection of barriers outside a book fair in Jerusalem as forms of "security," because all responded to "Palestinian threat," or, more accurately, to Israeli anticipation of Palestinian violence. Even left-wing media sources presented the IDF's collective punishments of Palestinians as necessary reactions to Palestinian "terror" and tended to conceal that Palestinian violence was often a reaction to Israeli force (Korn 2004). When something was designated as *terror*, it was as if it already necessitated and legitimated a "security" response.

Particularly after 9/11, Israeli discourse of security refracted global rhetoric on security and counterterrorism. As Joel Beinin (2003) argues, Sharon's government harnessed the George W. Bush administration's rhetoric on security in an attempt to legitimize its repression of Palestinians and align itself with the United States.[12] Security, nonetheless, already had local resonance in Israel, where it has long referred to a broader ideology of Jewish strength and power. Over the course of many decades, security practices in Israel became synonymous with Israeli sovereignty and national identity. The state harnessed security not only as a military strategy but also as a politics of identity to delineate a self and another in time and in space. Security came to connote a desire for the normal, whether the normality of a comfortable, routine life or the normalization of Jewish politics.

In Hebrew, security is generally spoken about with two words, *avtaha* and *bitahon*, both deriving from the same root (b-t-ḥ). *Avtaha* refers to the act of securing, while *bitahon* refers to the resultant state of safety. *Bitahon* is used most commonly, often in both senses, to speak of security. *Shmira* refers to guarding, distinguished in everyday parlance from *avtaha* in that the latter is assumed to be armed. The term *hagana* can also be translated as "security," or "defense," but it tends to refer to full-scale war and military efforts to maintain national borders. In daily conversation, *bitahon* evokes imaginaries of "internal" Palestinian threat while *hagana*, or defense, evokes an "external" threat from neighboring Arab states. *Bitahon* refers to ongoing conflict with Palestinians while *hagana* refers to circumscribed war. Frequently, however, these designations shift and overlap. With the invocation of *bitahon*, senses of "inside" and "outside" threats impinge equally on people's senses of political, bodily, and emotional security.

National discourse in this period depicted the nation as fighting less for expanded settlement than for personal security, that is, for the safety of people's bodies and minds as they moved through their day. Security had not always instantly implied personal bodily safety. In the first half of the 1990s, for example, early proponents of a barrier between Israel and the West Bank defended the barrier in terms of economic security, as something that would keep Palestinians from stealing Israeli cars and Israeli jobs. By 2002, however, both support for and criticism of the barrier depicted it as a wall against fear, something that could calm national hysteria and provide Israeli Jews with a sense of security, hope for peace, and calm. Israelis perceived IDF operations, likewise, as battles for the quality of their daily lives. We might view the nation's focus on personal security as evidence of the success of Palestinian violence in making Israelis afraid even in their homes and on their streets. The frequency and severity of Palestinian suicide bombings led Israelis to feel uncomfortable in spaces and activities they most took for granted. But although Palestinian violence assaulted Israeli civilian realms, the Israeli government also harnessed the nature of this violence to remind Israelis that they were under personal threat and to portray "national security" as a necessary protection of daily life. As much as the penetration of terror into urban life made the conflict's violence personal, Israeli reactions to Palestinian violence made "security" itself more familiar and indeed palatable to Israelis. It removed security from a realm of critique and questioning.

As a political discourse in Israel, security was both confining and productive. It not only constrained movement and people but also constituted knowledge, spaces, persons, and relationships (Foucault 1980, 1994a). It produced its own regime of truth and authority, and it materialized across the landscape. Security was, indeed, everywhere. Layers of mesh fencing surrounded school playgrounds and portable police barriers enclosed pedestrian malls, arranged in a somewhat different configuration each day. State-employed armed guards regularly jumped on and off city buses, scanning them for signs of suspicious activity. Guards, gates, closed circuit televisions, and hand-held metal detector wands accumulated in the landscape, and new traffic patterns and constant bag inspections created and constricted everyday routine. In response to bombings or to senses of threat, spaces of public consumption turned into checkpoint-like spaces. Walls and blockades zigzagged in and out of city spaces as if every building or road was a border. Long lines of cars snaked through the parking lots of shopping malls, as security guards checked trunks for explosives. Gates and walls turned cafés into fortresses and, with their railings and barriers, restaurants appeared to have the political weight of state lines. Outdoor public events were gated or moved indoors, and open-air pedestrian malls provoked plans for enclosure.

Security generated new forms of consumption: literally, new modes of eating behind walls and at home, and also a new consumer culture of security services. Israel's Yellow Pages contained listings for over 375 security companies. They offered guard services and *technologiyot miggun*, or "technologies of protection," which ranged from intrusion detection systems to bulletproof briefcases to the "Magshoe," an automatic metal detector for shoes. Security was bought and sold, developed, invented, implemented, and circulated. Not unlike other ways of establishing "observable empirical" so-called facts on the ground, material technologies of security were thought to give "credible form to a Jewish nation" (Abu El-Haj 2001: 129).

Security was ubiquitous, but it was also itinerant. Fortification was portable and ephemeral, fickle and unpredictable. Open spaces were suddenly barricaded and established gates suddenly disappeared. The Tel

Aviv police set up roadblocks within the city during a suicide-bombing alert only to remove them hours later. The Jerusalem police enclosed a summer street festival with armed guards and fences one night and left it unenclosed the next. In its portability, security also transcended military, state, and civilian domains. Soldiers moved fluidly from military service to security-guard jobs, and private architecture firms worked together with local police departments to rebuild bombed cafés. However capricious, impromptu, or temporary, forms of security still splintered the nation and overlay public space with political gravity.

On a different scale, security materialized in everyday artifacts and took the form of minute and nearly indiscernible details. There were security surcharges added to restaurant bills, noted in fine print at the bottom of small slips of paper. Barely conspicuous to begin with, they became so commonplace that they were often overlooked. Small notes were sometimes added as a courtesy in the corner of wedding invitations—"security will be provided"—which calmed some guests and often receded into nuptial chaos. Though subtle and fleeting, these signs of security delineated experiences of security as powerfully as looming artifacts like walls, gates, and guards. In addition to tangible forms of surveillance, national discourses of threat and practices of alertness manifest themselves in intimate practices and personal relationships. There were grandfathers, for example, who assumed new roles as chauffeurs for their grandchildren so that they would not have to ride the city buses, which were susceptible to Palestinian suicide bombings. There was the high-school girl on the Jerusalem bus who whispered to her friends, "My parents would kill me if I got killed!" Having been forbidden by her parents from riding public buses, she enlisted her classmates to look out for passengers who appeared "suspicious." Her alertness was a reaction to fear, yet it was also a mode of bonding with her peers and a response to parental discipline. The gaze of her parents appeared to be more significant than her own gaze for Palestinians.

Fences and finer-grained practices of fortification placated some Israeli fear, but they also corroborated anxiety and anger toward Palestinians. Rather than truly soothing its citizens' anxiety about Palestinian threats, state institutions transvalued fear and validated it, transforming emotions of suspicion into traits of good citizenship. People developed exceptional states of alertness and hypervigilance to supposed signs of danger and to signs of security itself. Walls and guards affirmed the sense of disorder they purported to prevent, eliciting the very vulnerabilities they claimed to temper. It was a self-fulfilling process, a phenomenon that anthropologists of violence have studied in contexts in which those identified as the state and those perceived as terroristic come to mirror each other; where acts called counterterrorism create the very reality they contest.[13] The second intifada was a time of fierce interaction between security and fear, one fueling the other without resolution.

People often speak of a cycle of violence and security, but security was very often tantamount to violence. Security was violence in other terms, "the logos of war expressed as a logos of peace" (Dillon and Lobo-Guerrero 2008: 275). Simultaneously a form of biopolitical and sovereign control, security was depicted in state discourses as a way of managing a population through its protection rather than through its death, a way of regulating people's lives through techniques and technologies rather than through juridical power.[14] However, when the state used its military and legal power to preserve its territory and population through the subjugation of Palestinians, security became indistinguishable from sovereignty. Palestinians were "disciplined" or subjugated by the violence and suppression of Israeli security, while Israeli Jews were "disciplined" to be a panoptical population that, in turn, scrutinized Palestinians. Israel thus exemplified the contradictory nature of the modern state, promising safety while coercing and controlling (Edkins 2003: 6).

In their pledge to protect Israelis against "threat," Israeli state officials conceived of national security broadly as any response to whatever infringed on the survival and certainty of the state (Hajjar 2005: 31–32). State discourse invoked "security" in all-encompassing and self-validating ways to identify all military acts, all practices of occupation, all forms of state violence, and all expansions of Jewish settlement. Public policy on Israel has tended to echo the state's own discourse, using phrases such as security risks, security facilities, security needs, security assets, security techniques, natural security, effective security, security guarantees, and security implications. The connotations of and referents for these terms, however, are ambiguous. Are "security risks" hazards to human safety or dangers shaped by "security" itself? Does the idea of "security needs" leave any room for discussion as to the necessity of military action? For whom is "effective security" effective? Do "security implications" implicate state sovereignty or human rights? I hope this book will offer new ways to think about the security terminology that is often used without explication. To set my own use of the term "security" apart from its applications in Israeli political rhetoric and to try to move away from the state's own analytical categories and perspectives (Blom Hansen and Stepputat 2001: 5), readers should imagine quotation marks around all my uses of the term in this book. This is not to suggest that security is unreal, but rather that its meaning is always contextual and in flux.

As an ethnography of embodied practice, this book does not search for understanding solely in people's minds and speech, but rather it locates knowledge within the quotidian, the personal, and the plural practices that constantly make and renovate people's lives (Mol 2002: 32). For all the talking with, interviewing, and living with my informants, I only fully gleaned how security circumscribes the lives of Israeli Jews when I attended to people's "movement, gesticulating, walking," the focus of Michel de Certeau's study of the practices of everyday life (1988: 130). For de Certeau, the world in which people live is not a discursive circumstance that precedes the subject but rather is the product of subjects' practiced interaction with it. People both actualize a matrix of fixed possibilities and interdictions and also invent possibilities by either transforming or abandoning certain spatial signifiers. Everyday practices do not necessarily order the world in purposeful, self-defined, or strategic ways, but the minutiae of daily life, be it walking or cooking, contains the substance of subjectivity and of cultural logic. In Israel, everyday practices of security in daily life were thus not ancillary to military expressions of power and sovereignty but rather part of the same reality. People encountered national security not only in West Bank checkpoints, Palestinian refugee camps, or the hallways of the Knesset but also in homes, cafés, and magazines, spaces of consumption and intimacy where security had particular resonance precisely because of its seeming innocuousness. State power and political belief materialized in individuals' use and interaction with (and, equally, avoidance of) particular streets, corners, and barricaded spaces. These everyday practices also implicated a politics of exclusion and separation.

Attention to everyday manifestations of security requires a phenomenological lens, for security is an embodied phenomenon, carried in physical bodies as well as in their dispositions and routines. In the cultural phenomenology of Thomas Csordas (1999), one of the most sustained applications of phenomenology in anthropology, Csordas draws on Maurice Merleau-Ponty, according to whom people are their bodies and bodies exist in a reciprocal relationship with the environment around them. Csordas also draws on Pierre Bourdieu's (1977) concept of habitus, wherein social life is generated and regulated by an embodied, socially conditioned system of dispositions. Csordas thus studies embodiment not as a process of inscription but rather as itself the "existential condition" of cultural life (1999: 143).[15] In daily life in Israel, security involved perception, imagination, and intersubjective experience. Security constituted gesture, movement, and "the phenomenon of habit" (Merleau-Ponty 2005 [1962]: 128) as much as it constituted knowledge and power.

In a book on the Israeli-Palestinian conflict, readers often expect one of three kinds of works: a psychological study of Israeli anxiety, a side-by-side comparison of Israeli Jews and Palestinians, or a critique of the State of Israel through a study of its effects on Palestinian life. This book does not fall into any of these categories. Particularly since the first intifada, it has become common among Israeli scholars of psychology to study Israeli "trauma" and Israeli behavior and emotion as forms of "resilience" and "coping."[16] These, however, are themselves terms that tend to presume the designation of Israelis as victims. My own study is ethnographic rather than psychological, examining the political discourses and cultural politics that become entangled with feeling and consciousness. This book adopts a critical approach to Israeli politics and practice, not by suppressing Israeli voices or avoiding Israel as an object of study (Stein and Swedenberg 2005: 11)[17] but rather by focusing intensively on Israeli subjectivity and experiences. Why does the Israeli population persist in supporting an occupying government? What are the forces that perpetuate Israeli desires for separation from Palestinians? Answering these questions demands an understanding of Israeli state discourses and everyday practices of security and surveillance. Studies of Palestinian life have certainly been vital to grasping the detrimental effects of Israeli occupation and colonization, from the ways Israeli bureaucracy conceals Palestinian humanity and suffering behind layers of legal documents (Kelly 2006a) to the Israeli legal practices in the West Bank and Gaza that function as an apparatus of Israeli control to reinforce national boundaries and accentuate Jewish-Arab distinctions (Hajjar 2005).[18] Yet the very nature of security itself—its assumptions about what is inside and what is outside, its binaries of safe and dangerous, us and them— must be approached, at least in part, from the perspective of those whom security claims to protect.

The first chapter of this book introduces the political economy of security in Israel. It organizes a brief genealogy of security as a state preoccupation and national culture in Israel around a chronology of Hashmira Security Technologies Ltd., now the largest public company in Israel. Beginning with the company's founding in 1937, the settings in which Hashmira guards worked and the roles they played reflect the interdependence and even indistinguishability of "private" and "state" security in Israel. We see that the Israeli military complex responds to Palestinian violence, but we also see that nationalist desires for Jewish territory and power themselves propagate violence in the form of "defense." The close relationship in Israel between civilian and military institutions, and the often indefinite boundaries in daily life as well as on the front line between security and violence, demand particular ethnographic sensitivities. The second half of this chapter describes my own fieldwork methodologies for the study of everyday security.

Each subsequent chapter in this book is an ethnographic study of one moment or expression of everyday security, including rebuilding a bombed café, experiencing fear and resilience, enacting terrorist profiles, commuting to work, organizing one's home, and touring the separation wall. Specifically, Chapter 2 offers a micro-history of a popular Jerusalem café destroyed in a Palestinian suicide bombing. In the thirty days over which the café was rebuilt, Israelis secured, consecrated, and then normalized the site. This is a study of security through architecture and aesthetics, for, in the café's rebuilding, built form mediated particular notions of national strength. The solidity of bricks and fragile transparency of glass became not only structural elements but also signs of political perseverance. Israeli police, government officials, and security guards engaged in this aesthetic of security as much as did the café's customers and managers, all working to render material their desires for political and social normalization. Even those who expressed cynicism about security's efficacy held tightly onto its ideas and practices. Skepticism and symbolism of security both relied on strong imaginaries of the state and its power.

The desire for defense in Israel has long been undergirded by fear and a sense of Jewish vulnerability. Chapter 3 studies the fear that, during the second intifada, assumed particular rhetorical and material forms. Referring explicitly to suicide bombings and implicitly to Palestinians, fear circulated as an Israeli code of social knowledge, harnessed to express anger at Palestinian violence or to criticize government tactics. Fear was a political discourse, but it was also intensely intimate and bodily. People's personal sensations of fear conveyed "I am an Israeli Jew" or "Israel is under threat"; their feelings of fear not only commented on the political conflict but also became part of their attachment to the state. This chapter analyzes the concurrently political and affective significance of fear in Israel.

Israeli Jews so internalized and normalized fear of Palestinians and state discourses about suicide bombers that they felt they could trust their instincts of suspicion to identify potential threats. Discourses of suspicion generated a host of state technologies and bodily habits. Chapter 4 studies Israeli alertness for so-called "suspicious people," comparing police and government profiles of "suspicious people" with individuals' everyday practices of suspicion. Through fleeting gestures and wary glances, pedestrians and security guards alike not only embodied state perceptions of danger and modes of seeing Palestinians, but also proliferated state blindness to Palestinians. Despite the ubiquity of suspicion, Israeli Jews rarely apprehended suicide bombers. It was not so much the presence of "suspicious people" as their absence that enabled the discourse to persist as part of daily life.

The next two chapters describe everyday fantasies of normalization in which Israeli Jews imagined ways for life to go on "as usual" during conflict, and indeed even acted as if things were normal, even as any semblance of the normal became ever fainter, even as the new normal had itself become menacing. Chapter 5 studies security through spatial stories of people's daily commutes to work in Jerusalem. For the four commuters I describe, deciphering media information and popular conceptions of safe and dangerous space to determine a morning itinerary was less a calculation of risk than a negotiation of memory, emotion, faith, and subjectivity. People's paths through the city were superimposed with memories of past bombings, private experiences, theological beliefs, and intimate relationships. As personal creativity and military logic coalesced, everyday projections of security reflected and reproduced national discourses of security in daily life. The matrix of routes people selected or avoided reflected not only their fear of *terror* but also their confidence in the ability to "cope," that is, to surmount Palestinian violence. The idea of coping, we see, can function like other practices of security to proliferate exclusive notions of us and them, inside and outside.

Chapter 6 studies how homes were physically redesigned and socially reconceived during the intifada as sites for safe sociality. Israelis sought solace through domestic purchases, such as DVDs and coffee machines, and domestic fantasies, such as those afforded by design magazines and furniture shopping. Drinking cappuccinos at home or leafing through glossy home design magazines, however, produced an uncanny comfort. This incongruity echoed other ways the state entered the Israeli home, such as in the outfitting of basement bomb shelters with gas masks or the cycling of military uniforms in and out of home washing machines. Through domestications of security, excessive enclaving facilitated blindness to violence and Palestinian suffering. Even when Israeli Jews tried to distance themselves from Israeli politics, fantasies of escape at home subdued the urgency of resolving conflict.

Israelis conceived the state, like the home, as a comfortably fortified enclave when they imagined the emergent separation wall between Israel and the West Bank. Three tours around the wall are the focus of Chapter 7. While the sensors, video cameras, and panoptic watchtowers of the wall claimed to survey and illuminate Palestinians on the other side, tours of the wall purported to scrutinize the wall itself, offering tourists privileged views, both visual and political. These tours, however, ultimately did less to evaluate the wall than to extend the wall's fortifying qualities. Circumambulation of the wall embodied a form of surveillance that did not truly see Palestinians on the other side, but rather, like the wall, reinforced fantasies of a safe and bounded Israeli homeland.

In this everyday life saturated with security, Israeli Jews generally remained aware of security's inefficacies and contradictions, whether questioning the ability of the separation wall to thwart Palestinian suicide bombings or cynically implying that the state pantomimes superficial protection. Even those apparently critical of Israeli violence against Palestinians, however, still craved not just national security but also everyday security. People tended to see their desire for well-being as outside politics: they did not, for example, want the separation wall to define Israeli borders, but they did want it to keep their children safe. This, regrettably, was the politics of security at its most powerful. People experienced their daily engagement with security as benign, nonviolent, and politically inconsequential, and yet it was firmly woven into a larger Israeli political fabric of occupation and exclusion. This is not to say that desires for protection inevitably reproduced the conditions of state policy or that experiences of fear necessarily led to the proliferation of state discourse.[19] The affective side of security, that is, the role of emotion, intimacy, and the body in reproducing state notions of safety and threat, suggests that critiques of state discourses of security can truly reverberate only when they are sensitive to the multiple guises that state security assumes in the form of escape, fantasy, and desire for the normal.

Vered's wedding convoy that opened this Introduction was an ephemeral domain of security in which vision coexisted with blindness, the familiar with the foreboding, and fantasy with materiality. So too does everyday security thrive in the junctures of these seeming incommensurabilities. Actions taken in the name of security by the State of Israel or by individuals, in their seemingly innocuous desire for comfort and often-subconscious everyday practices of suspicion and exclusion, did not resolve the binaries of safety and danger, private and state, self and other, or peace and violence. Rather, security held these binaries in tension, becoming an end unto itself, creating its own authority, its own truths. Ultimately, the illusion of normalization that security provided in moments like the drive to the wedding in Jerusalem precluded ardent efforts to get out of conflict. Providing comfort in its very enactment, security prompted only resistance to meaningful resolution to conflict.

Chapter 1

A Genealogy of Israeli Security

With intrusion-detection systems and metal-detection archways, Elite Professional Units and Shopping Mall Units, Hashmira Security Technologies Ltd. is Israel's largest security company and the largest private employer in the country. Its employees, veterans of IDF combat units, guard Israeli ports and military defense-related institutions across the country. The company provides monitoring technologies to the Israeli prison system and to Israel Railways and calls its "Moked 99" unit Israel's largest private police force. With earnings that grew from $60 million in 1995 to $185 million in 2003, Hashmira's revenue and scope reflect the expansion of Israel's security industry in the 1990s, itself tied to the global proliferation of security corporations working within and across national borders.[1] The second intifada further bolstered Israel's military industrial complex, and, with it, Hashmira's earnings.[2] Recent expansion notwithstanding, Hashmira's roots are deeper than this period of Israeli and Palestinian violence. Hashmira was founded more than a decade before the State of Israel, a company spurred by Jewish settlers' desires to lay claim to land and prevail over the protests of native Palestinian inhabitants. In many ways, to tell the history of Hashmira is to tell a history of security and defense in the State of Israel. The growth of the company delineates the details of Jewish settlement, Israeli land seizure, and state panopticism. In order to contextualize the ethnographic chapters that follow, this chapter structures a brief genealogy of Israeli security as a state preoccupation and national culture around a chronology of the Hashmira security company. My focus is the history of Israeli state security, but I use the security company as a lens to show how an economy of security has been integral to Israel's history and to demonstrate that security is a discourse and set of practices generated jointly by civilians and the state.[3] Security, as this history intimates, is a technology of nationalism rather than its fate.[4]

Histories of Israeli defense frequently depict Israeli practices of security as inevitable outcomes of historical circumstance. Even scholarship critical of Israel's relations with Palestinians and neighboring Arab countries renders Israeli defense an unavoidable reaction to Palestinian hostility toward Jewish settlement. Scholars portray Jews in Palestine as "forced to defend themselves" and present force as something to which Jewish settlers need to "resort" (Shapira 1992: 367, 122). Studies of Israeli politics that present the "threat of annihilation" (Shalit 1994) as a purely material reality describe security as an inexorable, inescapable response to danger. These ideas about the inevitability and necessity of force can risk corroborating and naturalizing actions in the name of national security. This chapter's genealogy frames Israeli security not only as an outcome of long-standing conflict with Palestinians but also as a set of institutions and dispositions grounded in the Jewish nationalist aspiration to create Israel as a "normal" nation with desires for territorial expansion. It recognizes that Israeli discourses of "security" generate their own logic and sources of justification that are independent of "real" threats, and that defense is not an inevitable reaction but a condition of possibility for Israeli statehood and national identity. In studying security in contemporary Israeli life, as in historicizing security, national discourses of defense and threat can all too easily attract attention to the domains of political life, such as military institutions, that themselves presume the presence of threat and the necessity of defense. The second half of this chapter outlines the fieldwork in everyday life that informs this book's focus on agents other than "threat"—such as family and fear—that perpetuate desires for security.

National Security Before the Nation-State

Although Jewish immigration to Palestine grew steadily beginning with the First Aliyah from Europe and Yemen to Palestine in 1881, it was not until the mid-1930s that large-scale conflict between Jews and Arabs in Palestine began to take shape (Dowty 2005: 77). During the period of British rule (1920–48), the Jewish community in Palestine swelled from one-sixth to nearly one-third of the population of Palestine, sparking riots by the Arab majority in 1920 and 1921 and from 1936 to 1939. Violence and defense were often blurred and cyclical, with settlement spurring uprising and uprising spurring enclosure. Fortification and defense became an increasing focus of Jews' settlement project. Jewish settlers began to conceive of their existing *kibbutzim* and *moshavim*, the collective agricultural communities founded in ideals of socialism and Zionism, less as pastoral cooperatives than as paramilitary outposts (Troen 2003: 3–4; Kimmerling 2001: 209). They also constructed *ḥoma U-Migdal* (literally stockade and watchtower) settlements with central towers, trenches, and high walls that were intended to shield Jews from Palestinian resistance riots and also from British opposition (Weizman 2007: 100; Rotbard 2003). "This form," according to Anita Shapira, "was designed to permit colonization in frontier areas while safeguarding the settlement from attack" (1992: 237). As pre-state forms of architectural security, these outposts carved out space from Palestinian land and, as Ilan Troen argues, functioned as unilateral borders in calculated places (2003: 76).

Moshe Shermister, formerly a Jewish member of the British colonial police, capitalized on Jewish settlers' desires for protection from local Palestinians. On July 30, 1937, Shermister incorporated a new company under the British Mandate of Palestine.[5] Hashmira Company, LTD, which might be translated "The Guardian," set out as an association of independent and private Jewish police to guard the growing Jewish community in Palestine.[6] Shermister opened his first office in Tel Aviv and announced his company in a local notice:

> We are delighted to inform you that our company has received the permission of the [British] Mandate to begin operations. We hereby undertake to guard banks, offices, stores, storage areas, apartments, factories, etc., in accordance with the company's fees. The company's management were officers in the police force of the Land of Israel, and the guards also served in the police and are experienced professionals in the field.

With an initial payroll of just two guards, Hashmira started small but grew steadily over the coming decades.

By 1939, Hashmira had a force of seven guards who wore badges with the company's emblem—two intersecting keys and a large, radiant eye beneath the words "The independent police in the Land of Israel." Armed with clubs, flashlights, and whistles, they guarded Jewish settlements in the Tel Aviv area. The company helped to police the nation-in-formation in ways not unlike Jewish paramilitary organizations, such as the Haganah, which acted in state-like ways for the growing Jewish community. Jewish settlers formed the Haganah, meaning "defense," after the Arab riots of 1920 and expanded it further after the 1929 riots.[7] Although officially outlawed by the British Mandatory Authorities, the Haganah provided its members with arms training, engaged in armed violence against Palestinians, and established central arms depots. By the time of the 1936 Arab Revolt, it was a full-fledged army.

When Haganah's soldiers and Hashmira's guards fashioned themselves as sentinels of Jewish settlements, they were not only laying claim to the idea of a Jewish biblical homeland but also embodying the political aspirations for Jewish power that began in Europe in the late nineteenth century. Jewish settlers' turn to defense in this period may have been spurred by Palestinian retaliation, as Almog (2000) and Ezrahi (1997) have shown, but the inclination to self-protect lay at the foundation of Jewish nationalist thought. Self-defense, according to early Jewish nationalist discourses, would enable the Jewish people to become a "normal" nation (Shapira 1992: 25–26). The desire to reverse the vulnerability of Eastern European Jews was particularly characteristic of Labor or Socialist Zionism, the dominant strand of left-wing Zionism, but revisionist Zionist thought and, by the 1930s, religious Zionism, also espoused a radical shift from a place of political weakness to one of sovereign strength. The "new Jew" was expected not only to settle the land but also to defend it from native Arabs (Almog 2000). Late nineteenth- and early twentieth-century Jewish settlers in Palestine, as Yael Zerubavel suggests, transposed the biblical conception of God as sentinel—"the guardian of Israel neither slumbers nor sleeps" (Psalm 121:4)—onto the new Jewish guards (1995: 24). From the 1930s onward, the idea of self-protection became almost an end unto itself. According to Uri Ben-Eliezer, "military practices gradually became institutionalized and habitual . . . until finally the idea of implementing a military solution to Israel's national problems was not only enshrined as a value in its own right but was also considered legitimate, desirable, and indeed, the best option" (1998: x). Jewish settlers crafted self-defense as a condition of possibility for Jewish national identity and, eventually, for the legitimacy of the nation-state.

On the eve of statehood, Hashmira employed 150 guards and Shermister, now working with his son Kadish, opened a new branch in Jerusalem. After the British government withdrew from Palestine, Jewish leadership led by David Ben-Gurion declared Israel's independence in May 1948. However, when Palestinian representatives and the Arab League rejected the 1947 United Nations Partition Plan (UN General Assembly Resolution 181) to divide Palestine into a Jewish and an Arab state and create Jerusalem as an international city, the armies of Egypt, Syria, Jordan, Lebanon, and Iraq attacked Israel. This was the start of the 1948 Arab-Israeli War, known to Israelis as the War of Independence and to Palestinians as al-Naqba (the Catastrophe). During the war, twenty Hashmira guards from the Jerusalem branch worked alongside the newly formed IDF to stand watch over ration warehouses in Jerusalem, a response to the blockade by Palestinian Arabs of food and water to the Jewish community of Jerusalem.

A year of fighting ended with the 1949 Armistice Agreement, which established the Green Line as the critical border between Israel and a theoretical Palestinian state. Jordan annexed what became known as the

West Bank and East Jerusalem, and Egypt took control of the Gaza Strip. The fate of an estimated 600,000–760,000 Palestinian Arabs who were expelled or fled the country has been one of the chief sources of controversy in the Middle East ever since (Morris 1987). Soon after the Galilee and the Negev, captured during the war, came under Israeli control, Hashmira opened new offices, as if in place of the displaced Palestinian residents.[8] Kadish Shermister established new branches in Jewish cities such as Haifa and Hadera, which the state was filling with Jewish immigrants from Eastern Europe and Yemen. A Hashmira office opened in Acre, an Arab city with a Palestinian population that Israel largely displaced when it captured the port city in 1948 (Pappe 2007: 100), and in development towns such as Kiryat Shmona, which Israel established in 1949 on the site of al-Khalisa, a Bedouin town (Khalidi and Elmusa 1992: 462–63).

Prime Minister David Ben-Gurion declared during the war: "I have to admit that I am not capable of seeing anything now other than through the prism of security. . . . Security is involved in all branches of life" (Ben-Eliezer 1998: 207). To the first prime minister, security meant not only military strength but also economic independence and a modern, densely settled landscape. In the early years of the state, the work of Hashmira was part of this broad vision of security. After Israel's invasion of the Sinai Peninsula in 1956, for example, when Israeli civilians and the military clashed with Palestinian militants, or *fedayeen*, primarily from the Egyptian-occupied Gaza Strip, Hashmira police worked alongside the IDF's infantry units and paratroopers to guard Jews from *fedayeen* attacks along the Lebanese, Jordanian, and Syrian borders. Security, in Uri Ben-Eliezer's words, "was no longer a pure state-bureaucratic project but the people's enterprise" (1998: 214).

The 1967 war "turned the Arab-Israeli conflict upside down. It marked the final stage in the reversal of power relationships" (Dowty 2005: 110). When Israel seized Gaza and the Sinai Peninsula from Egypt, the Golan Heights from Syria, and the West Bank including East Jerusalem from Jordan, Hashmira guards assumed position in the newly annexed Golan Heights and Sharm-El-Sheikh in the Sinai Peninsula to assist the government in establishing Jewish settlements outside the Green Line. If the decades between 1948 and 1967 were a period of interstate conflict between Israel and its neighboring countries, Israel's 1967 war with Egypt, Jordan, and Syria, which Palestinians call al-Naksah (the Setback), initiated Israel's direct negotiation with Palestinians. Roughly one million Palestinians clung tenuously to two small tracts of land now under Israeli military occupation. Israel's occupation of the West Bank and Gaza subjected the majority of the Palestinians living there to Israeli military administration without Israeli citizenship.[9]

Palestinian resistance to Israeli occupation galvanized. The Palestinian

Liberation Organization (PLO), formed in 1964, became stronger, and Fatah became the dominant force of the Palestinian national movement (Baumgarten 2005: 30; Kurz 2005). Largely under Fatah's leadership, Palestinian militants carried out bombings and hijackings against Israeli civilians, such as in July 1969 when two members of the Popular Front for the Liberation of Palestine commandeered an El Al airplane. Hashmira guards were part of Israel's arsenal against Palestinian resistance. When Israel stationed Hashmira guards at seaports and at the Lod Airport (renamed Ben Gurion International Airport in 1973), the private guards served not only as an overt response to Palestinian hijackings but as a covert and broader effort to assert Israeli territorial control. During this period, military and civilian security came to assume, according to Oren Barak and Gabriel Sheffer, "a hegemonic position in the country" (2007: 15).

The Labor governments of the late 1960s and early 1970s were not committed to a single vision for settlement in the newly annexed territories. Conflicting government guidelines and competing proposals by government officials reflected a range of territorial ambitions and settlement ideologies (Weizman 2007: 90–92). However, when the right-wing Likud Party led by Menachem Begin came to power in 1977 amid the growth of religious nationalism together with the expansion of business corporations and the amplification of Mizrahi voices (Ram 2004), Jewish settlement in the West Bank became an organized state project. The Likud government regarded settlements as a human border of defense, a precaution against future invasion, and a way to expand Jewish territory into Palestinian areas. At the same time, the messianic civilian settler movement that organized in 1968 and formalized as Gush Emunim in 1974 was determined to establish Jewish presence throughout the Land of Israel, thereby making Israeli withdrawal from the newly captured territories impossible (Dowty 2005: 117). As these religious Jewish settlers established their own residential outposts, the state created an infrastructure of Israeli-built roads and bridges that began to crisscross the West Bank, circumventing Palestinian spaces while interconnecting Jewish settlements. Scholars debate the extent of the change in government policy toward the settlements during this period, but the demographic shift is undeniable. The government sent thousands of Jewish settlers into recently annexed and heavily populated Palestinian land such that, in the first four years of Likud's leadership, the number of Jewish settlers in the West Bank quadrupled, growing from about 4,000 to more than 16,000 (Weizman 2007: 92).

As settlements grew, so did the Israeli security lexicon, with terms such as *surveillance, security needs,* and *security principles* entering political rhetoric in the late 1970s.[10] The Israeli concept of a "security zone" came to the fore after the 1982 war in southern Lebanon. (When Israel withdrew its troops from Lebanon in 1985, it left a residual contingent of IDF units to patrol a "security zone" that Israel considered a necessary deterrent against attacks or infiltration into the north of Israel.[11]) Hashmira embodied the growing vocabulary of security. In 1971, Hashmira created a new division called Hashmira Security Technologies, expanding its electronics division from fire- and smoke-detection systems and patrol and monitoring services into electronic surveillance systems, and later magnometric gates and closed-circuit televisions. The division grew in the years after the October 1973 war with Egypt and Syria (called the Yom Kippur War or the Ramadan War). When the 1979 Egyptian-Israeli peace treaty stipulated Israel's military and civilian withdrawal from the Sinai Peninsula, Hashmira guards began to work at Taba (an Egyptian town), Rafah (split between Gaza and Egypt), and Nitsana (in Israel), Israel's international border stations under the jurisdiction of the Israel Airports Authority (established as a public corporation in 1977).

In December 1987, Palestinian nonviolent and violent resistance against Israel's occupation swelled into the first Palestinian intifada. Demonstrations and attacks directed at Israeli soldiers and civilians using Molotov cocktails, hand grenades, and stones protested Israel's interrogation methods, house demolitions, extrajudicial killings, and mass detentions. Over the course of the six-year conflict, Israel increased its social and spatial regulation of Palestinians in the West Bank and Gaza.[12] It issued Palestinian identity cards, extended Palestinian curfews and border closures, and confiscated Palestinian land for what the state called "buffer zones" around Jewish settlements. The first intifada sparked the genesis of Islamic militant groups such as Hamas and Islamic Jihad, but it also cemented Palestinian identity and global support for Palestinian self-determination.

The conflict led to mainstream Israeli and Palestinian championing of a two-state solution to the conflict and the willingness to take risks for peace. The Oslo Accords, signed by PLO leader Yasser Arafat and Israeli Prime Minister Yitzhak Rabin in September 1993, were one such risk. For the first time, two figureheads of the conflict established mutual recognition and openly negotiated a comprehensive peace treaty. The Accords outlined Israeli withdrawal from parts of the West Bank and Gaza and provision for the creation of a Palestinian National Authority, which kindled optimism among Israelis and Palestinians. The early 1990s, as a result, were a period of relative moderation and broadmindedness, not least because support for the peace process led to foreign investment in the Israeli and Palestinian economies. Economic deregulation led to a rise in private consumption, to a new ethics of personal responsibility, and, in turn, to a new economy of security.[13] The Hashmira Company expanded dramatically in this period. In 1993, the security company began to be publicly traded on the Tel Aviv Stock Exchange and, by 1999, Hashmira's revenue reached $137 million.

Despite an ethos of peace, violence eventually prevailed. Beginning in 1994, Hamas and Islamic Jihad, who opposed Israel's very existence, claimed responsibility for a series of suicide bombings against Israeli soldiers, settlers, and civilian centers. The Israeli government attempted to limit attacks through measures such as building a wall around the Gaza Strip, which was erected under Rabin's leadership beginning in 1994 (Weizman 2007: 143). Israelis' fears of Palestinian terror and the state's focus on counterterrorism grew in tandem. Benjamin Netanyahu, who ran for prime minister in 1996 on a platform of "security and peace" (Ram 2008: 172), promised to restore a sense of "personal security" to Israeli citizens by subduing what he called Palestinian terrorism. A spate of Palestinian bombings in 1996 and 1997 in places such as the the the Central Bus Station in Jerusalem, Jerusalem's Maḥane Yehuda market, and outside Dizengoff Center in Tel Aviv, reinforced Israeli support for Netanyahu's right-wing government and its militaristic approach. It is no coincidence that, as a more conscious culture of security developed, Israeli scholars began to analyze and classify the culture of security. In 1995, political scientist Asher Arian wrote about security as a "pervasive preoccupation" and as tantamount to a religion (1995: 164). Sociologist Baruch Kimmerling described the "civil religion of security" in Israel (2001: 212), and geographer Maoz Azaryahu described Israeli security as "a tenet of collective faith" (2000: 103). Daniel Bar-Tal, Dan Jacobson, and Tali Freund (1995) studied the "security feelings" of Jewish settlers.

During the second intifada, Hashmira's guards epitomized the nation's reliance on emblems of security. At least one hundred Hashmira guards worked alongside Israeli soldiers in Jewish settlements and at West Bank checkpoints in the early 2000s. According to a 2002 report in the *Guardian*, along with other security companies operating in the West Bank, Hashmira benefited from subsidies that the government issued to settlements to fund their security operations (Lagerquist and Steele 2002). Hashmira's guards, many of them settlers themselves, "routinely prevent[ed] Palestinian villagers from cultivating their own fields, traveling to schools, hospitals and shops in nearby towns, and receiving emergency medical assistance." In Qedumim, for example, a Jewish settlement established in 1976 alongside the Palestinian village of Kafr Qaddum, Hashmira guards carrying submachine guns worked in conjunction with the IDF to prevent a Palestinian minibus from driving through the settlement. Whether acting as a private army or as a paid extension of the IDF, Hashmira's "private" guards buttressed Israel's military occupation. The assimilation of privately employed security guards into the engine of Israeli occupation blurred the private and public, state and civilian faces of security.

When the Danish security conglomerate and private prison contractor

Group 4 Falck acquired a 50 percent stake in Hashmira in 2002, Hashmira's work in the occupied territories was opened to new scrutiny.[14] Following international criticism in the fall of 2002 that Hashmira guards were working in settlements the UN considers illegal, Group 4 Falck (which had since been renamed G4S and fully acquired Hashmira) removed Hashmira guards from the West Bank. Even when Hashmira guards ceased to work as settlement soldiers, however, the company continued to uphold Israeli military experience as the source and model for Hashmira's professionalism and proficiency. All guards, the company claimed on its Web site in 2006, were veterans of IDF "combat units" and "senior security forces." The company not only invoked the IDF to bolster its guards' authority but also depicted its divisions as akin to military units. Their Elite Professional Units, for example, provided "security services at restricted and sensitive installations" such as the port of Haifa and Israel Railway trains. The company lauded its "fleet of operational vehicles" and its "logistic command and control network." In the company newsletter and in statements by its current president Yigal Shermister, terms such as missions, recruitment, risk factors, and enemy population evoke government concepts of counterterrorism.

As the history of Hashmira lays bare, despite the normative distinction between public and private that is implied in the term "private security company" (Neocleous 2007), security in Israel has long been a collaboration between government and civilian institutions, an enterprise elemental to state sovereignty yet still assumed by civilian bodies.[15] It is a domain of state authority even as it is enacted and molded by organizations that predate the state. The alliance between civilian and military bodies is often obscured or normalized. This is exemplified, for example, by the Hashmira Company's Shopping Mall Units, which provide security services and entrance inspections at shopping centers around the country, including the Azrieli Mall in Tel Aviv and the Malha Mall in Jerusalem. The army rhetoric used gives imagined authority to the guards work and militarizes the civilian space, while the pedestrian title of the unit normalizes the guards' state-like surveillance. "Security," as Ben-Gurion said in 1948 and as has remained germane since, "is involved in all branches of life" (Ben-Eliezer 1998: 207).

Fieldwork in Security

Hashmira's vacillation between state and civilian domains not only characterizes contemporary security but also informs the ethnographic study of security. Just as a history of Israeli security cannot assume that actions in the name of national security are always carried out by the state in a formal or bounded sense, so too must a study of Israeli security look beyond prescribed state institutions of security. In a country where self-defense is a locus of national identity in addition to a strategy for state-building, Israeli citizens do not easily enact and make sense of national discourses of security. Israelis constantly negotiate and generate discourses of fear, threat, and safety with their minds and bodies, as individuals and in relationship with others. In what follows, I describe the fieldwork I conducted in Israel between July 2003 and August 2004, and again in the summer of 2005. My research focused on everyday security in two rather different Israeli cities—Jerusalem and Arad—whose residents' fears, imaginaries of danger, and engagement with national discourses of security were ultimately more similar than the cities' diverse histories and national symbolism would suggest.

As the capital of the country and the most divisive piece of land in the Israeli-Palestinian conflict, Jerusalem is the most natural place in the country to study security.[16] Jerusalem, the heart of Israeli civic ritual and religious pilgrimage, is also the heart of Israeli security, the Israeli city most palpably saturated by security guards, Israeli soldiers, border police, and municipal police. Israeli Jews and Palestinians both claim Jerusalem as their national capital, and both lay claim to land in East and West Jerusalem. In many respects, the line between East and West Jerusalem, between the Israeli state and a prospective Palestinian state, is a palpable ethnic, religious, cultural, and economic border. And yet with Palestinian-populated towns in West Jerusalem and Jewish settlements in East Jerusalem, it is impossible to call East Jerusalem a strictly Palestinian city or West Jerusalem a Jewish one. In fact, the Jewish population within the municipal borders of Jerusalem makes up approximately three-quarters of all Jewish settlers in the occupied Palestinian territories (Weizman 2007: 26; Savitch and Garb 2006: 156). A city where contemporary barriers and borders overlay and intersect with ancient fortification, it is the place in which, more than any other Israeli city, Israeli Jews are fretful and fearful about the integration or mere presence of Palestinians.

Arad, a small city 60 miles south of Jerusalem, served as a second field site, a place where I could study how fear and desires for security affect daily life even when political tensions did not so overtly dominate life. Arad was established in 1961 by a team of Israeli architects, economists, demographers, and politicians driven by a nationalist devotion to settlement and determined to create a successful and economically viable development town in the desert. After its population swelled with a surge of Russian Jewish immigration in the late 1980s and early 1990s, Arad was designated a city in 1995. By 2003, its population had grown to 28,000 due to the influx of Ethiopian and Argentinean immigrants whom the state settled there, a size comparable to many of Israel's other small cities and large settlements. Although Arad was a place where, as many of its residents told me, "nothing happens," it experienced many of the problems common to other Jewish cities and towns at the time, such as the recession of 2003 and the recurring emotional and economic reverberations from Palestinian suicide bombings elsewhere in the country. The city lacked Jerusalem's internationally contested borders but sat ten miles from Palestinian towns in the West Bank and abutted several Bedouin villages. Jewish residents' talk of the "Palestinian threat" often focused on their anxieties about these neighboring Palestinians. As I realized over the course of my fieldwork, despite geopolitical differences between Arad and Jerusalem, people in both cities conveyed a similar range of political affect. This book draws on insight from interviews and life in both Jerusalem and Arad.

I began my fieldwork in Jerusalem by living in an apartment on a street in Talbiyya, a Jewish neighborhood that was home from the 1920s until 1948 to affluent Palestinian Christians (Bisharat 2007: 88). I lived on Hovevei Zion Street, literally translated "lovers of Zion" and referring to the Zionist organization formed in Eastern Europe in the 1880s that assembled some of the earliest Jewish settlers of Palestine.[17] It was not uncommon for Jewish residents of this neighborhood to volunteer in Israel's Civil Guard (Ha-Mishmar ha-Ezrahi), a branch of the Israel Police and the largest volunteer organization in the country. The Civil Guard was founded in 1974 as a civilian apparatus to monitor Palestinian "terrorist activity" in towns near the Lebanon border and soon became a division of the Israel police.[18] In the fall of 2004, I too became a volunteer in the organization. Presenting my U.S. passport, my student visa, and the phone number of the police station in my hometown in Virginia gave me the "security clearance" necessary to volunteer. Authorization is generally granted only to permanent residents but exceptions are often made for Jews visiting from foreign countries. In my case, approval was facilitated by the head of my local base, who was sympathetic to my desire to conduct graduate research. Once clearance was granted and I sat through a training session, I was allowed to don a yellow reflective vest on weekly pedestrian patrols of downtown Jerusalem, the crackling reports from the police radios we carried mingling with fellow volunteers' reinforcement or dismissal of reported threats.

Living alone for this early phase of fieldwork, I quickly sensed my distance from the essence of the daily life I had come to study. After all, family networks, parental responsibility, and intimate relations were the units through which Israelis tended to express their fears of Palestinians and anxieties about ongoing violence. Alertness, for example, was seen as a trait of good parenting. Mothers and fathers discussed whether it was safe for their child to take a particular bus, walk a certain route, or go on a school field trip. Fear and violence also set family networks in motion, particularly cell phone networks. In many families, after a Palestinian suicide bombing, it was the formal or default task of one individual to make a round of cell-phone calls. The calls were streamlined and rote: "Are you okay? Okay, bye" sufficed. One family I saw regularly announced several weeks after meeting them that I would be part of their family list of post-attack phone calls. I took this as a sign of my integration. Israelis saw such calls less as an obsessed concern with death than as a "binding force,"[19] a sign of friendship. One woman in her late twenties even broke up a relationship with a man who didn't call her after suicide bombings. Israelis mocked these cellular chains but still clung to them. At a bar in Arad, one soldier home for the weekend recounted to a group of friends that, once, he was sitting with friends when a Palestinian suicide bombing occurred nearby. The phones of these friends began to ring as their parents checked in, but his phone stayed silent. He later asked his parents why they did not call and they said they knew he doesn't take the bus that was blown up. Everyone hearing this story laughed. With a facial expression that said, "What, they don't care about me?!" he divulged his mild offense at his parents' lack of overprotection.

To make family life and space a more important focus of my research, I divided my time between the homes of four families I met through my small social network, three in Jerusalem and one in Arad. Israeli Jews are a heterogeneous group in terms of country of origin, date of immigration, religious observance, and political belief. While the families I lived with are not statistically representative of Israeli society, they do represent a demographic range within the country, encompassing the observant and secular, high-school-educated and Ph.D.s, Ashkenazi (Jews descended from Jewish communities in Eastern Europe) and Mizrahi (Jews from the Middle East and Central Asia).[20] All these families had at least three generations who had lived in Israel and, by and large, served in the IDF (unlike, for example, ultra-Orthodox Israelis or recent immigrants above drafting age), enabling me to consider how military knowledge extends into daily civilian life and how experiences of this period of violence compare with earlier periods. My intent when I refer to Israelis or Israeli Jews is neither to generalize or homogenize them nor to eclipse formal and informal acts of true political dissent and critique. Rather, my aim is to discern, through their daily lives, some larger patterns of seeing, experiencing, and speaking about political life. The insights and experiences of these families—as family units and as individuals—reverberate through this book, alongside a range of other voices. I introduce these families here, with their names and identifying details changed.

Shlomit and Ilan Maimon lived in Ramat Eshkol, a neighborhood built in East Jerusalem after 1967. Their three-story attached stone home was recently renovated, with space for children and grandchildren, always coming and going. Shlomit's father came to Palestine from Germany in 1933 at age fifteen, and her mother came from Germany in 1939 at seventeen with the Youth Aliya.[21] Both were founding members of a religious kibbutz in the north of Israel, where they met before moving to Katamon in Jerusalem in 1948 and then, in 1972, to the Jewish Quarter of Jerusalem's Old City. Ilan's family came to Palestine in the late nineteenth century from Russia and settled in Safed and then moved to Haifa in the 1920s, where Ilan was born. Shlomit, sixty when I began my fieldwork, was a paralegal and Ilan, sixty-four, was a professor of physics at Hebrew University. They considered themselves *dati* (religious), which meant that they abided by Jewish dietary laws, were Sabbath observant, and observed the festivals of the Jewish calendar. They had three daughters, one son, and five grandchildren. All their children served in the IDF and received college degrees. Two daughters lived with their families in Jerusalem, the other lived in a Jewish settlement outside Jerusalem, and their son lived in Haifa. Shlomit and Ilan watched their grandchildren at least once a week after school, and frequently hosted their children on the Sabbath.

Closer in age to the Maimons' children, Noa and Gil Shahar lived at the westernmost edge of Jerusalem in Motza, a quiet neighborhood more affordable than those closer to the city center but still within the Green Line. This was important to Noa and Gil, who considered themselves left-wing Israelis lapsed in their Zionism and attuned to their government's repression of Palestinians. The area they lived in was not without its own complicated history. In the 1890s, Motza became the first Jewish village outside Jerusalem when it was established on farmland purchased from the nearby Palestinian village Qalunya. In 1948, Qalunya villagers attacked upper Motza, and the Palmach, the military branch of the Haganah, destroyed the village, from which many residents had fled following the massacre at the nearby village of Deir Yassin (Benvenisti 2000: 113–14; Segev 1999: 324). Noa and Gil lived in a small house dating, they believed, from the late Ottoman era, on top of a steep hill. Gil's parents emigrated from Afghanistan as children in the early 1950s. Noa's father came to Israel from Syria with his parents in 1964, and her mother emigrated from Poland in 1949. In their early thirties and with an infant son, Noa and Gil were, in a number of ways, representative of the middle-class, secular couples that lived in their neighborhood. Gil commuted to work at an office in Tel Aviv for the Israel Airports Authority, a government-owned corporation, and Noa taught math at a high school in Jerusalem. They had recently purchased an apartment in Modi'in, a rapidly growing Israeli city between Jerusalem and Tel Aviv. They would move there in 2005, following a larger trend of young Jerusalemites leaving the city for peripheral suburbs and settlements, attracted to easier access to jobs in Tel Aviv and more affordable real estate, and repelled by the increasingly ultra-Orthodox population of Jerusalem. After 2000, security became an additional impetus.

Unlike the Maimon and Shahar families, I met Sheri and Yinon Kashani, twenty-two and twenty-four respectively, through my volunteer work for a Jerusalem-based nonprofit organization called ATZUM. Established in 2002, ATZUM was one of a new genre of nonprofit organizations that began to proliferate in Israel shortly after the beginning of the second intifada. Privately funded, these "terror victims' funds" saw themselves as supplements to or substitutes for government welfare services and offered financial and psychosocial support to individuals and families affected by Palestinian suicide bombings (Ochs 2006). In April 2002, Sheri's mother had been one of seven killed by a Palestinian suicide bomber (al-Aqsa Martyrs' Brigades claimed responsibility for the attack) who detonated a bomb at a bus stop on Jaffa Road near the outdoor market Maḥane Yehuda. This made Sheri and her family "terror victims" to the Israeli government, and a social worker for Bituaḥ Leumi, Israel's National Insurance, eventually referred them to ATZUM. The two institutions helped Sheri and her husband secure money and loans to purchase a two-bedroom basement apartment in Pisgat Ze'ev, a Jewish settlement within the Jerusalem municipality, where they lived with their two daughters, aged two and four. Sheri worked as a receptionist at an ophthalmology office in Jerusalem and Yinon worked for a Jerusalem-based security company installing home security systems in Jerusalem and in Jewish settlements in the West Bank. Both Sheri and Yinon's parents were Iranian Jews who emigrated from Iran in the early 1980s in the wake of the 1979 Revolution. Their families were traditionally observant, although Sheri and Yinon, who were both born in Israel, had themselves become even more so over the course of their years in religious state schools and the religious Zionist youth movement B'nei Akiva.

In Arad, I lived with Naomi and Arieh Bergmann, who had moved to the city as a newly married couple in 1978. They first lived in an apartment and then moved into a home their parents had purchased for them, a *villa*, as they called it in Hebrew, with three bedrooms and a small yard overlooking the desert. Naomi was a social worker for the local school system and Arieh worked as a mechanic for the city. Arieh, born in Poland, escaped in 1943 and moved to Israel in 1947. Naomi's father was born in Hungary in 1919 and in 1935 fled through Prague to Israel with the Zionist youth organization Ha-Shomer Ha-Tsa'ir, or the Youth Guard, and with the help of Haganah. Naomi's mother, also from Hungary, survived the Holocaust and fled to Israel soon after the war. Naomi and Arieh had two sons; the older son generally lived in Tel

Aviv but was traveling with his girlfriend for a year in Australia and the younger was still in the army. Both had grown up in Arad. As residents of Arad for nearly all their adult lives, Naomi and Arieh had a large circle of friends in the city, but they often spoke of leaving, now that their sons were grown, for a more cosmopolitan place.

Even though none of the families I lived with called themselves Jewish settlers, two families lived in what the United Nations considers Jewish settlements. The Maimons' neighborhood of Ramat Eshkol was the first Jewish housing project built on land Israel took from Jordan during the 1967 war. The Kashanis' neighborhood of Pisgat Ze'ev was also built east of the Green Line on land de facto annexed in 1967. The government calls it a Jewish neighborhood, part of the Jerusalem municipality, but the United Nations, which did not recognize the 1967 annexation, considers it an illegal settlement. The government started construction there in 1982 to create so-called Jewish continuity between Jerusalem and Neve Ya'akov, a more northern settlement where Jews have lived since the 1920s. Both Ramat Eshkol and Pisgat Ze'ev are part of the Jerusalem municipality, but neither is legal under the international law of the Fourth Geneva Convention.[22] Israeli Jews generally refer to Ramat Eshkol as a neighborhood of Jerusalem and Sheri called Pisgat Ze'ev, a suburb of Jerusalem. The reference to settlements outside the 1949 borders as Israeli neighborhoods or suburbs rather than settlements (*yeshuvim*) is a means of naturalizing the settlements as legitimate Israeli spaces (Weizman 2007: 8).[23] Noa and Gil Shahar were the only of my informant families to regularly use the term *shtaḥim* to refer to settlements in the occupied territories. Most others not only tried to dodge the contentiousness of their residential space but also rarely mentioned their proximity to Palestinian towns.

The families I lived with resided within a few miles of Palestinian homes, close enough to glimpse everyday activity, and yet personal interaction was scarce.[24] In Arad, for example, the only contact Naomi Bergmann had with Palestinians was with the Israeli Bedouin she hired for small construction jobs. "Last month," she told me once, "we had an encounter with Arabs because the builders of the porch were Arab. . . . They worked well . . . I gave them water and coffee and cold drinks. But all the time the house was closed." Naomi's contact with "Arabs" was a strict business agreement and her description made clear that she was the one to set its terms: She offered them coffee, and she maintained social and physical borders by keeping the house closed to them—as much an expression of her desire for control as it was of her mistrust. The Maimons lived across the valley from Shu'afat, a Palestinian neighborhood in Jerusalem that Israel occupied after 1967. Residents of Shu'afat, some holding Israeli citizenship and others only permanent residency status, frequented the supermarket, bank, and post office down the street from the Maimons. From the Maimons' living room, the family could see Shu'afat's minarets and hear its multiple *muezzin* and made periodic comments, excitedly or with irritation, about wedding noises drifting across the valley. And yet aside from these passing comments, Palestinian inhabitants of Shu'afat never came closer to the Maimons' lives than a view from their window. It was similar for the Kashanis, who lived not far east of Shu'afat and adjacent to 'Anata, a Palestinian town in the West Bank. Their daughters' playground sat almost directly beneath a row of 'Anata homes, and their young girls possessed a banal acquaintance with these neighbors' daily life. Once, while walking to the park, we heard the *muezzin* from 'Anata; Sheri's five-year-old daughter Nava said to me matter-of-factly, "The Arabs are praying." When we heard fireworks from 'Anata, three-year-old Hadar said, "The Arabs are getting married." To the young girls, Palestinians were their prayers and marriages. To the parents, their Palestinian neighbors were largely a source of irritation and a symbol of danger, even as they were effectively excluded from their line of sight. Signs of security, such as fences and walls, as we will see in the next chapter, were more blatant components of Israeli Jews' field of vision than the Palestinian population.

Chapter Two

Senses of Security: Rebuilding Café Hillel

At 7:30 on a September morning in 2003, a middle-aged man wearing red shorts and sport sandals stood across the street from the popular Café Hillel in the German Colony, an upscale Jewish neighborhood in West Jerusalem. His head turned downward, he was reading the cover article of the daily newspaper *Ma'ariv*, which described the previous night's suicide bombing of this very café by a Palestinian militant. The article's large color photograph reflected the shattered storefront he now stood opposite. In the image and before him, the café's sign had been swept off and a blown-out roof left only a dangling black awning. Beside the man, two middle-aged women each holding a dog on a leash stood quietly facing the shell of the café from across the narrow but busy city street as they scrutinized the remains. These women soon joined three others leaning against a stone wall. As they gazed in horror, concern, and curiosity, the bystanders' very scrutiny of the scene became part of the spectacle of the bombing.

The five women debated the order of the previous night's events, exchanging hearsay and speaking as secondhand witnesses. "I heard that the bomber tried to get into Pizza Meter next door," said one, "but the security guard blocked his entry, so he moved on to Café Hillel." A second added what she had learned: "The security guard at Café Hillel tried to prevent the bomber from entering the café but was killed in the explosion." A third woman reminded the others that the street is called Emek Refa'im, "Valley of Ghosts." The street's biblical name, she implied, had augured the calamity. A mother in the group focused on the seemingly mundane details that undergirded disaster: "It was a loud explosion, but

Figure 1. Onlookers across the street from Café Hillel the morning after the bombing.

it wasn't very big. See, the bottles on the [café's] bar are still standing! My kids did not even wake up. Did yours?" She saw her children's unbroken slumber as an indication of the bombing's relatively diminutive scale, her minimization of the explosion exemplifying what Stanley Cohen calls, in his study of indifference and denial, a "dulled routinization" (Cohen 2001: 82). Reacting as if nothing had changed, or unconsciously protecting her own emotions, she readily normalized the disaster. These women were able to place the ordinary things of life, such as dogs and children, alongside a newly disjointed reality without deflating daily life itself, maintaining seemingly "orderly surfaces that deny fragmentation" (Mertz 2002: 378 n. 26).

Able to speak of the attack with facility and ease, the bystanders became, as Allen Feldman did when he studied the militarized Belfast of the 1980s, "ensnared by a dialogical nexus where acts of violence had an everyday coherence and banality" (2003: 59). With numerous Palestinian suicide bombings in recent years and with marked investments of state resources and emotional energy into vigilance for Palestinian violence, when a bombing did occur, people found themselves making sense even of a sudden and dire tragedy. In the logic of daily security, bombings seemed to corroborate suspicion and substantiate hyperalertness.

Only hours before this morning assembly, the café had been a scene of chaos. At 11:30 P.M. on September 9, 2003, a Palestinian militant linked to the East Jerusalem-based Hamas group exploded himself at the entrance to Café Hillel. The large Starbucks-like café, with bold, eye-catching menu boards, trendy baristas, and vegetarian sandwiches, had opened that summer, the third branch of a successful Jerusalem chain. The bombing struck to the core of Israeli fury and fear, not only because of the ten deaths and many injuries but also because it targeted a residential area away from the city center that people saw as impervious to bombings. The suicide bombing, attributed to Hamas, came during a crumbling of the peace process. Palestinian Prime Minister Mahmoud Abbas had resigned amid a power struggle with Yasser Arafat, creating an upsurge of Palestinian violence, and Israel's hunt for Hamas leaders entailed numerous deaths, injuries, and intensified restrictions on Palestinian movement.

During the night, as soon as those killed and wounded in the bombing had been removed from the site, and even before the last ambulance siren faded, ultra-Orthodox volunteers from ZAKA, with heavy beards, large black yarmulkes, and orange fluorescent vests, searched for and removed remaining body parts strewn throughout the site. The male-only civilian organization ensured that Jewish death rites were observed by collecting and later identifying and matching every scattered piece of flesh and drop of blood.[1] Working alongside this civic religious presence were the municipal cleaning crews, who swept the window shards, hauled off splintered tables, and mopped puddles of blood. By morning, the remaining shell of the café was emptied of the fragments of disaster. Only small shards from the large glass windows that had formed the walls of the building were scattered amid the intermingled groups of rescue workers, municipal police, injured individuals, and onlookers. By the time the sun rose, the floors were clean and the tables were stacked. A peculiar kind of calm seemed to settle over the space, like the "uncanny silence" that Thomas Blom Hansen observed amid the Bombay riots (2001: 12). Though in ruins, the bombed Café Hillel was sanitized, as if a quick cleaning could prevent the bombing from becoming permanently etched into the civilian psyche.

By late morning, Emek Refa'im Street was lined with state and civilian personnel, each group "overcoming threats to disorder" in its own way (Mehta and Chatterji 2001: 234). Television vans with cameras and journalists with microphones had been stationed since daybreak. Bulldozers carried wreckage and police directed the mounting traffic. Three tall

Figure 2. Near the café, Israeli Border Police cluster around their jeeps.

soldiers in gray uniforms and two city police officers leaned on a parked police car, looking silently upward toward the café. Nearby, twelve male and female *magavnikim,* or "Border Police," the Israeli border gendarmerie, stood between two heavy military jeeps. They wore olive-green uniforms, rifles slung over their shoulders. The role of this military presence at the café that morning was unclear: they were neither clearing the area nor inspecting passersby, but their uniforms and conspicuous weaponry nonetheless invoked the power of state sovereignty. Although the nature of the state's authority was indistinct, performances of law and order still reified state power. As Jean and John Comaroff write in their reflection on images and perceptions of lawlessness in postcolonial South Africa, "So it is with the spectacle of policing, the staging of which strives to make actual, both to its subjects and to itself, the authorized face, and force, of the state—of a state, that is, whose legitimacy is far from unequivocal" (2004: 805). Indeed, even the quiet presence of the Israeli authorities simultaneously displayed and normalized the bombing. With a relaxed posture and muted conversation, they conveyed with uncanny reassurance that this had happened many times before and that they knew what to do. Despite its seeming passivity, the military presence enacted what Don Handelman calls in a description of Israeli emergency response the "state-owned and state-sponsored ways of remaking order from chaos" (2004: 12).[2]

And yet, attempts to reclaim order at this bomb scene and even efforts to embody the state were hardly the sole task of the state. Intimate practices also permeated the site that morning. Standing next to me and staring into the bombed space was a young woman wearing a white bandana and smoking a cigarette. Next to her was a male newspaper photographer, seemingly distracted in quiet solemnity. I was tied to the site in my own way. I had been at Café Hillel the night before, sitting at a small table by the entrance and near the security guard as I waited for a fellow student from my Hebrew class to arrive. When she did, we moved inside to a seat near the back, which was her preference. After finishing our coffees, I returned home and as I crawled into bed, I heard one ambulance siren, then another, and a third. There is an intifada aphorism that one siren signals a pregnant lady, two signals a heart attack, and three a suicide bombing. A quick check online at the *Ha'aretz* Web site confirmed that there had been a suicide bombing—at Café Hillel. I immediately called the friend I had just met; even without family in the country, there is the impulse to call. We spoke briefly, our "what if's felt redundant. My return to Café Hillel the next morning was as much cathartic as analytic.

The woman in the bandana, the photographer, and I stood for nearly an hour without speaking. The photographer snapped a picture every few minutes. I periodically made a note in my notebook. The woman continued to gaze and smoke. We were joined for a few moments by a middle-aged man who wore a yarmulke and carried a small prayer book, with which he prayed quietly to himself before joining us in our staring and then moving on. In this space of death, Jewish ritual was summoned and performed and Jewish objects, such as candles and prayer books, were mobilized. Two religious high school girls dressed in long denim skirts and sneakers approached next, each carrying a pocket prayer book and a cell phone, each object, presumably, a conduit for a different kind of communication. Mobile phones, in fact, dotted the landscape that day. Inside the café, an interior space even without walls, rotating groups of men spoke as much on their phones as with each other. Barking into the speaker, they negotiated with insurance companies and made plans for the rebuilding.[3] Several passersby arrived at the scene only to call a friend or relative to tell them they were here, and then moved on. Some took photographs with their cell phones. Others cried into their phones; words were superfluous.

While we stared and as the neighborhood woke up and began to go

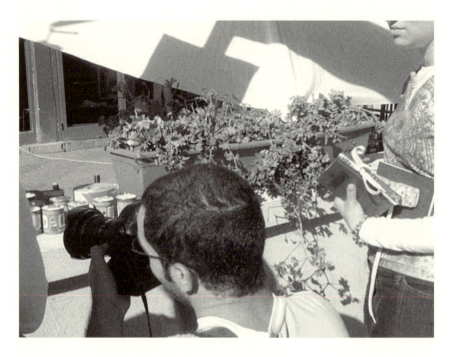

Figure 3. A newspaper photographer and a high school girl with a prayer book and cell phone look into the shell of the café.

to work and to school, the bombed site was first cordoned off and then enclosed. Heavy red plastic barriers replaced the red-and-white tape of the night's temporary cordons. Behind the barrier sat male and female security guards wearing fluorescent yellow vests emblazoned with the name of their security company and the label "Security and Guarding." By late morning, at least eight of these hired guards stood shaded by two large orange sun umbrellas advertising Straus, the ice-cream company. If the red barrier shielded daily life from a messy public space thrust into conflict, the guards, too, functioned as a kind of border. They buffered the bombed landscape with a human face that provided a security that was both commanding and compassionate.

While a range of civilian spaces had been targets of Palestinian bombings during the second intifada, Israeli Jews tended to see cafés as the primary index of Palestinian violence. This was because Israeli aspirations toward cosmopolitanism and secularism were embodied in the country's café culture, an ethos that selectively obscured the legacy of the Arab coffeehouse in favor of the European café (Stein 2002: 17). Bombed cafés thus stood as emblems of a precarious nation, symbols of the ways Palestinian violence transformed Israeli daily life, assaulted normative consumption, and threatened Jewish nationalism (Stein 2002). Thus when Israelis maintained that morning coffee and al fresco dining lay at the crux of conflict, they did so with little sarcasm. The normalization sought in cafés was as imperative as national order sought through pioneers' shovels or soldiers' guns. The idea of the normal has special resonance in Israel, a country where Jewish nationalism aimed to "normalize" the Jewish people and make them into a nation like other nations. During the second intifada, Israeli Jews in their twenties and thirties often conjured a different kind of normal, one that entailed veiling Zionism with a cosmopolitan busyness. The café culture somehow simultaneously signified this post-Zionist normal as well as the nationalist concept of Israel as a normal nation. It was not surprising, then, that the act of rebuilding and returning to a café after a bombing was, for many Israelis during the second intifada, a decisive act of normalization and perseverance.

Everything about the reconstruction of a building destroyed violently amid conflict is contested and fraught with meaning. Who does the rebuilding and where, whether it is rebuilt the same as before, whether there is an overt memorial plaque—all are open to question. Much of the literature on the rebuilding of structures ruined during war or conflict focuses on postconflict settings, contexts in which a victor has often been declared, large-scale relief work has begun, and national narratives have begun to coalesce. Nicholas Saunders's study of the meaning contained in the landscape of the World War II Western Front, for example, shows that some landscapes of conflict are deliberately maintained in a state of destruction to serve as a testament to past aggression (2001: 42). In contrast, in the case of Israeli establishments destroyed by Palestinian bombings during the second intifada, rebuilding occurred while conflict persisted. This endowed the reconstruction efforts with significance—as modes of retaliation more than forms of memorialization, as symbols of perseverance rather than closure. Rebuilding itself became a form of participation in the conflict, tied up with discourses of violence, notions of nationhood, and strategies of security. The Israeli public expected and the state ensured the expedient renovation of bombed sites. Every café or restaurant destroyed in a suicide bombing during the second intifada was rebuilt, often in the same location. Not only the fact of rebuilding but also the process of rebuilding became routinized, with a protocol shaped by responses to prior bombings and by discourses of perseverance and swift returns to "normal."

This chapter describes the rebuilding of Café Hillel and shows how discourses of security materialized in particular aesthetics. As the café was remade, its built forms were imbued with the politics of nationhood, and Israeli discourses of security generated their own explanations for the space's safety and danger.[4] Assertions of Israel's strength and well-being sedimented themselves in the café's walls and windows while its physical spaces and patrons' movements through them embodied concepts of Israeli sophistication and normality. My focus on the interplay between discourse and fortified architecture follows scholars of material culture who examine translations between cultural knowledge and materiality or, as Victor Buchli explains, "the terms by which discursive empirical reality is materialized and produced" (2002: 16). In describing the rhetoric, actors, and imaginaries involved in Café Hillel's rebuilding, this chapter introduces the ways security works in everyday life in Israel through personal rationalization, through symbols, and through cynicism, as much as through walls and certainty. Even when security takes the form of senses and signs, it generates Israeli identity and state authority.

The Public Space of a Bombing

Bombs attain a "shadowy, mysterious presence in the life of the city," as Vyjayanthi Rao states in his ethnographic history of the 1993 bombings in Bombay and, in their immediate aftermath, constitute a particular kind of public sphere (2007: 570). Sites of suicide bombings in Israel also became instantly mythical spaces where the nation viewed itself as under threat but able to endure, spaces where conflict was simultaneously reified and normalized. After its September bombing, Café Hillel reentered the public domain as a national, state, and religious site, a process mediated by artifacts, practices, and discourses of security.[5] The site was consecrated by religious practices, whether in the form of ZAKA's work or individual prayer, and by performances of security. Security introduced feelings of nationalism not through force or formal pronouncement but through subtle inflections of ritual and sociality.

Hired by Café Hillel from a private security company and directed by the Jerusalem police, six security guards lined the inside of Café Hillel's red barrier on the first morning of rebuilding. I asked one vested worker why there were so many guards. He explained, in a voice suggesting I should have already known, that bombed sites are immediately bolstered following an attack for fear that a second bombing will strike soon after. As I observed in the ensuing hours, however, the guards' role was not just preemptive; their function was undoubtedly social. The security guards kept the pedestrian public at a safe distance from the site to enable the clean-up crews and insurance appraisers to do their work. More than keeping danger and intrusion from the barricaded area, they worked to prevent the terror and tragedy from seeping into a busy Israeli workday. The guards were attentive to their own comportment and monitored that of their coworkers. Amid a mid-morning mix-up regarding the placement of the barrier, one guard commanded another: "Don't yell. Speak quietly," suggesting their attention to calm. The guards were conscientious about their role in projecting to the many passersby that the situation was under control and that official bodies were efficiently restoring order to the street and to daily life.

In many ways, the post-bombing scene exemplified what Baruch Kimmerling has called an "interrupted system" to describe how Israeli society can fluidly mobilize military and civilian domains during times of intensified conflict without allowing war to transgress the boundaries of ordinary life. Kimmerling focused on the sinuous transitions Israeli society is able to make between a "time of interference" and "routine time," although at the Café Hillel site, the emergency was so routinized that calamity could have easily been mistaken for routine (1985: 11). An hour after I arrived, workers surrounded the damaged café with a tall metal frame overlaid with light-blue wooden panels, which shielded the building from view. In the coming weeks, this wall, like the security guards, not only enclosed the café as it was rebuilt but enabled the bombed space to become fleetingly a nonplace, an ambivalent space temporarily removed from the realm of the familiar (Augé 1995: 78). As the café underwent restoration and reconstitution, it became a space out of time that pedestrians perceived only partially and in fractions, even as it was a public space fully entrenched in the ongoing political conflict.

The red barricades concealed but also drew attention to the disorder that morning. Bystanders congregated and security guards worked to move the mass of people across the street. By this point, the woman in the white bandana sat on the ground, her teary face in her hands. The photographer, worn out, leaned against a wall. I, emotionally exhausted, was in tears as well. The guard must have noticed the emotion of the three of us who had been there all morning, and when he cordoned off the site, he quietly let us remain behind the barricade. He seemed as attentive to our emotional needs as to the need for social order, or perhaps he recognized that those needs were inseparable. In this way, he acted like the Parisian Metro police that Patricia Paperman describes, who were experts in social emotion, discerning affect "in subtleties of social interaction" (2003: 399). The security that the private café guards provided when they calmly answered questions, when they erected barriers, and when they cordoned off people was a security more sensitive and considerably less tangible than one might expect from armed guards at the site of a Palestinian suicide bombing.

Figure 4. A woman from the neighborhood lights memorial candles.

Artifacts of memorialization immediately filled the site. In the hours after the bombing, almost as soon as bodies had been carried away, people began to fill the concrete railing adjacent to the café with traditional Jewish memorial (*yahrtzeit*) candles in blue tin holders. When candles blew out in the wind, new visitors rekindled their flames. Over the course of the next day, the entire wall overflowed with candles and discarded matches. Soon, the floor beneath the wall and, later, a table set up specially, was studded with more candles as well as with flowers, small notes, and prayer books left for others to use. The bombing space became not only highly charged but also sacralized. Soon, a large Israeli flag hoisted by neighborhood residents flew from the security guard stand. The blue-and-white flag fluttering in the wind seemed to avow that rebuilding was a national duty.

In the weeks of rebuilding, the assemblage of ad hoc memorial artifacts developed more permanence. The pale-blue wall concealing construction became a backdrop for traditional Jewish Israeli bereavement-announcements mounted by family members. Printed in stark black letters, they publicized the name of the deceased, provided information about the funeral and house of mourning, and sometimes contained an inscription or biblical verse. Large colored photographs and smaller black-and-white newspaper clippings were mounted on the wall. Soon, two small tables were set up to hold large floral wreaths, some with the names of national and international charitable and political organizations, and others with individuals' names handwritten on ribbons. These stood for days, until they withered and were replaced by new wreaths. Care for these mounted objects was the impromptu duty of the security

Figure 5. A security guard sits inside the red barricade, chatting with a passerby. On the temporary blue wall behind him hang memorial posters and floral wreaths.

guards, who hung up photographs given to them by visitors, taped on personal blessings, and kept the candles near the wreaths lit. These guards, employees of a security company contracted by Café Hillel and paid by the hour, were the custodians not only of the café and the crowds but also of a community's mourning. Their "security" was far reaching, sensitive to emotions, and visibly relational.

The Aesthetics of Security

With workers on ladders still adding final touches, Café Hillel reopened exactly one month after the bombing, the timing linked significantly to the end of *shloshim*, the traditional thirty-day Jewish mourning period. At a quiet but well-attended memorial ceremony, participants lit candles and a Jerusalem rabbi mounted a *mezuzah*, an entryway amulet containing passages from scripture. In the café the next morning, a steady trickle of patrons entered, resuming their routine, this time in a distinctively politicized space. As one customer explained to me that day, "You want to show some solidarity. Because you identify yourself with the place, with the losses. Because you're thinking about what happened there, about all the people that got killed and injured, about the people that you've read about in the papers." For some, sitting in the café now had a valence of patriotic defiance, seen as unwillingness to give in to Palestinian violence and its efforts to disrupt daily life.

As I observed time and again, people who entered the reopened café lingered by the doorway to survey the new space before proceeding to the counter. They scanned the entirety of the space, seeming to look as much from curiosity as from concern. Was the café rebuilt as before? Was it safer now? Many patrons ordered their coffee to take out, something considerably more common after the bombing. People who sat down with their coffee tended to sit along the back wall, a common safety-minded practice of positioning oneself as far as possible from the potential entry-point of a suicide bomber. Israelis sometimes used the term *omek estrategi*, "strategic depth," which in military terminology refers to the distance between the front lines and key inner population centers. In specifically Israeli military discourse, there is the idea that Israel must attack Palestinians first to ensure that military activities take place on enemy territory, something that Ariel Sharon long advocated. When the concept was transplanted to civilian urban space, the doorway to a downtown Jerusalem café becomes the buffer zone and the space outside that, enemy territory. There was always a combination of cynical humor and gravity when people used "strategic depth" to describe where they wanted to sit. They recognized the absurdity of their depiction of cafés as war zones, but they still really experienced public spaces as zones of lurking threat and everyday risk calculation. It was as Allen Feldman wrote about the polarity between the observer and the observed: "that relations of domination are spatially marked by the increase of perceptual (and thus social) distance from the body of the Other" (1994: 92).

Perhaps the gawking patrons noticed what I had observed: that the café appeared much the same as it had before the bombing. The newly rebuilt Café Hillel was fronted, as it had been before, with large plate-glass windows lined inside with a long wooden bar and a row of stools. Adjacent to the cashiers' counter, a glass display case of cakes and sandwiches still greeted patrons upon entering and small round tables still stood in the large indoor space. But what had been a large outdoor seating area was now enclosed like a greenhouse with tall glass windows. The enclosure seemed to stand as a shield against future bombings, yet with its planked wooden floors and a black cloth awning overhead, it retained an outdoor feel and did not revise the atmosphere of the café as a whole. Why was the café rebuilt so similarly to its pre-bombing form? One would have thought that the café's owners, not to mention its patrons, would want the café to feel more fortified, to be enclosed in brick, perhaps, instead of defenseless glass. But the politics of rebuilding during conflict combined with the psychology of security to create a unique set of aesthetic values.

During the height of the second intifada, in 2002 and 2003, it was generally only venues with security guards that could attract enough patrons to remain open, but only successful venues were able to afford guards in the first place. Cafés and restaurants around the country were responsible for hiring and paying for their own security guards. Similarly, as systematic and state-driven as post-bombing reconstruction appeared, the owners of bombed commercial venues were largely accountable for the completion, though not the entire cost, of rebuilding. Although the state, generally in the form of the local municipal police, gave case-specific guidelines for rebuilding with increased fortification, the implementation of those guidelines and the course of the place's securitization was a collaborative process.

Six months after the bombing, I sat at a small table in Café Hillel with Itzhak, one of the managers of the branch. Itzhak began to work for the café with the opening of this branch; he had previously owned a fleet of taxicabs in Jerusalem. He was in his early forties and wore jeans and a black t-shirt. Having been overexposed in recent months to media questioning, Itzhak was not interested in small talk and allotted me only thirty minutes to interview him. I began by asking Itzhak how the rebuilding of the café was affected by the bombing, but he interjected before I even finished the question. "No, that is the point! The café looks the same as it was before, to give the impression that nothing happened. This is the motive everywhere in Israel. If we recreate it as it was, then we tell them [Palestinians, he meant] that you are not going to win with terror. We even put up the same pictures again, because this is what is good for the public." Itzhak underscored the purposeful architectural continuity between the pre- and post-bombed café structure, explaining that he and the other café managers consciously devised all details of the café's reconstruction, from picture frames to menus, to be exactly the same as they had been before the bombing. He privileged the emotive reasoning of his patrons: with spatial sameness favored over amplified fortification, he imagined they would feel confident a bombing would not happen again. Excessive fortification, Itzhak warned, could have elicited fear and foreboding. Itzhak was not interested merely in making his patrons comfortable. He attributed his desire to normalize space to an ideological logic he claimed all Israeli Jews shared. "We don't want to give in to terror," he said, reiterating an oft-cited assertion. Replicating the café's pre-bombing appearance was how, Itzhak maintained, Israeli Jews could convey to themselves and to Palestinians that they were resolute; they were too strong and determined to be thrown off course. To re-create space, for Itzhak, was to reassert Israeli national and economic confidence in that space.

Surely there were *some* changes in the new café, I asked as I pointed to the enclosed patio. Itzhak explained that just two weeks before the bombing, he and the two other café managers had, in fact, begun to develop plans to close the outdoor seating area for the winter. "All this was done exactly as our plans had shown before the suicide bombing occurred. Nothing changed because of the suicide bombing. I can say with an open heart that we will never let terror beat us. I will not put a concrete wall here instead of this glass pane. I will not block the view or close this open space." The manager persisted ever more resolutely to affirm architectural sameness, intermingling discourses of Israeli ascendancy over Palestinian "terror" with discussion of certain building materials. He suggested an inherent correlation between materiality and ideology: Concrete meant closed and, in turn, defeatist. Glass, in contrast, connoted open and thus patriotic, its candid vulnerability expressing confidence and resolve (even as the new shatterproof variety of glass offered concealed reassurance). With this, architecture became a moral discourse, embodying those very notions of power, perseverance, and protection that lie at the heart of conflict.

The idea that material continuity connoted national continuity played out similarly in the United States after September 11, 2001. Michael Sorkin, analyzing attempts to secure Washington, D.C., after the attacks, describes the bollards and benches around the city that doubled as covert barricades. Although they appeared benign and familiar, they allowed "an unaltered view of the world to abide on the surface, the elaborate stage machinery of deterrence artfully hidden from view" (2004: 259). In Israel as in the United States, the materiality of security was expected to conceal the conditions of its own creation. Places rebuilt in the name of security were supposed to reveal order while concealing the need for order.

Despite Itzhak's insistence that nothing had changed, there was an area of significant architectural adjustment that arose from a collaboration among the café, the police, and an architect from Tel Aviv whom Café Hillel had used previously. In the days after the bombing, Itzhak and the café's other managers met several times with representatives from the Jerusalem municipal police. The police, responsible for ensuring that renovated buildings meet basic safety requirements, stipulated that the rebuilt café eliminate the side entry and have only one door to serve as both entrance and exit to enable guards' closer monitoring of patrons' coming and going. The café's managers themselves decided that entering should become more layered and guarded than before. In Israel, the progressive layering of security is not unique to bombed cafés. Tiers of gates, fences, barricades, and pathways form the entrance to bus terminals, malls, and schools throughout the country. At Café Hillel, the entryway was repositioned to place seating at a greater remove from the door, lest a bomber detonate immediately, and the architect designed an outdoor entry that progressed from gate to fence to door. This allowed a security guard, stationed by a gate, to inspect each patron, swing open

Figure 6. On the morning of the reopening, a guard with his metal detector wand is stationed beside the ornate, layered entrance.

the gate with an electronic release, and only then allow customers to walk along a fence and through a glass door.

Café Hillel's new entrance imparted an air of distinction, and not just defense, with an elaborate ironwork gate and bronzine planters filled with low shrubs that matched planters on the café's side patio. This design was installed simultaneously at Café Hillel's other branches in order to create uniformity, as Izhak put it, among the venues. Teresa Caldeira has used the notion of "an aesthetic of security" in her study of privatized, fortified, residential enclaves in São Paulo to describe how security elements such as fences and walls make statements about status and class at the same time that they work to segregate and protect (2000: 291). The ornamentation of Café Hillel's entrance, which exceeded the augmented fortification stipulated by the Jerusalem police, attested to the managers' prioritizing of aesthetics as tantamount to and indeed part and parcel of physical protection.

There were Israeli architects who attended specifically to this concern. Zalman Enav, for example, was president of the Tel Aviv-based Enav Planning Group. Having already worked on projects for Israel's military, Enav formed a subsidiary firm during the second intifada called S+A+F+E, standing for Security + Architecture + Foreplanning + Engineering. The company, a regular consultant to the IDF, sought to draw on architectural design and engineering services for the sake of security and counterterrorism. According to the firm, the projects of S+A+F+E integrated "urban planning, landscaping, architecture, civil engineering and anti-terror techniques to formulate a complete public safety solution."[6] Following the Palestinian bombing of the Park Hotel in Netanya in March 2002, where thirty people were killed and more than sixty wounded, Enav reflected on how architecture might be used to minimize the casualties of a bombing. "Cafés today have their windows all the way down to the ground and then they put the tables next to the glass. . . . If somebody blows himself up outside the café, then the glass hits the customers' legs and lower body. If the window began 70 centimeters from the ground, it would protect the lower body" (Winer 2003). Interested in protective design, he sought absorbent materials and "protective partitions" for restaurants and other buildings that could shield patrons from flying debris. Although Enav wanted to mobilize design to prevent injuries from bombings, he also acknowledged that excessive buttressing has its faults. "Nobody wants to sit in a bunker; they want to sit in a restaurant. They need the sense of security as well as a friendly environment" (Winer 2003).

Indeed, it was this "sense of security" that guided Café Hillel's renovation. Its new entrance, as Itzhak described it, offered a sense of security without placing patrons in the trenches. The extended threshold combined human and architectural buffers to ensure passing patrons that the café had improved its security. At the same time, the visual appeal of the ornamental gating reassured in a different way, confirming that the café had not turned into a garrison. The architecture of the rebuilt café thus embodied particularly Israeli conceptions of security. The combination of vulnerable glass windows and impervious steel gates conveyed that security is simultaneously fortification and normalization, a means to assert Jewish national power while concealing the very need for force.

Everyday Security Knowledge

In 2002, an exhibition and catalogue entitled *A Civilian Occupation* by Israeli architects Rafi Segal and Eyal Weizman (2003) was censored by the Israeli Association of United Architects for its criticism of the politics of Israeli architecture before it could represent Israel at the World Congress of the Union Internationale des Architectes (UIA) in Berlin. The public denouncement brought widespread attention to growing critiques and self-censoring from within the Israeli architectural community about the role of architecture and planning in the construction of national space (Cohen 2004). It was around the same time that, because of the upsurge of suicide bombings around the country, Israelis more generally became conversant in a different but related architectural politics, a focus on the role that built forms can play in symbolizing and enacting protection. If those making decisions about the new Café Hillel were attentive to the integration of security and design, those who sat in the café were equally conscious of an aesthetic of security. I encountered many Café Hillel patrons in the period after the bombing who were acutely focused on the correlation between the café's physical appearance and its safety.

Two days after the bombing of Café Hillel and only a few streets away, I sat with a woman named Rachel in the living room of her modern four-story home. She was a typical patron of Café Hillel, a fifty-five-year-old woman born in the United States who moved to Israel in 1968; she was a social worker and mother of three who had lived in downtown Jerusalem for thirty-five years. Rachel's home had a private, gated entrance, and, as we sipped herbal tea, I felt we could not have been more cocooned. Nevertheless, Rachel spoke frenetically in English: "I wonder if Aroma [a café near and similar to Café Hillel] is going to do something about their security. Because right now it is glass. And I wonder if they are rethinking their security arrangements. Does that other one also have a glass front? Oh, no, it's metal. Maybe because it's newer and they were already thinking about that in the design." Not only was Rachel keenly aware of the materiality of Jerusalem cafés, but she confidently entered the mind of a café architect assessing the correlation of substance, psychology, and security. Like the architect of S+A+F+E, Rachel posited a direct correlation between glass and its susceptibility to suicide bombings, and between metal and its armor-like quality. She also revealed an underlying sensitivity to business strategy as she suggested, like Itzhak, that the signs of security conveyed through built form had marketing value. She was aware as she went about her day that public spaces should appear and feel and not just be secure.

Several days later, I sat with another woman, Dina, across town on the balcony of her apartment. In her sixties, she was a writer and a mother of three. Thinking of Rachel's fixation on the materiality of security, I steered our conversation toward local cafés, and Dina quickly took the lead. She analyzed Café Hillel's security by envisaging the space from the perspective of an imagined suicide bomber. "One of the problems with the Hillel restaurant," she said, "is that it's right off the street, so if he [a suicide bomber] comes and rushes in, you don't have time." Dina spoke in shorthand to convey the role that ample distance plays in keeping café patrons away from potential bombers and giving them time to evacuate. Dina's ideas about secure space tumbled out; she was confident and her ideas were remarkably similar to Rachel's: "It is logical that if there's enough space between street and the place where people sit, and their guard checks you with enough space, then the people inside are safe. . . . For instance, there's a restaurant [in Jerusalem] that we go to often . . . because it's convenient and it's pleasant to sit in the garden or in the old building. . . . There I feel quite safe because it's an old house, with a big fence around." Dina's reference to "enough space" was a common way of stressing the importance of sitting at a remove from the entrance to a public space. In addition to wanting distance from potential explosives, Israelis such as Dina sought real and perceptual separation from the Palestinians whom she imagined to be lingering at the portal.

Rachel and Dina were mindful of the ways space is bisected and bound. Not only could they articulate what a secure space should, in their mind, look like, but they also possessed, like Itzhak and Enav, a particular "aesthetic" of security.[7] We could delineate this aesthetic: It included layered entrances, cafés set back from the street, and seating at a remove from the entrance. It featured stone and metal but accommodated, or sometimes preferred glass; it deemed distance a kind of barrier in itself. The ways Rachel and Dina spoke about security was so well versed, so easily and thoroughly articulated, that it assumed a degree of expertise. This acute attention to safe aesthetics is a form of everyday security thinking. Everyday security thinking turned the abstract notion of security and the elusive and illusive concept of personal safety into material forms and spatial strategies that could be touched and identified, like the "observable empirical facts," which, in Nadia Abu El-Haj's analysis, Israeli archaeology provides for Jewish nationalism (2001: 129). So routinized was Rachel and Dina's attention to security that personal experiences and perceptions of safety blurred seamlessly with state-like ways of assessing threat. Almost any thought they had about public space involved imaginaries of Palestinians or Palestinian suicide bombers. It was what Michael Taussig describes as "the apparent normality of the abnormal created by the state of emergency" (2004: 270). Individuals' everyday security thinking and seeing were an integral part of the larger political apparatus of security in Israel.

Where Is the State? Accounting for Security

An authoritative air prevailed at Café Hillel during the month of renovation. Uniformed guards, layers of fences, and still-lingering police and military vehicles lent a palpable sense of state surveillance and sovereignty. When one got closer, however, to chat with a guard or to examine building decisions, this "stateness" (Blom Hansen and Stepputat 2001: 9) was more indeterminate. Private guards and café employees were clearly running the operation: erecting barriers and inviting or excluding patrons. Although the state (in the form of conflict and discourses of security) created the context for security companies to do their work, as it had for the Hashmira company described in Chapter 1, private security guards were constantly generating their own material presence and their own explanations for their work. I wondered as I watched security guards at Café Hillel, day after day, answering the questions of probing pedestrians: was the state creating these forms of security, or was security creating the state? Did the distinction even matter to anyone? Just as the state is a set of "distant and impersonal ideas as well as localized and personified institutions" (Blom Hansen and Stepputat 2001: 5), so too is security an unbounded entity constantly created and reified through everyday practices.

At Café Hillel, it was not "the state," certainly not in any bounded sense, that generated belief in national order.[8] In their study of biosecurity, Stephen J. Collier, Andrew Lakoff, and Paul Rabinow assert that to understand the process by which danger is turned into calculable "risk," one must adopt "an approach that distinguishes among the specific roles played by technical experts, political figures, moral authorities and 'big thinking' forecasters" (2004: 5). In the context of reasserting security at Café Hillel after the bombing, however, it was difficult to differentiate between categories of actors, difficult to determine who the security experts were. The café managers acted as much like "technical experts" as did the municipal police. The families of those killed in the bombing were presumably as qualified as the Jerusalem Municipality to be "moral authorities" when debating whether there would be a plaque memorializing the victims of the bombing. Where architecture was so thoroughly ideological, even an architect from Tel Aviv can be a "political figure." Security expertise and state authority transgressed, as Helga Nowotny puts it in her theorization of distributed expertise, the "boundaries between specialized knowledge" (2003: 152). In what follows, I describe a dispute between the café and the city of Jerusalem over whether "security" justified private claims to public place. Who was accountable for security in the public domain and what were the physical and legal boundaries between "public" and "private" space? Although a range of individuals enacted discourses of state security, the security they perform ultimately swelled larger than the state.

Building hurriedly after the bombing, Café Hillel enclosed its large outdoor seating area without gaining written permission from the Jerusalem Municipality, effectively placing a glassed-in patio on city-owned sidewalk space with no purchase or review. The café was able to accomplish this because, as had been the practice in Jerusalem following bombings in recent years, the city sped up the approval process for necessary reconstruction and suspended its otherwise strict building codes. Not just Café Hillel but also a host of other bombed and rebuilt restaurants, cafés, markets, and malls circumvented municipal property laws in the name of security. Although some business owners criticized a government that

Figure 7. Café Hillel's new glassed-in seating and fenced patio.

expected them to provide their own security guard and thus to assume the economic burden of national security, others resented the freedom that "security" gave their competitors, paradoxical as it was. When a tapas bar in downtown Jerusalem erected a fence around its outdoor tables in 2002, the city did not dispute the enclosure because, as the owner said, "they knew we needed it for security reasons" (*Kol Ha-Zman* 2004). The city took pride in its allowances for security. As Deputy Mayor of Jerusalem Yigal Amedi stated in October 2004, "We were the first municipality in the country to allow places to close off their seating areas on the street. This closure makes those sitting inside feel safe, and also lets businesses set up a few more tables to make money" (Lis 2004). In the name of security, the municipality allowed businesses to appropriate state-owned land for commercial use, which it saw as a way to quickly raise morale as well as capital.

As the years of the intifada waned, however, the Jerusalem Municipality became less sympathetic toward struggling cafés and anxious customers. When the rebuilt Café Hillel had been open a month, the Jerusalem Municipality censured its owners for building on city land, alleging that the café enlarged its commercial space at the expense of public space. According to local news reports, city officials accused the café of taking advantage of the municipality's sympathy. The case was never straightforward, as the café had, in fact, operated its outdoor seating area without the requisite business permits even before the bombing. Nonetheless, the municipality promptly fined Café Hillel for its illegal land use and required that the café apply for building permits *post factum*. Apparently, the café's claim to be rebuilding in the name of security did not justify a right to state space. The local Jerusalem paper *Kol ha-Ir* reported on this local scandal in an article provocatively entitled "Hillel Kovea Uvda ba-Shetaḥ," or "Hillel Is Setting Facts on the Ground" (S'idov 2003). The notion of "facts on the ground" refers to the Jewish nationalist ideology wherein the act of settlement reaffirms Jewish historical presence in Israel/Palestine and actualizes Jewish political power. The phrase is often used critically to describe how the state and Jewish settlers appropriate land in the West Bank and establish illegal settlements in Palestinian territory. Abu El-Haj's ethnography of Jewish archaeology in Palestine depicts excavation as a form of conquest that establishes "facts on the ground that instantiate particular histories and historicities" (2001: 13). She depicts archaeology, not unlike more overt forms of Jewish settlement, as a nationalist means of permanently seizing land through naming, planning, and building. In describing Café Hillel as establishing facts on the ground, the newspaper likened the café to settlers making unlawful claim to land in the name of national security.

The contested process of building, enclosing, and securing Café Hillel made it difficult to discern who was responsible for creating an environment of security in the city. On the one hand, the Jerusalem Municipality was initially willing to lend space to private establishments for the sake of security, suggesting that security entails cooperation between all urban forces, private and state. On the other hand, the city's fines and building permits made the café financially and organizationally responsible to secure itself. The Jerusalem police may have established the contours of the new entrance, but a security company hired and paid for by the café guarded it. When it comes to security, the domains of responsibility are not fixed, its authorship surmounting and subsuming the boundaries of civic and state.

If security companies, savvy cafés, and hyperattentive individuals together enacted security by defining how space is used, by imposing meaning on securitized artifacts, and by taking responsibility for order, this is not to say that the state disappeared. When claims were made about architectural design or customer base, the state always lingered as an imagined authority. Itzhak saw himself as acting on behalf of the state, for example, when he asserted that he reinstalled glass windowpanes "because of terrorism against me and against the state." In the enclosure of the patio, it appeared at first that public or state space was turned into private space, but, in fact, the café entered the domain of the state all the more so through its instantiation of discourses of national power and fortification. Describing the everyday micropolitics of the postcolonial state, Thomas Blom Hansen and Finn Stepputat explain that the state is created from a range of localized and seemingly unofficial interfaces. In the dispute over Café Hillel's enclosed patio, the state was enacted through "localized political struggles" (2001: 9). As the café managers enclosed that space, imaginaries of national security prevailed; and as they rebuilt the café with a mind toward customer morale, they asserted the value of Israeli perseverance during the fight against terrorism.

Café, Not Checkpoint

Since 2000, a rotation of male and female plainclothes guards had stood in front of Café Hillel. They greeted patrons with a cheerful if perfunctory "hi" or "shalom" and then inspected them, peering into opened handbags and scanning pockets and bodies with a handheld magnetometer wand. When patrons said "hello" in response, guards would take note of people's accents, listening for any trace of Arabic accent, interpreted as a marker of threat. They would certainly not be correct in assuming correlation between accent and nationality because many Palestinians are Israeli citizens with accents comparable to those of Israeli Jews and many Israeli Jews are native Arabic speakers born in Middle Eastern countries.[9] Still, in their examination of bodies, the café's guards imitated military modes of surveillance, acting like soldiers at a checkpoint. Their presence was supposed to incite a moment of uncertainty—How will you be inspected? How will your identity be interpreted? Will you be let through?—and at the same time to instill a sense of order and well-being. The continuities between military checkpoints and cafés were also a matter of training, for with few exceptions Israeli security companies only hire men or women who have served in the IDF. The military training was also thought to vet for guards' professionalism, but this practice effectively excluded Arab Israelis, who are not allowed to serve in the IDF.[10]

Although former soldiers brought combat experience to public spaces, the entrance to the Jerusalem café was a world apart from the Palestinian experience at a checkpoint, a crossing so precarious that Palestinians had the saying "You were given a new life" for when they returned home safely after passing through a checkpoint (Abdulhadi 2003: 93). At a café, a place where there is what Begoña Aretxaga describes as "uncertainty about the outcome of the encounter" (2003: 399), risk and insecurity are alluded to but are not present to the extent that they are at checkpoints. At the café, violence existed in the form of a fantasy, a potential that is rarely realized. Guards were alert for Palestinians, but patrons were never treated as "others" and their privacy was not threatened. In fact, security guards themselves were aware of stark experiential and symbolic differences between their role at a checkpoint and their role at a café. The difference was not a matter of "private" versus "state" security, here immaterial categories, but rather whether an Israeli guard experiences the space as one of "self" or "other," "inside" or "outside."

Shai, the younger son of Naomi and Arieh Bergmann, worked at the Qalandia checkpoint between Jerusalem and Ramallah, where southbound Palestinians needed to carry Jerusalem IDs and holders of Palestinian Authority IDs could pass without special permits. He was in the last year of his military service when I talked with him in Arad in March 2004, during one of his weekend visits home. To save money for post-army travel, Shai planned to work as a security guard in Arad or Beer Sheva that summer after he completed his military service. I asked Shai if he thought he would draw on his army experience in his work as a security guard. "No," he said. "There's no connection. They're totally different. There [at a checkpoint] you are surrounded by a different population, by Palestinians." He explained that if he sees a person at a checkpoint he suspects might be intending to explode himself, his role is to send him back away from the checkpoint. As he said it starkly, "Then if he blows up, other Palestinians will die, not me." Working in Jerusalem entails a concern for those he is inspecting. "If a terrorist goes to the mall and I'm the guard, I'm responsible to jump on him and deactivate the bomb, because it's in a Jewish population. Because it's my population, I think first about the citizens and only second about myself."

Even beyond a polarized concern for who gets killed, Shai was aware of the differences in mannerisms between the two spaces of inspection. At a checkpoint, in his estimation, soldiers are guarding the nation; he saw café security guarding, in contrast, as a service job. "In the army, even if it were an old [Palestinian] woman who approached me, I would tell her firmly to open her baskets and wait by the side until I get permission to let her pass. If I were working in a Jewish population, I wouldn't tell anyone what to do. Among [Israeli] citizens, you are giving a service. You have to be polite. You have to be nice. Or else they'll fire you!" Shai was right: café customers and owners expected guards to revise their disposition for the Jewish, urban, and capitalist context. It was crucial to Itzhak that security guards at Café Hillel be "pleasant and gentle." He wanted them to chat with people when they came in and even get to know them over time. Guards, he explained, should remain "mindful of the mood of the place" and know that patrons come to a café expecting "easy social interaction." At that time, guards had become the face of public eating establishments, so patrons and business owners alike expected guards, like waitstaff, to be hospitable. Aware of these expectations, security guards even exceeded the requisite affability. Whether flirtatious, sociable, or bored, guards would often, I observed, chat with regular customers—something patrons would either enjoy or bemoan. One university lecturer told me of the university's dining hall, "I always hope David is the guard." Indeed, as we approached the cafeteria, David not only greeted her warmly but, even more desirably, let her pass through inspection quickly. It was ease, after all, as much as safety, that people craved. Café entrances mimicked and alluded to military borders but they remained performative spaces offering fantasies of protection, safety, consumption, and normalization.

The cross-referencing between café and checkpoint enabled Israelis to envision checkpoints as humane and fluid points of entrance even as they surely were not. I asked Shai whether security guards' politesse reduced the protection that Israeli establishments could provide. "Of course it does," he said. "But in the end, you can't turn your nation into a military nation. Every entrance can't be a checkpoint, and you can't ask every citizen to strip and open his or her bags. It interferes with their human rights. You can't do that." Lacking political self-awareness, Shai privileged Israeli "human rights" to easily enter a café over human rights for Palestinians to freedom and dignity. Veena Das and Deborah Poole present the checkpoint as a metonym for the state and as a space where the state is encountered and produced; it is a place that unsettles "the security of identity and rights" (2004: 9).[11] Security at a café, in contrast, reaffirmed Israeli identity and rights. Sitting on a stool under a red sun umbrella, Café Hillel's guards exuded the authority of military expertise while instilling a sense of familiarity and normality. They did this even as they subtly reminded passersby that this is a state of exclusion, a state where there is "us" and "them" and where there is an "inside" and "outside" to the state just as there is to the café.

Security in Logos

In the shift from checkpoints to cafés, from soldiering to guarding, signs of security prevail over physical force. Café Hillel switched from one security company to another after the bombing. It was not that the managers held the previous guards responsible for the attack, but that the Jerusalem police advised them specifically to employ guards from Jerusalem's biggest private security company. Itzhak hired the company "because everyone knows that [the new guards] have a better reputation." It was not that their track record was better than any other large security company. The new guards, Itzhak affirmed, were not necessarily better trained or more attentive; they were not more likely to deter bombs in the future. But Itzhak felt that his café patrons would be reassured to see the company's ubiquitous and familiar name. The name of the security company was announced through its bold logo on guards' t-shirts and luminous yellow jackets. "Everyone knows that this is a very professional security company. They know the logo," as Itzhak put it.

When Itzhak referred to "everyone," he meant not only café patrons but also Palestinian suicide bombers. Whereas earlier Itzhak had been attentive to the psyche of his café patrons, now he imagined and described the tactics of a Palestinian bomber who, seeing the name of a security company known to have powerful guards, would be deterred even before attempting entry. "Terrorists choose their sites by observation," Itzhak told me. "They use their intelligence, and choose the location by how [the establishment] looks. They decide if it will be easy or hard to get in. They will talk to the guard to get a sense of whether he is professional or not." Itzhak presented security and bombing as occurring through a succession of "intersubjective gazing," as Adam Reed says in his study of sight and subjectivity in a Papua New Guinea prison, an "imagined reciprocity of gazes," where the hypothetical bomber is imagined as scrutinizing the competence of the guard and the guard is thought to be able to identify a bomber through scrutiny of patrons' features (1999: 50).

The company logo, even more than the guard's gun, was the sign and agent of deterrent power. Their fluorescent vests were, in Daniel Miller's words, "simultaneously the sign of what they can do and the means to do it" and in this sense, seemingly banal objects like security guards' clothing, sun umbrellas, and sunglasses were also artifacts of security (Miller 2005: 33; Kuchler 2005). As signs, guards work through their embodied reference to a larger body of sovereignty and protection, such as the state or the IDF. At the entrance to a café, the company logo signified repute, while the guards themselves indexed the more forceful military practices of checkpoint guards and military soldiers. Logos were vital for patrons' sense of safety in this space where security guards performed reassurance at least as much as deterrence. Guards, or their jackets, lured patrons from other cafés that did not have guards. (This was generally a matter of whether the establishment could afford a guard and whether the area was popularly considered a place that needed guarding.)

Guards were "investments in public appearance" and even "symbol[s] of status" (Caldeira 2000: 292). Like an attractive sign, an enticing menu board, or a sale poster, the guard's presence said to the passing public: "Come in here!" This is, in Setha Low's words, the "psychological lure of defended space" (2003b: 390). Literally, security was an object of consumption. Mark Neocleous argues in his critique of security as a political technology for liberal order-making that "the ideology of security has been governed as much by the process of capital accumulation as by state strategy against this or that enemy" (2007: 340). At Café Hillel, as at other similar establishments in Israel, security was as much a commodity as it was a state strategy. The value Itzhak placed on perseverance may have reflected a commitment to the state, but it was also an economic decision. Civilians' sense that order had been restored ensured that patrons would return to his café to order a latté or sit for a sandwich. Thus when the café manager asserted that architectural continuity is "good for the public," this was a multivalent "good," one simultaneously political, psychological, and economic.

"It's still a safe place," Itzhak said plainly as we stood up from our conversation, which had run longer than the time he had originally allotted. This simple statement conveyed overtly what he had been implicitly asserting all along in our discussion of architecture and terror, namely that the café and with it the state are still secure places, even after the bombing; the only difference is that patronage has become defiantly nationalistic. Security may have been less about corporeal protection than about a shared reading of signs, but convivial civilian gestures and eye-catching logos still conveyed the power and authority of the state. Private security guards infused the public domain with nationalist feelings in a way that even more blatant state agents could not. Guards' surveillant gestures and constant presence gave pedestrians and patrons the calming impression that the guards' role was purely protective, that security was about public safety and well-being. They let passersby see security as affable and uncomplicated rather than as an expression of a larger political system of expansion and rule. The guards themselves, however, were acutely aware of security's contradictions.

Cynical Security

By April 2004, Café Hillel had replaced the ornate bronze fence at its entrance with an expandable fence made of shiny steel, taller than the one before it and with an industrial feel. I eventually learned that the fence was changed at the demand of the Jerusalem Municipality, which had formed new guidelines for the securing of public places. The bronze fence that previously fortified Café Hillel was now classified as unsuitable, a household fence, and the new police-issued railing was thought to be more difficult to break through. As I inquired into the reason behind the fence's replacement, I learned more about how Israelis mock and dismiss security than I did about the ways the city dictates fortification.

At the café one morning, soon after the changing of the fences, I asked my waiter about the gate's replacement. He responded hastily but confidently. "The café rotates its fences with each season, and now it's spring," he said before moving to the next table. Whether teasing me, appeasing me, or being genuinely erroneous, the waiter spoke about the fence as an ornamental artifact, attributing its substitution to seasonal aesthetics. He did not directly deride my curiosity about the fence, but neither did he take me seriously as I dwelled on a facet of his daily landscape that he had ceased to notice or be concerned about.

I asked the same question of the security guard sitting outside the café on a barstool near the gate, wearing dark sunglasses and a black jacket. My question only seemed to annoy him. He retorted: "It doesn't matter. It's bullshit. It doesn't do anything," alluding to the futility of the fence or of security more generally. I then asked him what *is* effective, what *does* matter when it comes to protecting the café. Still with irritation and skepticism, he pointed upward: "Only *Allah, Elohim*," using the Arabic and Hebrew words for God, clearly more intent on debunking his current vocation than on declaring his faith in God. The guard not only wrote off the new ostensibly stronger fence as "bullshit" but also went on to doubt his own ability to prevent the entrance or detonation of a suicide bomber. As I stood next to the guard, he asserted that the new fence might be more robust, but "Still, it won't do anything." He shook his metal detector wand in the air. "I myself can't do anything. If a terrorist comes, what can I do? He can just push by me, blow himself up. . . . Anyway, a truck can come, park right here in front of the café, and blow itself up. And what could I do?" Echoing what Itzhak had told me weeks before, the guard stated bluntly: "There's no one who can protect you. Not me for you, not you for yourself. Only—" and he again pointed up to the sky, leaving open whether security remains, in his opinion, a matter of chance, fate, divine will, or diplomacy. Before returning to a growing line of customers, the guard concluded with the following: "Look, everything is about money," and he pointed to the fence, to his wand, to himself. "Security is only cover for the state."

As the guard waved his magnetometer wand in the air for ironic emphasis, he expressed his own powerlessness—despite his technologies, training, and authority—to prevent the café from being bombed or its patrons from being hurt. Not only did the guard suggest that his own work was inadequate, but indeed the entire institution of urban security, he argued, existed only for the sake of the economic prosperity of the café and the city. The state and the café, he claimed, present the paraphernalia of security as matters of immediate bodily protection, when they are in fact acts of consumption and deep social violence. His stance resonated with scholarly critiques such as Avram Bornstein's argument that Israeli security works less to defend the state than to protect the position of government officials. "Violence, especially at borders, worked to conjure the authorial power of the state" (2002a: 214, quoting Taussig 1992: 137–38). The café's security guard saw his own job, the artifacts he uses, and the security he ostensibly performed as "a front" for the state, meaning either (it was not clear) that security performs for the world Israeli Jews' fear of Palestinians or that security is compensation for the state's imposition on its own citizens.

The guard subverted the very institution he enacted every day and yet he not only continued to publicly perform security but in the process was clearly willing to stand every day as a symbol of state power. Following Slavoj Žižek's (1989) depiction of political subjects as conscious of false ideology, Yael Navaro-Yashin (2002) has proposed cynicism as a way of experiencing and perpetuating the political. She argues in her study of a culture of statism in Turkey that political subjects' cynicism may appear as a critique of state violence or power, but it is in fact the engine that permits statism to persist (2002: 159). Indeed, Israelis, like this Café Hillel guard, seemed to "know very well," in Zizek's term (1989: 29), that security technologies are not fail-safe. They knew that larger-scale acts of diplomacy had more significant influence on violence in urban space. And yet the guard's "critical consciousness" did not preclude his dogged enactment of security (Navaro-Yashin 2002: 180). He stood as an emblem of security, as if he didn't deem it ineffective, as if he weren't aware of its contradictions. Despite his cynicism about security's efficacy, he continued to practice it, crave it, and convey knowledge of it. Mockeries of security were hardly rare during the second intifada. In typical fashion, one columnist in the Jerusalem newspaper *Kol Ha-Ir* mocked a combination of security excess and inefficiency: "In order to get to [the clothing store] H&O, you have to pass the security check at the entrance to the mall, and then a check at the entrance to the store. If you need to use the bathroom, God forbid, you will need to pass another check. It doesn't end there" (Lansky 2004)

Daily security nonetheless retained presence and potency in Israeli life. In fact, these critiques seemed almost to bolster security's power. To Café Hillel's security guard, guarding appeared to sustain a fantasy of security's protectiveness, a "habitual performance," in Navaro-Yashin's definition of fantasy, "of everyday life practices that is done in full consciousness of their counterproductive (or self-destructive) quality" (2002: 162). Among Israelis, there was a constant performance of security "as if"—as if the guard could prevent another bombing, as if Itzhak could enter the psyche of a suicide bomber, as if Rachel in her living room had true knowledge of the correlations between architectural materials and bomb safety. These fantasies about security, far from illusions about daily life, came to regulate social reality (Navaro-Yashin 2002: 161). Even as charades of protection, they thrust security into the political domain.

In the rebuilding and reinhabiting of Café Hillel, everyday security experts did not rely solely on the physical efficacy of gates and guards. Security worked through symbols, aesthetics, feelings, and skepticism. A politics of safety and danger gained potency not only through its enunciation but also through imaginaries of safety and material practices of perseverance. Fantasies of security worked in tandem with security's tangible materiality to achieve senses of fortification and differentiation, normalization, and routine. Here, and as we will see throughout this book, Israelis erected walls and desired security even as they questioned security's efficacy. In oblique but potent ways, practices and discourses of security constantly created ideas about Israel and Israeliness. Rather than simply emerging from the state, security generated state power, and perhaps even exceeded the parameters of the state.

Chapter 3

Paḥad: Fear as Corporeal Politics

Fear in Israel was elusive but palpable, inexplicable but shared. Israeli Jews commonly assumed that Palestinians caused fear, that Israelis felt fear, and that suicide bombings reinvigorated the circulation of fear. People spoke about fear without a referent, expecting the listener to already comprehend their anxiety about Palestinians and their fear of bombings. The second intifada was not the first time that fear was an omnipresent trope that saturated political rhetoric, steered public opinion, and seemed to unite Israeli Jews through shared senses of physical and national threat. But fear's most recent incarnation was particularly pervasive. Israeli ideas about fear reinforced long-standing narratives of Jewish suffering, but fear also came to life as a tangible entity that flowed through public space, so seemingly conspicuous and ubiquitous that observers could apprehend it and depict it. Israeli Jews experienced Jerusalem, in particular, as a place of routinized fear where civilians homogeneously and consistently assimilated national fear. Government ministers formulated military operations as responses to national fear as often as television comedians mocked the country's anxieties. Fear was itself an object of journalistic reporting. Following the Palestinian bombing of a Jerusalem city bus en route to Hebrew University, a Jerusalem newspaper reported: "Look at how people internalize feelings of fear, and what relief you see on their faces when they get off the buses" (*Kol Ha-Ir* 2004). Fear was seen as an enveloping entity that came from outside individuals and encased them as bodies and as a collective.

Israeli Jews experienced fear as a pervasive cultural force, but fear was a more grave way of life for Palestinians living under Israeli occupation. Israeli military checkpoints instilled in Palestinians deep uncertainty about their ability to move and endure, and government curfews and the indeterminacy of Palestinians' legal status induced constant insecurity (Kelly 2006a: 106).[1] As genuinely afraid as Israeli Jews were of Palestinian bombings, laying claim to fear by depicting Israel as a fearful society and a dangerous setting also served as a veiled way of legitimizing the value and virtue of Israeli daily life as a political struggle. Fear was one of the masks (Ben-Ari 1989) Israelis wore to cope with the unease of their implication in the policing of Palestinians, to deal with unspoken guilt about Israel as an occupying power while still seeing themselves as members of a democratic society. Expressing fear was a means to diffuse discomfort about Israeli occupation without overtly acknowledging either the violence or their own moral quandary.

In recent years, much has been written about the ways fear, whether of natural disaster, environmental catastrophe, crime, foreigners, or terrorism, pervades social life and political agendas.[2] Scholarship on fear often depicts fear as a self-generating phenomenon with a force of its own. Zygmunt Bauman, for example, writes that "fear becomes self-propelling and self-intensifying; it acquires its own momentum and developmental logic and needs little attention and hardly any additional input to spread and grow—unstoppably" (2006: 132). Bauman's argument productively probes the social construction and cultural effects of popular anxieties, but the depiction of fear as self-propelling can tend to conceal the agency and political strategy behind fear as well as the daily work that goes into fear's perpetuation. Discourses of fear circulate and persist because they enter the crevices of people's daily lives and bodies and because emotion is transvalued to have political significance. This chapter first studies the manifestations of a discourse of fear in Israel that circulated in social life and assumed tangible and corporeal form in the public domain. This chapter then suggests that everyday engagement with fear in Israel did not simply reiterate national discourses. Even when political subjectivities were conditioned by Israeli notions of fear, and even when people consciously rallied fear to bind themselves to the state and nation, they also experienced fear in personal ways by ascribing it to particular spaces, places, and body parts. People wore fear on their bodies and in their gestures, and this very embodiment of a discourse of fear gave the public life of fear in Israel particular power and momentum.[3] The meanings Israelis ascribed to fear and the ways in which they attached it to their bodies were part and parcel of how they defined themselves as Israelis and commented on Israel's relationship with Palestinians.

Fear Embraced and Denied

One Sunday morning in December 2003, I rode along with Merav Bentsur in her white Peugeot while she showed me apartments in the Jerusalem residential neighborhoods of Rehavia, Baka, and the German Colony. Merav was a real-estate agent and I was posing as an interested client in the hope that her tour of local rentals would offer me insight into how Israelis represent and market urban space. Merav treated me like a foreigner who needed reassurance. The Jerusalem neighborhoods we traversed were friendly and tranquil, she assured me. "Look, children as young as six walk by themselves to the corner market. People often leave their apartment doors unlocked." People feel safe and at home here. Soon, our conversation turned, as it often did during my fieldwork, to the reason I was in Israel and to the topic of my research. Upon offering Merav a précis of my interest in security, she quickly substituted a saleswoman's white lies for more candid and personal revelations: "I grew up all my life in Jerusalem, in the city, but for the last three years, or four already, I'm afraid. My friends and I, we're afraid. No matter what, we're afraid."

Merav, in her early forties, was born in Jerusalem and now lived with her husband and two children in Tzur Hadassah, an Israeli suburb fifteen minutes west of Jerusalem. She told me about the stress of driving on "bypass roads" from her real estate office in Jerusalem to her home,[4] and impressed on me the magnitude of her fear in the city. "Let's say we're sitting in a coffee shop at night, you think: look it's so busy here, and it's crowded, and so easy to put a bomb here, with the windows, and you sit there and you're afraid. I once took a bus to Haifa and for two hours, I was petrified." Merav's anxieties filled the small space of her car. When she was offered the opportunity to portray her experience to an attentive foreigner, Merav's fear swiftly came to the fore. Her perspective had shifted, but Merav was still, in effect, making a promotion: she offered a rationalization of fear couched in patriotism. "Look, I love this country," she said. "I won't leave this country. But there's fear. I can't say it's comfortable living here."

Not all Israelis delved into the intensity of their fear. Some pointedly refused to do so, although this, in its own way, became a conversation precisely about fear. Several weeks before my drive with Merav, I had dinner in the Katamon apartment of Esther Shenhav, a physical therapist in her mid-sixties, and her husband Shimon, a retired linguist in his mid-seventies. After a meal of fish and salad, as we stood to stack dishes and clear the table, Shimon spoke to me, firmly, as if offering his conclusive perspective on my subject of study. "I can say one thing. We realize that there is always danger, but that doesn't mean we live with fear. I know that the [Israeli] newspapers claim some children have constant fear and so on. Not us. We know we have to be careful, and we know that it is always dangerous, but that's it. That is life." Speaking in the third person plural (it was not clear whether his proclamation was made on behalf of all Israelis or if he spoke just for himself and his wife, who in fact later divulged her own fears), Shimon refuted the sensationalist fears swelling in the Israeli media and underscored his belief in perseverance despite adversity. He looked down on those who wallow in fear even as he spoke for them, suggesting that fear is something one must recognize and then shake off. The intensity and confidence of his refutation of fear appeared to be an attempt to do this very shaking off.

As we moved to the living room for tea, Shimon turned to me and added, "I have no fears here [in Israel], only anger," referring to his enmity toward Palestinians. "Perhaps it is because I know that my people fight for me," he said, asserting his confidence in the IDF and its soldiers. Shimon, born in Czechoslovakia, survived the Holocaust, immigrated to Israel by himself in the 1950s, and served in the IDF. His grandsons were currently serving in the army. The more Shimon attempted to distance himself from fear, the more I sensed his fixation on it. It was not so much his anxiety about Palestinians or bombings as his concern that any expression of fear would signal—to me the researcher or perhaps to Palestinians—that the nation was weak.

I was well aware that my presence as a foreigner and an anthropologist may have incited Merav and Shimon to embellish their emotive state. Ethnographers' presence can always confound informants' emotion, and fear, particularly in contexts of conflict, is no exception. Kay Warren, studying Mayas after years of war and state repression in Guatemala, interrogated the effect of the anthropologist in contexts of political violence: "Does our presence as outsiders—no matter how familiar—cause people to shift to a politically ambiguous language or to exaggerate uncertainty?" (1998: 111). Avram Bornstein, studying Palestinian prisoners incarcerated by Israel during the first intifada, cautions against the power of ethnographic empathy when imagined international scrutiny is at play (2001: 550). In my presence, both Merav and Shimon indeed appeared to amplify their unease, perhaps imagining me as an embodiment of international scrutiny, aware that personal narratives of fear and its refutation would do a certain kind of political work. Shimon presented himself as he hoped I might perceive of the entire nation: stoic and indomitable. Merav depicted Israeli life as a noble struggle by affirming her devotion to Israel while depicting the obstacles of everyday life. By invoking fear, they designated an enemy, defined themselves in opposition to threatening others, and reinforced a narrative of Jewish Israeli suffering. Merav and Shimon harnessed fear to bind themselves to the state.

Despite Merav and Shimon's rather different perspectives on fear, they evinced comparable comfort in talking about it. Speaking easily and succinctly, they both displayed a certain connoisseurship of fear; they were familiar with the way fear moved through their minds and through public space. They seemed to know what fear was and what it meant, where it came from, and who had it. Once invoked, fear was already known. The pervasive fear that Linda Green describes in her study of Mayan Indian women's lives amid the totalizing violence of revolution was "invisible, indeterminate, and silent," hard to detect, and veiled (1999: 55). Fear in Israel, by contrast, appeared to be known in multiplying, concrete, and public ways. It was patent and observable, treated as a self-evident, circulating object. The intense coherence of Merav and Shimon's trope-like statements about fear was not a product of their sensitivity to emotion but a quality of the Israeli discourse itself. Israelis readily identified fear, easily invoked it, and readily situated themselves in relation to it, as if fear were a revered national treasure. The next two sections outline the antecedents and multiple guises of the contemporary Israeli discourse of fear.

The Reiteration of Fear

Israel's first prime minister, David Ben-Gurion, may have been paraphrasing Plato when, during his second term in office, he defined courage as "the knowledge of how to fear what ought to be feared and how not to fear what ought not to be feared," but his veneration of fear also expressed a sentiment at the core of Israeli national belief: that fear and senses of impending threat were formative experiences for the Jewish people and catalysts for the creation of a Jewish state; that fear is dynamic rather than destructive. Even before Israel became a state, Jewish leaders invoked historical events, from biblical stories of exile to the siege at Masada, to reinforce a collective memory of fear and suffering and to give meaning to new generations' experiences of victimhood.[5] The Holocaust, in particular, has served as a trope to express fear at the core of Jewish existence. Idith Zertal (2005) contends that national narratives conceptualized every war in Israel, from 1948 through the intifada, in terms of the Holocaust, using Hitler's extermination of the Jews as rallying points for military action and as metaphors for opposing states. The Holocaust stood as a prime symbol for Israeli vulnerability and isolation, a "moral justification," in Ronit Lentin's critique, "for the occupation and its excesses" that persists despite the strength of Israeli military power (2000: 145). As Avi Shlaim argues, as much as the Holocaust spurred Israeli Jews to seek safety and security, it also enabled them to ignore the fear they instilled in Palestinians and to overlook the magnitude of Palestinian suffering (2000: 423).

Anthropologists Michael Silverstein and Greg Urban (1996) use the term *entextualization* to describe how particular discourses remain continuously emblematic of a culture, even when they are only periodically performed, by being repeated and re-embedded. The Holocaust is so embedded in Israeli culture that present fear becomes, not like the past, but experienced *as* the past. During the second intifada, accounts of Holocaust suffering were used to explain, stand for, and foretell Palestinian violence.[6] In April 2005, between the Jewish holiday of Passover and the national celebration of Israel Independence Day, the nonprofit organization Mishpaḥa Eḥat (One Family), which assists "victims of terrorism in Israel," ran a pop-up ad on the Web site of the newspaper *Ha'aretz.* The advertisement conjured an ongoing cycle of Jewish suffering by juxtaposing iconic images of Passover, the Holocaust, and the current intifada. With the words "In every generation" the pop-up began by flashing a refrain of the Passover text. "They rise against us. To annihilate us." The ad referenced the oppressions of Jews by Pharaoh in Egypt, but the accompanying photo was of the Auschwitz concentration camp. In the final screens, a flash of images juxtaposed the shell of a Jerusalem bus destroyed in a suicide bombing with an Israeli flag. Equating the intifada with the Holocaust and blurring distinctions between Ancient Egyptians, Nazis, and Palestinians, the ad transposed and re-embedded multiple generations of fear. It aimed to make communal memories of past Jewish suffering relevant to Israelis in the present by fashioning the present as a reincarnation of a history of threat. When fear is not only a reaction to danger or consequence of conflict but the connective tissue of a society's memory, fear itself becomes a domain of political conflict.

A Discourse of Fear

Although belief in the tenuousness of Israeli existence conditioned Israeli depictions of looming danger during the second intifada, the discourse of fear also portrayed the contemporary Palestinian "threat" as unprecedented. There were three particularly distinctive expressions of this discourse. "Fear of terror" was constantly reified as a component of daily life, "Palestinian threat" and "security threat" were invoked to incite civilian fear, and "existential fear" encapsulated anxieties about the viability and longevity of a Jewish state. I elaborate upon these below.

The most common colloquial expression of fear during the second intifada was the phrase "fear of terror" (*paḥad mi-terror*). This referred specifically to people's fears of Palestinian suicide bombings, but it also came to refer to a condition that plagued Israelis. School trips were cancelled because of "fear of terror" and festivals were postponed or moved indoors because of "fear of terror". The notion of "fear of terror" was so familiar that it was considered to be quantifiable. In October 2000, Haifa University's National Security Studies Center launched the Index of National Resilience to monitor, in the words of the center, the ability of the Israeli population to cope with conflict. Notions of threat and of fear comprised the basic language of its surveys and also conditioned its interpretive logic. One poll conducted in April 2004 collected data on "fear of terror" by asking respondents to gauge their fear by responding to four descriptions of terror: "terror that will shake the foundations of the political system"; "terror that will harm me or my family"; "terror is a strategic threat to Israel's national security"; and "terror disrupts daily life in Israel." Results indicated that Israelis' level of fear was 75 percent overall, similar to the 80 percent at the start of the intifada in October 2000. The Index of National Resilience, whose very name seemed to forecast its research findings, reported that chronic civilian fear coexisted with a continued high level of trust in state institutions. It concluded that the nation, undeterred by Palestinian violence, is decidedly resilient, which referred to citizens' commitment to the state despite fear (Rudge 2004). Here, the presence of fear was a crucial factor in corroborating Israelis' patriotism. "Fear of terror" was a trope of political belief, a quantifiable political category through which citizens, consciously or not, were thought to express their commitment to the state. The very enunciation of fear was thought to make claims and do political work.

When Israel's political leaders recognized the country's "fear of terror," they were more likely to acknowledge its incisiveness rather than to placate it, more likely to underscore anxiety about Palestinian suicide bombings than to offer comfort. Prime Minister Ariel Sharon, addressing the Knesset in August 2002, commended all Israelis "who in spite of the worries and understandable fear, still continue our lives." Sharon's statement, like Shimon's stoic stance described earlier, exemplified a classic tension in national imagination between a narrative of persecution and the post-Holocaust ethic that "never again" shall Jews be powerless or defeated. The result was a positive configuration of fear, as in Ben-Gurion's adage decades earlier. Sharon appeared to establish his power as protector not by promising to ameliorate violence but by sympathizing with Israelis' fears. It was as if by recognizing fear, rather than eradicating it, the prime minister attested to his political authority. Acknowledging the nation's fear did political work. In recognizing civilian trepidation he distinguished an enemy and in observing a timid populace he justified an uncompromising Israeli government that deemed "security," from checkpoints to "targeted killing," necessary and unavoidable.

The Israeli discourse of fear treated "threat" not as an indication or a warning of possible danger but as an already extant menace. Politicians persistently invoked a range of looming political threats in addition to Palestinian terror, including the growing Arab birthrate (Morris 2004), missile attacks from Syria, and Iran's development of nuclear weapons. In 2003 Israel declared the elimination of any "Iranian nuclear threat" a top national priority. Iran denied Israel's right to exist, supported Hezbollah, and severed diplomatic and commercial ties to the country, but Israel saw Iran's nuclear potential as most menacing.[7] Iran's nuclear weapons program was not as advanced as Israel had feared, but in any case, in the early years of the second intifada it was not so much concern with nuclear capacity as less specific and all-encompassing "security threat" and "threat of terror" that contributed to public perceptions of Israel's vulnerability.[8] The Israeli media tended to use "Palestinian threat" and "security threat" interchangeably, speaking of "threat" without delineating the nature of that threat. For example, in an editorial in July 2005, Ari Shavit (2005) described Israel as "under threat" and "a threatened nation," as he argued that the Israeli-Palestinian conflict was generated by a Palestinian threat to Israel and not by Israeli occupation, and, furthermore, that Israelis accept the occupation because of their fears of threat and not because of any disregard for Palestinian fate. When Shavit spoke about "the threat," he presumed without specification that Palestinians are the referent source of danger.[9] Appeals such as this made "threat" appear not only ubiquitous but also inexorable, as if unprovoked threat was the landscape in which Israelis lived.

National narratives often framed threat to the state as "existential threats" to Jewish nationalism, and during the second intifada talk of "existential threat" and "existential fear" were especially pervasive. Anthropologist Don Handelman characterized existential fear as "the greatest of ongoing, pervasive fears among Israeli Jews—the terror that the State could cave in upon itself, either because of threat from without or because of weakness from within, or one leading to the other"(2004: 7). Poet Eliaz Cohen, who considers himself a religious Zionist, described his recently published book of poetry as an exploration of how "the current events [of the second intifada] have infused the individual Israeli Jew with existential terror at a level never experienced before" (Halkin 2004).[10] Trepidation about the demise of the Jewish state was not a trait only of the Right. Novelist David Grossman, who is a member of Israel's Leftist political party Meretz, asserted in an interview that the first two years of the second intifada created an Israeli population forever imagining their state's failure: "I think that everyone who lives here also lives the alternative that maybe Israel will cease to be. That's our nightmare. . . . What has happened here in the past two years is that suddenly the possibility that Israel will no longer exist has become concrete" (Shavit 2003).

Cohen and Grossman depicted fear of the demise of a Jewish body politic as a dread both visceral and instinctive, as a "nightmare" that "infused" individuals. This discourse of existential fear blurred the political and the emotional as well as the self and the state. Likewise in my conversation with the Jerusalem real estate agent, Merav extended her discussion of personal fear into a questioning of Israel's longevity: "I don't see Israel continuing for very long. The economic situation is getting worse, and the pressure that Israelis are under—it's crazy. It's crazy. You can't live like that for long." Merav superimposed fear for the state onto fear for herself; she transposed state survival onto personal survival. The discourse of existential fear bound concern for the state with unconscious anxiety and embodied angst in ways that made fear appear beyond politics, rather than deeply bound with an Israeli ethos of power and perseverance.

In some ways, fear in Israel worked in the way anthropologists writing in the 1980s described the social construction of emotion. They argued that affect is public and relational, that emotions are always "*our* emotions" (Lutz 1988: 71), "*in* and *about* social life" (Abu-Lughod and Lutz 1990: 11).[11] They wrote against an understanding of emotion as personal, subjective, selfish, or unknowable and instead treated emotion as communal and public, accessible and discernible. Setting this constructionist approach to the emotions apart from psychoanalytic approaches and denying an unconscious basis of emotions, their interests lay in the ways emotion words were reactions to and themselves social actions. In the mid-1990s, anthropologists began to suggest that this discursive approach to the emotions explained away rather than accounted for experience. They argued that studying emotion as culturally constructed obscures the inner states of affect and the ways emotion is expressive of the self and highlighted the unconscious life and the embodied nature of feeling. Emotions, according to John Leavitt, are "experiences learned and expressed in the body in social interaction" (1996: 526).[12] Indeed, fear in Israel was not only a function of discourse, public and political, but also had an interior life, felt in people's bodies. But this is not to say that fear was simply concurrently discursive and embodied. There were times when Israelis did not so easily tap into the public discourse of fear, times when they found it hard or inappropriate to describe their fear in ways that cleanly reiterate national narratives. In these cases, as we will see, recourse to relationships and to bodily feelings became alternate means of expressing a fear that hovers between the intimate and the discursive.

Embodied Fear

Fear of terror, fear of Palestinian threat, and existential fear were aspects of the Israeli discourse of fear that pervaded Israeli media airwaves and state rhetoric, but the fear people experienced in their daily lives was more veiled, its expressions more masked, and its manifestations more malleable than the enveloping rhetoric suggested. As many times as Israeli Jews like Merav presented their fear in a straightforward and succinct a manner, and as many times as people like Shimon carefully qualified fear to elevate Israeli nationalism, others recoiled from engaging with their own fear. Routinizing fear by obscuring it, as Green states, "allows people to live in a chronic state of fear behind a façade of normalcy, even while that terror permeates and shreds the social fabric" (1999: 60). Many Israelis I knew were intent on facilitating a sense of their lives' normalcy and tended to defer discussion of their emotions among friends and family.

Talk of fear did seep into mundane discussions of daily schedules, although I found that people were more likely to talk explicitly about fear with me than with their friends. After months of conversation with Noa Shahar about the intersecting strands of anxiety in her life, she mentioned that she does not usually talk about "these things" with her friends or family:

> These are things that I don't usually tell people because they're not doing research. Because they're such heavy conversations, and very unpleasant. But because it's for research I allow myself to talk about all these unpleasant things . . . There isn't one day I don't think about something like this. But I don't always want to start to talk about it, because sometimes it's just useless to talk about. What can you say? What will it change?

To Noa, who lived in Motza outside Jerusalem with her husband and son, airing anxieties felt ineffectual at a time when conflict felt endless and when her acquaintances, she sensed, shared the same worries. There was a self-censoring, not unlike the Delhi Sikhs studied by Joyce Pettigrew, for whom emotional displays of fear were "regarded as indulgent" (2000: 213). Talking about fear, Noa suggested, only ruptured the fantasies of normality so tenuously maintained. Although I avoided naming fear explicitly as a focus of my fieldwork, my presence as an outsider caused people to respond with an emotive appraisal of daily life enveloped in fear. To them, I was an unburdened listener without the same relentless fears and with a detached research interest in the subject.

Women were more likely to tell me about their fears, in part the result of the more intimate relations I naturally developed with women during my fieldwork and in part because of the lingering gendered typecast of Israeli men as stoic. On the one hand, the culture of machismo in Israel (Almog 2000) has been on the wane for decades and, as Edna Lomsky-Feder and Eyal Ben-Ari explain, Israeli society became more open to psychological language and therapeutic perspectives after 1973 as "combat reactions" became medicalized by the IDF (Lomsky-Feder and Ben-Ari 2010).[13] On the other hand, as Noa Shahar once explained to me as we sat on her front stoop, Israelis still tended to see fear during the second intifada as a gendered phenomenon. "Men talk about fear less," Noa told me, "because that's how men are educated, to talk about it less, to express their feelings less. Even nowadays, although we encourage them to express emotion, they still talk less about it." Her assessment commonly played out in other women's comparisons of their own emotions to their husbands'. The Maimons' oldest daughter said that she is "very, very aware of my fear, and engage in it," while her husband "is afraid, but he succeeds in putting it aside."

People often expressed anxieties about bombings through stories of parental concern.[14] One woman, a resident of a Tel Aviv suburb and the mother of two grown children, told me, "I am not afraid for myself, but when my daughter wants to meet with friends, I make sure she doesn't sit in a café that is on the sidewalk of a main street. I always check where they are going, and I interfere." She experienced parenthood as something that sanctioned fear and made expressions of fear more socially acceptable. This was one contemporary expression of the ways the nation has long enlisted Israeli women's bodies, or emotions, to serve the needs of the national body. Susan Kahn (2000), for example, describes how Israeli Jewish women's use of state reproductive initiatives implicates Holocaust discourses and Arab-Israeli demographic disputes.[15] Expressions of fear were also, to some extent, a way that mothers and, to a lesser extent, fathers bound themselves to the nation at this time.

When a culture of security is itself fueled by a trenchant belief that the nation is under threat, it is a challenge to write about Israelis' desires for protection and safety without reifying their fears of Palestinians and without perpetuating a discourse of Israeli victimhood. Objects of anxiety and foci of fortification need to be studied obliquely, without naming the emotions under scrutiny, reifying people's imaginaries of danger, or sanctioning their perceptions of threat. In the three individuals' expressions of fear that I describe below, fear emerges gradually out of conversations about other aspects of life and work. Despite streamlined narratives and political discourses of fear in Israel, in comfortable settings, in the context of long-term relationships, people narrated their experiences of fear in ways that were, if not divorced from discourses in the public domain, then not fully of them. Without full recourse to political rhetoric, their fear was embodied: a set of dispositions to activity, nonlinguistic ways of knowing and being. The emotion hovered between the corporeal and the discursive, not yet fully converted into or infused with national narratives of fear.

In Arad, I met with an urban planner to talk about recent building projects in the city. Roni Gavish was in her mid-thirties and had lived her entire life in Arad, where she had a large extended family. A discussion about Arad's distance from Jerusalem caused our conversation to digress, and Roni began to talk about how her unease had swelled since the beginning of the second intifada, which coincided with the birth of her first child. "There is fear (*paḥad*)," she said, speaking of her own emotion. She continued to speak, using different synonyms for fear to describe her emotion: "There is fear (*ḥashash*). Look, I have little girls. I used to go through East Jerusalem to the Western Wall or to hike freely. But, now, my daughters still have not been to Jerusalem. There is anxiety (*ḥarada*), and so I do not like to go to malls with them. It's a matter of safety." For Roni, fear was temporal as well as spatial. She distinguished between a time when she used to hike and travel to East Jerusalem or the Old City without restraint and the "now" in which she travels to malls or Jerusalem cautiously or not at all.

Roni used different words for fear to describe what seemed to be the same phenomenon and the same word for "fear" in different contexts, but the seeming interchangeability of the terms indicates less their equivalence than their nuanced semantic difference. The first term Roni used, *paḥad*, is akin to the English "fear" not just in terms of its connotations of apprehension and insecurity but also in terms of the frequency of use and its occurrence in noun, verb, and adjective forms: fear (*paḥad*), to fear (*lefaḥed*), afraid (*mefaḥed*), frightening (*mafḥid*). *Paḥad*, as opposed to *bitaḥon* (meaning security in a national or personal sense, or confidence), expresses both a tense anticipation of physical harm and, more abstractly, a sense that order and stability are being threatened. "There is fear (*ḥashash*)," Roni also said. The word *ḥashash*, more so than other fear-related words, is most likely to be translated "anxiety." In biblical Hebrew, the word *ḥashash* means simply to feel a sensation or feeling or the capacity of an individual to feel. In its contemporary usage, *ḥashash* tends to refer to private, personal affect rather than to social or political senses of threat. Roni also expressed her experience of *ḥarada*, a word derived from the biblical root *h-r-d*, referring to emotive movement such as trembling and shaking in the face of God. The modern term *ḥarada* generally conveys a fear of greater magnitude, but it can also express a particularly embodied fear.[16] In daily secular conversation, Israelis tended to shift as Roni did from one term for fear to the other, each expressing different facets—physical, intellectual, communal—of this emotion. This linguistic shifting was a manifestation of the simultaneity of different modes of fear in Israel, sometimes discursive and other times affective, private and public, personal and political.

In March 2004, Naomi Bergmann and I were sitting in the kitchen of her home in Arad, talking about the vacation time she has more of now that her sons are grown. She would love to visit the Czech Republic and Argentina, she said, and she had noticed some recent package travel deals on the Internet. After several moments of travel reverie, Naomi cut herself off: her fear of bombings, she acknowledged, has deterred her from traveling both within the country and abroad. She said: "I look in the newspaper, I say, 'Oh great, there's a nice place to travel to,' or 'There's a good deal!' But you always have here, here, the fear (*ha-ḥashash*)." As she spoke, she poked her index finger into different points on her forehead. She explained further: "It's all fear about a bombing (*ḥashash mi-pigu'a*). On the one hand, I am happy that I have many opportunities to travel. But every time we prepare to travel, I have—I need Arieh [her husband] to calm me down. Usually, it is enough for me to hear him say, 'It's okay, nothing will happen.' But my worry (*ha-de'aga etsli*) is simply—well, it is as if you have your skin, and then your clothes, and then there is another something. It's another layer we are wearing. The fear is just there. It is like there is another layer of skin." Naomi situated fear on her body in a number of ways, first pointing to spots on her forehead as places where she both locates and feels fear and then depicting her worry about bombings as an outer "layer of skin" that encases her flesh and presses in upon her. In experiencing fear as a layer of skin, Naomi sensed fear as a mediator between her body and the world. Constricting her body such that it became part of it, fear was a mode in which Naomi related through her body to the world. Far from an abstract concept, Naomi's fear was a physical and an intersubjective experience—a way of "comporting oneself towards objects and others" (Crossley 2001: 85)—as she depended on her husband Arieh to soothe her worries.

For Shlomit Maimon, fear was similarly somatic and intersubjective. As we walked one evening through her neighborhood of Ramat Eshkol, Shlomit spoke about her older son's army service in the early 1990s, which led her to reflect on the contingencies of her fear during the current period of conflict. "I don't feel preoccupied all the time with suicide bombings," she told me. "You can't always be afraid." Still, there were times that Shlomit felt fear, which she expressed this way: "If I need to go to a bustling place, like the mall, or if Ilan [her husband] goes to the outdoor market, then there's something in me that goes like this—" Still walking alongside me, Shlomit proceeded with her explanation using hand gestures. She made a wringing motion with both hands held in front of her stomach, conveying that she feels the worry of going into crowded places in her abdomen. She felt the same twisted stomach when she or her husband went to spaces she feared might be bombed, her fears for self and for an intimate other similarly embodied. What Shlomit said about her fear and the bodily way she expressed it were prompted by and entangled with each other. While speaking, she continued to wring her hands in front of her stomach. "I feel that until Ilan comes back home—. Well, I do worry." Linda Green notes in her study of Guatemala that "One cannot live in a constant state of alertness, and so the chaos one feels becomes diffused throughout the body" (1999: 60). In Israel, the emotion conditioned the way people carried themselves and encountered the world (Crossley 2001: 85). Shlomit's alertness and fear assumed a constant presence in the form of bodily feelings. Her fear of Palestinian bombings, like Naomi's, were deeply corporeal, binding her to her own body and expanding outward to bind her in a reciprocal relationship with her son or her husband.

Fear as a Corporeal Politics

Narratives of victimhood and of Palestinian threats sedimented themselves in Israeli Jews' gestures and habits, in their perceptions of place, and in their sensitivities to others. State discourses of fear were instantiated in people's perceptions such that what Israelis said about fear and their bodily feelings of fear were inextricably intertwined. Shlomit and Naomi relied on their bodies to depict their fears, and their inextricably relational fears were entwined with national discourses. When Naomi encapsulated her fear as a fear of bombings, she elided specific reference to Palestinians, in a manner common to the Israeli discourse of fear. She also spoke of fear as "just there," resonating with media reifications of fear as an object seemingly detached from the context and narratives that produce it, an artifact that sits and circulates in the Israeli environment. Shlomit's embodied fear also resonated with national discourses of fear. She prefaced her fear by upholding an ethic of resilience: "You can't always be afraid." Even embodied fear had a politics that concealed Palestinians and that was thought to circulate autonomously; a fear that was alternatively revealed and concealed, embraced and denied. Fear was a corporeal politics that many Israeli Jews carried in their bodies and their daily routines.

And yet, fear was not a mere construction of or by the nation-state that inevitably propagated state discourse. Shlomit's stomach did not feel twisted only because Israeli discourses of fear were inescapable; her stomach did not twist simply because she wanted to demonstrate the effects of Palestinian terror. Fear, this wringing in her stomach, was where Shlomit experienced the collision between her identity as an Israeli who wanted to defend her country and a mother who wanted to protect her son; it was where she negotiated the tension between her political commitment to perseverance and her deep concern for her husband. When Naomi engaged in and negotiated national narratives of fear through her body, biography, and psyche, she actively experienced and expressed emotion in ways distinct from those of Shlomit or Shimon. Each harnessed political discourse and rendered it intimate. Fear was thus not only a mode of attachment to the state but also a constantly negotiated form of connection to family. Within a corporeal politics, political and affective fears intersect, diverge, and realign.

Chapter 4
Embodying Suspicion

At 8 o'clock on a Thursday evening, wearing a reflective yellow Israel
Police vest, I and my fellow volunteer, thirty-five-year-old Aharon, set out
from the Rehavia neighborhood of Jerusalem on our weekly patrol as
members of the Civil Guard (ha-Mishmar ha-Ezraḥi), the national vol-
untary division of the Israel Police. As we entered the courtyard of the
Evelina de Rothschild School, I carried a flashlight and Aharon his Civil
Guard-issued World War II era carbine rifle. We walked the perimeter
of the school and turned the handle of each door to make sure they
were locked. I shone my flashlight into an alleyway and peered under a
garbage can lid, looking, as we had been directed, for bombs or items
out of place. We were dutifully alert for "suspicious objects" (ḥafatsim
ḥashudim)—objects, as I had recently been told and as Israeli-born Aharon had known since kindergarten, that were unfamiliar or incongruous,
whether weapons or ammunition or innocent items left behind. Aharon
gazed into the windows of the small booth that housed the school's security guard during the day, making sure that what was leaning against a
chair was really just a forgotten umbrella. As we inspected the last corner
of the basketball court, the police scanner in Aharon's vest pocket began
to crackle. It was Osnat, the officer in charge of our volunteer base, reporting that we should be alert for a "suspicious man" who had escaped
from the Jerusalem police, driving what they believed was a stolen white
Subaru. Without discussion with Osnat or each other as to what exactly
this suspicious individual might look like, Aharon and I promptly shifted
our vigilance from suspicious objects to a suspicious person (anashim
ḥashudim), and continued on our beat.

In daily life as in the Civil Guard, alertness for bodies bearing suspicious signs was not only a national discourse during the second intifada but also an everyday ontology, an Israeli mode of being in and moving through space. Israeli Jews internalized state profiles of "terrorists" and fear of Palestinians such that they felt they could trust their instinct to spot suspicion. On buses and sidewalks, pedestrians' state-like panopticism invested otherwise ordinary encounters with the urgency of emergency. A study of codified profiles of suicide bombers alone would miss the nuance, the gradations of emotion, and the ephemeral impressions that characterize everyday suspicion. This chapter studies how Israeli Jews embodied discourses of suspicion in their daily lives in ways that reproduced state notions of threatening others and conditioned everyday interactions, generally without ever encountering Palestinians or real danger. After providing a brief historical context for contemporary Israeli suspicion, I describe suspicion as enacted by Civil Guard volunteers, by a security guard in Arad, and by pedestrians in their daily lives. More than a means of assessing risk or apprehending militants, the discourse of suspicion dictated particular ways of seeing and being as an Israeli.

Objects of Suspicion

Israelis have long been expected to have a gaze as sharp as their sword. In his oft-cited May 1956 eulogy for an Israeli settler killed by Palestinians from Gaza, IDF chief of staff Moshe Dayan depicted Palestinians as targets to be defeated through scrutiny. "Let us not be afraid to perceive the enmity that consumes the lives of hundreds of thousands of Arabs around us. Let us not avert our gaze, for it will weaken our hands" (Kimmerling 2001: 208). Watchfulness was a patriotic stance, although it was not until after the 1967 war that the government turned civilian alertness for suspicion into a national campaign. When Israel's occupation incited routine Palestinian bombings in and around Jerusalem, police began to warn civilians to be alert for "suspicious objects," that is, for the backpacks or garbage cans or watermelons that could be concealing bombs (Segev 2007: 499). In response to Israel's seizure of Palestinian land in the 1973 Yom Kippur War, Palestinians perpetrated bombings in Israeli public spaces. In July 1975, for example, a refrigerator holding five kilograms of explosives exploded in Zion Square in Jerusalem and, in May 1976, a booby-trapped motor scooter exploded at the corner of Ben Yehuda and Hillel Streets in Jerusalem. The Israeli government stepped up its campaign for alertness, placing ads on bus station billboards and in the commercial spots before movies.

One of the most widely circulated and well-remembered service announcements was an advertisement disseminated in the 1980s by the Ministry of Education and Culture's office for emergency and safety. The one-minute spot opened in a schoolyard filled with children wearing gym shorts playing soccer. As cheery Israeli folk music plays in the background, one girl notices a plastic garbage bag tied to the fence. "Yaron, don't touch! It's a suspicious object," the children warn her as she runs toward it. The music suddenly stops, and an authoritative male voice tells the listeners what to do in case of a suspicious object: "Clear the area. Notify the police." The ad closes with two schoolchildren saying solemnly: "I know and you know that you are forbidden to touch a suspicious object. And also forbidden to approach it." Through public announcements such as this and parallel instruction in school, alertness for suspicious objects became embedded in Israeli society and consciousness. For Israeli children growing up in the decades after the 1967 war, looking for metal cylinders with wires sticking out or refraining from picking up discarded dolls, buttons, or pencils was a way they learned how to be good citizens.[1] Israeli Jews who grew up in this period tend to see alertness wistfully, rather than with fear. "Oh, what nostalgia!" people often exclaimed when I referred to Yaron in the Ministry of Education's service announcement. Suspicious objects entered memory more as a part of childhood akin to playgrounds or dolls than as a repressive government order.

The discourse of "suspicious people" was a later development.[2] In April 1993, a Hamas militant detonated the first Palestinian suicide bomb in a Volkswagen filled with propane tanks and explosives at the Meḥola Junction on the Jordan Valley Highway. As Palestinians targeted Israelis with car bombs and suicide bombings throughout the mid-1990s, the Israeli media began to talk about individuals "suspected" of being suicide bombers and urged the public to be alert to both suspicious objects and suspicious people. The phrase "anashim ḥashudim," however, did not refer exclusively to potential suicide bombers; it also denoted prospective criminals. It was not until the second intifada that "suspicious people" came to refer specifically to Palestinian suicide bombers. It is impossible to separate Israeli suspicion from global surveillance of personal data and movement, especially its extension and intensification after 9/11. "In the 'war against terrorism,' the net of suspicion is being cast far and wide," David Lyon said in his analysis of surveillance technologies and systems of racial profiling that proliferated and also became more secretive after the events of September 11 (2003: 1). In fact, the phrase "suspicious person" became truly rife in the Israeli media only in the wake of September 11, 2001. In 1998, for example, Israeli newspapers used the term "suspicious people" to describe those suspected of an organized crime murder plot. Even in February 2000, *Ha'aretz* referred to Hillary Clinton as a "suspicious person" (Rosner 2000); the paper called Rabin a "suspicious person" in October 2001 (Hannah 2001). By November 2001, however, the term had ceased almost entirely to be used for anything other than suspected "terrorists." Israeli newspapers began describing "suspicious people" noticed in settlements, "suspicious people" intercepted in villages, and "suspicious people" inspected by soldiers. But if local media was influenced by post-9/11 discourses and international stereotypes of Arab Muslims, the discourse in Israel took on the particular nuances of a culture absorbed with security and mistrustful of Palestinians.

Archives of Suspicion

Israelis saw their stance of suspicious vigilance as self-protective, but the discourse of suspicion also functioned as a uniquely Israeli euphemism, a code used to signify stereotypical traits of Palestinians without referring to them, a veiled way to portray their fears of Palestinians in the oblique language of security rather than in the overt language of discrimination. Constantly alert for signs and markers of bodily threat, Israelis tended to presuppose the danger of any Palestinian or "Arab-looking" individual in the street. They relied on internalized catalogs of ethnic or racial stereotypes to determine whether a person was Palestinian or Jewish, threatening or familiar. Israeli Jews' suspicion went beyond a self-protective strategy to become a code of Israeli social knowledge that delineated particular notions of "threat" and Palestinians.

Vigilant Israelis relied on a combination of government-issued attributes and their own elusive but long-honed intuition to be alert (*'erani*) for signs that might connote impending "terrorist activity." Lists of the physical traits and distinguishing mannerisms ostensibly characteristic of potential suicide bombers saturated newspapers and government Web sites alike. Pedestrians, the thinking seemed to be, would embrace the role of the "official gaze," always scanning bodies for signs "in an attempt to render them transparent, to extricate the secret opacity of its uncanny familiarity" (Aretxaga 2003: 404). On one user-friendly Web site of Israel's Home Front Command dedicated to civilian preparedness for both natural disasters and "terrorist attacks," a page titled "The Suspicious Person" depicted an imminent bomber through a bulleted list of attributes. "The suspect shows signs of emotion and irritation, or perspires excessively," the Web site offered.[3] It continued:

> The suspect shows signs of being in clandestine collaboration and contact with other people, directing signals and movements towards them. The suspect's appearance is unusual, does not suit his personality, or his clothes are not appropriate to the season (for example: wearing a heavy coat when it is

hot outside should arouse the observer's suspicion). The suspect gives the impression that he may be concealing a weapon in his clothing.

The media often conveyed specific appeals by the Home Front Command and the Israel Police for civilian alertness. In March 2004, for example, amid news of a seven-hour high-level alert for a suicide attack in the Tel Aviv area, *Ha'aretz* reported that city residents should "be especially vigilant and look out for suspicious persons or vehicles" (Singer 2004). The same day, *Ma'ariv* stated: "the public was asked to show heightened awareness and report all suspicious objects to the police" (Yamin-Wolvovitz and Shlaider 2003). Whether intended to rally civilian vigilance to preempt violence or circulate a sense of civilian empowerment, the actual intent and authority behind these messages was never fully clear. Still, the urgency in each of the uniform issuings presented civilian alertness as a stance necessary not only for national security and civilian safety but also for the survival of the State of Israel. As Dani Arditi said in 2004 as director of the Counterterrorism Bureau in Israel's National Security Council, "alertness of the public is a vital part of the war against terror" (O'Sullivan 2004). When government bodies and the media called on Israeli citizens to be alert for "suspicious people," a sense of national responsibility was contained within these directives.

The contemporary framing of suspicion in terms of threat and danger presented suspicion as a technology of security, as if it were itself a military strategy in the Israeli war against Palestinian suicide bombings. But suspicion also extended other Israeli practices of obscuring and eclipsing Palestinian life.[4] Oz Almog wrote that "The Arab was not described positively or negatively so much as he was shunted aside, sometimes virtually obliterated from consciousness" (2000: 194) to describe a view held by Jewish settlers in Palestine during the pre-state period, although his description held true during the second intifada as well. Few Israeli Jews had engaged contact with Palestinian citizens of Israel or Palestinian residents of the occupied territories after the beginning of the second intifada. In February 2004, political columnist Ari Shavit interviewed the Hebrew author Aharon Appelfeld in *Ha'aretz* about his new novel *Priha Pir'it* (Wild Blossoming) and his strained sense of belonging in Israel. Shavit asked, "What is your take on the story of the Jewish-Arab struggle?" Appelfeld answered, "I am not familiar with the Arabs. For me they are an abstraction. But I met [members of] Arab intelligentsia at Oxford and Harvard and at other universities" (Shavit 2004). The everyday reality for many Israelis was not far from the scholarly drama of Appelfeld's response. In Arad, as Naomi Bergmann's son Shai said to me once, "There are Bedouin in our area. But they aren't connected to us. They are with them, we [Israeli Jews] are with us." In lieu of regular, informal contexts for interface between Israeli Jews and Palestinians, in place of engaged or meaningful interaction, suspicion became one of the primary modes through which Israelis engaged with Palestinians in their daily lives.

Alertness for "suspicious people" felt, to many Israelis, like a private stance. Suspicion was so imprinted on individual subjectivities and bodily practices that people tended to experience vigilance not only as self-protective but also as personal and instinctive. Thus through suspicion, Israeli racism toward Palestinians was perpetuated as something personal, part of people's bodies, emotions, and selves. The danger Palestinian suicide bombings posed to Israelis was a real one, not illusory and not a construction. But inventories of suspicion were less a repository of the traits of suicide bombers than an "archive," as Ann Stoler uses the word in her study of colonial governance: "sites of the imaginary and institutions that fashioned histories as they concealed, revealed, and contradicted the investments of the state" (2008: 49). Publicly circulated imaginaries of suspicion did not necessarily correspond to the appearance of Palestinian militants, and people's everyday vigilance rarely deterred Palestinian bombers. Profiles and practices of suspicion were domains in which racial categories were created and assigned even as they were contradicted, in which national solidarity was revealed and Israeliness upheld.

Suspicion in the Civil Guard

The Civil Guard, which had focused its volunteering efforts during the 1990s largely on neighborhood crime, shifted its attention during the second intifada to terrorism (*pe'ulot terror*). Volunteers ranging from retirees hoping to help their community to high school students enticed by weapons training saw their work as a way they could attain a modicum of control over "the situation" and give fellow civilians at least a feeling of safety. From my first day as a volunteer, it was clear that our primary role was to look out for all things suspicious. "What we do above all in terms of the security situation," Osnat told me as I signed my volunteering papers in the fall of 2003, "is look for suspicious objects, suspicious cars, and suspicious people." As much as the police leadership of Israel's Civil Guard presented suspiciousness as a set of traits that needed to be taught and learned, volunteers themselves relied in their alertness on preexisting stereotypes of what Palestinians look like. The result, as Civil Guards paced city streets wearing yellow vests, was an impulsive and racially inflected gaze overlaid with an air of authority.

In a large classroom at a community center in Jerusalem, about twenty volunteers from several Civil Guard bases gathered one December evening to receive specialized training (*haḥshara*) in how to recognize and report what the Israeli police call *samaḥim*. The term, a contraction of the Hebrew phrase *simanim maḥshidim*, "suspicious signs," referred, we were told, to all signals that would warn us of a suspicious person, suspicious object, or suspicious car. The instructor was a bomb expert (*ḥablan*), a member of the police bomb squad, or, in colloquial understanding, the person who coordinates the detonation of suspicious bags or boxes found in public spaces. Standing before us in a police uniform, the bomb specialist first described the protruding wires and rigged ignition that might divulge a suspicious car and then, with photographs and models, illustrated how bombs could be concealed in computer bags and guitar cases. He outlined the characteristics of a "suspicious person." He used male pronouns; even with the increasing awareness of female Palestinian militants, the stereotype of male suicide bombers persisted. "When you see a person who looks unusually nervous, if he has a big bag on his back, if he is wearing a long heavy coat in the summer, or if wires are sticking out from him, these are signs that he is suspicious." The bomb specialist spoke in police lingo and relied on ordered lists to describe suspicious people, but he also expected us to be attentive to considerably less tangible markers. He instructed us to watch for cars that, as he put it, "seem tampered with," for things that "look weird," and for particular mental states: "First of all, look at his behavior. They are not always so stable. They act nervous."

The Civil Guard educated the Israeli public more broadly by circulating a brochure that listed attributes of suspicion, with the expectation that civilians would become as adept at interpreting what Aretxaga calls "bodily diacritics" as trained security specialists (2003: 404). In 2003, the Israeli Police produced a three-panel brochure in both Hebrew and English, made available in print as well as in a PDF file available online. "Terror: Only Together We Can Stop It," the brochure announced. The cover icon showed a blurred photograph of the aftermath of a bus bombing, as seen through the crosshair of a rifle. This image was itself inset into a close-up detail of a human eye, wide open. The remaining panels of the brochure were filled with small photographs relating to bombings and bomb detection, including an explosive belt, a robot the police use to examine and defuse suspected bombs, a uniformed expert examining an electronic device, and an image of the Sbarro pizza restaurant in Jerusalem, bombed in 2001, an emblem for Israelis of Palestinian suicide bombings. The imagery illustrated the power of the gaze (the crosshair, the open eye) more so than the objects of surveillance. Surveillant technologies functioned euphemistically for those for whom Israelis were expected to be alert.

"How will you behave if you become involved in a suicide bombing or terrorist shooting?" the brochure asked. The leaflet divided "the suspicious signs of a suicide bomber" into three categories: external appearance, suspicious behavior, and suspicious equipment. To detect the physical appearance of a suspicious person, civilians were expected be attentive to "clothes unsuitable for the time of year (e.g., a coat in summer)" and to pay particular attention to "a youngster (usually) who is trying to blend in, by dress and behavior, with the surrounding population (on public transport, at entertainment places, amongst soldiers, or religious/Orthodox groups), even though he or she doesn't belong to that group." One should, according to the brochure, be aware of "anything protruding in an unusual way under the person's clothing." The list assumed that the suspicious other would be recognizably out of place, that people would plainly know a particular version of "usual" and "suitable," and that they could tap into common knowledge of what a person plotting a bombing looks like. The brochure's second list described "suspicious behavior," characterized by five manners of conduct:

- Nervousness, tension, profuse perspiration.
- Walking slowly while glancing right and left, or running in a suspicious manner.
- Repeated attempts to avoid security forces.
- Repeated nervous feeling for something under one's clothing.
- Nervous, hesitant mumbling.

The Civil Guard ascribed to civilians an expertise able to isolate gestures and emotions from a larger body to diagnose perspiring or mumbling as transparent, explicable indications of malicious intent. This decorporialization, as Kevin Haggerty and Richard Ericson have argued in their reflection on late modern surveillance, turns the human body into a body of data, pure information, "such that it can be rendered more mobile and comparable" (2000: 613). References to nervousness, tension, agitation, and uncertainty made the police archive of suspicion appear like a medical diagnostic system and Israeli civilians experts on terror with a seemingly innate ability to analyze symptoms of aberrant Palestinians.

In reality, the processes of decontextualization and categorization that constructed political and racial difference were not a matter of consciously applying codified government technologies as much as they were the result of acting on a hunch. This was the case for volunteers in Arad's civil guard, who worked in sprawling residential neighborhoods and expanses of desert, zoomed in jeeps through sandy hills, and drove police cars, lights flashing, through darkened back streets. If for the volunteers in Jerusalem Palestinian men embodied suspicion, in Arad—with its large surrounding Bedouin population and a weekly market shared by

Figure 8. An early morning temporary roadblock in Arad set up by Arad police and Civil Guard volunteers.

Jewish Arad residents and Bedouin merchants and customers—Bedouin men personified the local suspicious person.[5] One day in the spring of 2004, with the sun barely rising over the desert horizon, I joined two other volunteers in an early morning patrol: Arik, who was born in Israel, had lived in Arad for over thirty years. Mark, who had begun to volunteer more recently, came from Cincinnati to Arad after college in the early 1980s and never left. We rode in one of the small white police cars designated for Arad's Civil Guard, marked with the word Police (in Hebrew and English) and Community Guard (*shitur kehilati*). With Arik driving, we passed through a neighborhood of single-family homes and headed to the outskirts of the city, dotted with small factories and electrical stations and, in the distance, Bedouin homesteads. As we approached the municipal water towers, Arik began to accelerate. "That car looks suspicious," he said to me, pointing to a rundown vehicle about a hundred yards ahead. "Let's go see if there is something suspicious." Speeding up, Arik approached a beat-up white 1991 Subaru and pulled alongside it, his lights flashing. We all peered in, and an elderly ultra-Orthodox man and two younger yeshiva boys stared back at us. Arik waved to them, chuckled to me, and drove on.

It was nearly five in the morning when Arik decided we would set up what he called a *maḥsom,* a roadblock (the same term used for military checkpoints) near the main entrance to the city. Volunteers in Arad's Civil Guard were often called on by the Arad Police to assist in the temporary roadblocks that regular police officers set up on market days at the city's main entrance, complete with a traffic guard, flares, and traffic spikes. The roadblock this morning was more informal but no less imposing for those we stopped. Arik parked the police car just inside the main road, leaving the flashing lights on, and we stood on the curb. Over the course of the next hour, Arik stopped six cars and, together with Mark, asked the drivers for their national identity card and vehicle registration.

Israeli citizens carry a blue photo identity card (*teudat zehut*) that includes their name, national ID number, birth date, address, and national or ethnic identity (*le'om*). Until 2005, the permissible categories for nationality included Jewish, Arab, Druze, and Bedouin, as well as more than 100 other classifications, such as Circassian and "non-Jew."[6] There is no category for "Israeli." Palestinians displaced in the 1948 war but remaining in areas that became Israel are Israeli citizens, carry blue ID cards, and have civil and political rights in Israel, but they never received the same rights as Jewish citizens of Israel. They are what David Grossman (1993) refers to as "present absentees," recognized by Israel de facto but not de jure as full citizens. Israel is what Oren Yiftachel (2006) calls an ethnocracy, in that it privileges ethnicity (Jewishness) over citizenship and confers benefits and protections to Jews more than to Israeli citizens. The government uses military service, for example, as a requirement for public benefits such as housing loans and financial aid for higher education, but Palestinian Israelis are not allowed to serve in the IDF.[7] Although Jewish and Arab identity have never been autonomous or isolated (Lockman 1996: 363), as contemporary legal categories, Jew and Arab or Israeli and Palestinian are "absolute, categorical, inalienable, and official" (Lefkowitz 2004: 88). Indeed, to Arik, the ID cards and the identity label of their holders conveyed consistent, fixed, and official social categories, although as Tobias Kelly has shown, the rights bestowed on Palestinian carriers of blue ID cards could easily be revoked (2006a: 94). For Palestinians, identity cards are fateful even as they are indeterminate. At the *mahsom*, Arik was on the lookout for green ID cards, which are carried by Palestinian residents of the West Bank and Gaza Strip, issued by the Palestinian National Authority, and approved by the IDF.[8] We only saw blue ID cards that day, however.

My role at the roadblock was to sit in the police car and write down the license plate number of each car we stopped. As much as I explained to the base chief and to fellow volunteers that I was a researcher with no political agenda, I was aware that my presence was allied with the very practices of security—ethnic profiling, racism—that I was studying. I was, even transiently so, drawn into in a race-based system of interrogation. The Civil Guard expected me to embody the suspicious eyes of the state, and, from the perspective of those we scrutinized, I certainly did. My vest, my gaze, my body were symbols of the state. I recalled how Michael Taussig questioned the ease with which one can reproduce discourses of terror: "In talking terror's talk are we ourselves not tempted to absorb and conceal the violence in our own immediate life-worlds?" (2004: 270). How does one study, as Joseba Zulaika wondered in "The Anthropologist as Terrorist," "the ubiquitous yet almost unmentionable, the glorified yet heavily tabooed, political violence?" (1995: 206). Zulaika found his liberation by engaging Basque members of the ETA in debate about their own history. I never resolved my own bind of participant observation, but I tried to question fellow volunteers when they approached an individual simply because he or she "looked" Palestinian.

I asked Arik how he decided which cars to wave down. He strained to convey criteria he was not used to articulating. "Well, I just look at their faces, and at the cars." He thought for a moment, and then continued more authoritatively: "Also, two people in a car are more suspicious because drivers with permits [blue ID cards] try to bring in Palestinians from the territories who don't have permits and who might be terrorists." We never did encounter a car or person suspicious in the way Arik envisioned, although he did pull over three drivers wearing traditional Bedouin dress, all Israeli citizens according to their blue cards. In general, it was the shabbiness of a car or raucousness of a teenager's behavior that aroused Arik's suspicion. When it came down to it, he wasn't looking for the subtle signs of nervousness we had been taught to look for; he was looking for Bedouin and for some hazy concept of aberrance. As Civil Guard volunteers, we had all the authority of our flashing lights and police-issued rifles, and, yet, gut feelings and apprehensive impulses were what triggered action and produced state authority.

Security Guard Academy

Security guards in Israel during the second intifada tended to frame their work in terms of alertness for suspicious signs. They used language that echoed state inventories of suspicion, but alongside the codified profiles of nervous and covert bombers always sat personal intuition. Even armed guards with recent counterterrorist training for their job explicitly articulated their decisions as to who belongs, what fits, and what does not as matters of common sense and feeling. This was the case for Tomer, a twenty-three-year-old born and raised in Arad who worked four days a week as a security guard in the largest of Arad's three immigrant absorption centers. The Jewish Agency for Israel, the state organization in charge of immigrant absorption and economic development, ran the complex of apartments and social services for recent Jewish immigrants primarily from Ethiopia, Russia, and Argentina. The Jewish Agency outsourced its guarding work at this absorption center to a security company called Agudat Hashomrim (literally, Guards Union), which employed Tomer. This was Tomer's first job after completing three years of combat service in Nahal, an infantry regiment of the IDF. Because the Ministry of Defense considered civilian guarding a national priority, it offered an extra financial incentive, called *avoda mo'adefet*, to those who had recently completed mandatory military service and were going to begin work as security guards. Tomer's job, which paid $7 an hour, enabled him to save money (because he lived with his parents) and to have time on the side to prepare for university entrance exams.

Before Tomer could begin working at the absorption center, the Jewish Agency required him to attend a two-week course at Mikhlelet Ta'as, a school of Israel Military Industries, the weapons manufacturer, that Tomer dubbed "a security guard academy for the war against terror." There, he explained, "We learned how to deal with all sorts of situations: with a terrorist gunman or a suicide bomber. We also learned how to deal with situations within the absorption center like, say, two drunks brawling or a woman in labor. But if that happened, I would faint! I can cope with a terrorist but I don't know what to do with a woman giving birth!" Lucky for Tomer, he spent his time monitoring the building's gated doorways, observing people's entrances from his booth, and authorizing access for each entrant, one at a time, by pressing a remote access button. "If I already know them personally, then I let them straight in. If I don't know them personally, then I have to ask them about the purpose of their visit." In many ways, Tomer functioned as a doorman, screening entrances and giving residents a sense of belonging and safety. Still, when I asked him about his job, he depicted a considerably more grave assignment:

> First of all, my job is to guard against terrorists (*mehablim* or *terroristim*), whether it be a terrorist armed with a gun, or cold weapons, which means a knife or some other implement; or an attack from inside a car, or a suicide bomber. With a suicide bomber, it is more about spotting him or her at the entrance. We are supposed to have determination (*nehishut*), which is, like, always looking for something wrong even if there isn't something wrong.

I spent a day with Tomer inside the small security booth inside the building's entrance to learn what it meant to "look for something wrong." As I settled on a stool next to him, Tomer told me, "It's about recognizing someone suspicious before he even comes. For instance, if I see someone walking kind of funny, even if I know him from before, say he put on glasses and a scarf and now looks strange, then I'll approach him and ask who he is." While Tomer was talking, an employee of the absorption center approached the gate together with a curly-haired, middle-aged woman in shorts whom Tomer did not recognize. He buzzed them in after a brief glance, and I wondered how he decided to permit entry to the unfamiliar woman. He explained: "There are certain characteristics of people we have been trained to spot and be wary of. Say, an Arab-looking man. There are specific suspicious signs (*simanim maḥshidim*) we look out for."

What exactly did Tomer mean by "suspicious signs"? Resonating with the language and imagery of Home Front Command lists of suspicion, Tomer paid attention to gait and gesticulation as possible indicators of threat: "Say, for example, if someone arrives with a large bag, it means paying attention to how he carries the bag, where he looks, how he walks, if his steps are big or small, what he is doing with his hands, where his hands are." Unlike government lists of suspicion, Tomer's taxonomy explicitly invoked ethnic stereotypes. Tomer was particularly alert for Bedouin, but any "Arab-looking Israelis," in Tomer's words, gave him reason to investigate further. Tomer explained what it meant to look Arab: "It's the skin tone, his face, his clothes." His description of stereotypically Arab dress was even more specific:

> Usually jeans. A tricot shirt, maybe striped. You know, the usual Arab clothing. A *kefiyya* is of course straight away suspicious. If someone arrives with a *kefiyya*, I'll go out towards him immediately. Usually it's a Bedouin. It's not that when I see a Bedouin I immediately think he has come to do an attack. But I'll go speak to him. If I see someone who looks Arab, even if he isn't an Arab but an Arab-looking Israeli, then I'll approach and talk to him.

Tomer regarded attention to racial or ethnic characteristics as essential to his role as a guard,[9] but he did not regard his own practice as racial profiling. Israelis rarely use the word *geza'* (race) when talking about Palestinians or other ethnic groups and are more likely to substitute *leʾom*, which can mean nationality or ethnicity (Lefkowitz 2004: 88). Although the term connotes political allegiance rather than biological characteristics, Israelis still, in practice, construct nationality as genetic and corporeal, something into which one is born. Tomer classified skin tone, bodily habits, and ways of dressing, down to the stripes in a knit shirt, to be concurrently characteristic of Arabs, meaning both Bedouins and Palestinians, and of potential suspicion. Tomer had so internalized the racial discrimination pervasive in Israeli society that he could articulate, categorize, and label ethnic stereotypes at least as fluidly as he could the signs of suspicion he learned at Mikhlelet Taʾas.

Everyday Practices of Suspicion

Even when Israelis did not put suspicion into words, one could glean their suspicion from subtle gestures. Government categories inform the ways people see, think, and speak, as Tania Forte (2003) demonstrated in her study of the correlation between Israeli state classifications of identity and the analytic categories used by Israeli researchers studying Palestinians: "the seamless connection between patriotism and academic expertise" (2003: 221). So, too, in daily life Israelis embodied government classifications of the affect, dress, and gestures of "suspicious people." "All the time you think about it," said a high school boy who lived in Kiryat Menachem, a relatively low-income neighborhood in southwest Jerusalem still shaken by a 2002 bus bombing by a Hamas militant. "Every place you go, everyone is looking, all the time. All the time, you look and see if there's someone new. There's no time you're not thinking about it." Busy streets and city buses became stages for a choreography of covert peeks and shared gestures. People squinted, sidestepped, or altered their course, always on the lookout for the unfamiliar or unsuitable. Pauses in speech, more so than articulate narratives of identity or experience, revealed the nuances of Israeli vigilance.

On a morning bus ride on the 4A through downtown Jerusalem in the spring of 2004, a man wearing tattered clothing embarked. His tan suit was soiled, his untucked shirt hung down in threads, and his face was pallid. He sat in the seat in front of me and next to an Israeli Jewish woman in her late sixties, with dyed red hair and a floral blouse. As soon as the bus slowed at the next traffic light, the woman stood up and moved to the seat beside me. Meeting my eyes, she gestured with her hands and shoulder toward the man. "Suspicious, no?" she whispered. I shrugged in response and a woman on the other side of the bus aisle, looking on, nodded her head. The red-haired woman shrugged back. A shared glance, a synchronized shrug. Thoughts and assessments about bus bombings, suicide bombers, and Palestinians were articulated through unspoken signals. In this fleeting moment, civilian hypervigilance turned the bus into a nationalistic yet peculiarly intimate place. Shared imaginaries of danger and fantasies of otherness created closeness through assumptions about who "we" are and who the "other" is. As quickly as the intimate vigilance began, the three of us went back to staring straight ahead and continued our journeys in silence.

When the absence of Palestinians in the lives of Israeli Jews went unspoken, which it often did, it was transient glances and glimpses of suspicion that revealed the invisibility and evasion endemic to the conflict. Subtle, barely detectable, and often unconscious nods or blinks were a critical domain in which Israelis perceive and constitute Palestinians. What people experienced as out-of-place, however, did not always correspond to codified archives of suspicion. The scruffy man on the 4A bus looked atypical, but he would not qualify as suspicious according to the criteria laid out by the Home Front Command or the Arad Civil Guard. At this time of heightened vigilance, detecting simple aberration took on a nationalist

valence. Alert Israeli Jews took any sign of social deviation or simply varia-
tion into account as a possible indication of looming terrorism.

Late one Thursday evening in February 2004, I stood in Shlomit Maimon's Jerusalem kitchen as she pounded a kilogram of chicken breast to
make into schnitzel for the family's Sabbath meal. As Shlomit cooked, we
talked about the Palestinian suicide bombing on the 14A bus near Lib-
erty Bell Park in Jerusalem several days earlier. Shlomit dwelled on the
details of the event only briefly before diverging to reflect on her own
experience. "When *I'm* on a bus," she said, emphasizing the words as if to
suggest that she might have been more attentive than the passengers on
the 14A, "I look backward and forward, behind me and in front, to see
who's there." While dipping a strip of chicken into a plate of flour and
then beaten eggs, she turned her neck from side to side to demonstrate
how she scans a bus full of passengers. "When I'm on Emek Refa'im,"
the street in Jerusalem where Café Hillel is located, "I look around at
people and wonder if they're bombers." She again twisted her head back
and forth. Recently, she recalled, "I was on a bus and saw someone who
looked suspicious." She paused to begin frying the schnitzel in hot oil.
"So I got off the bus because I didn't feel safe, and hailed a taxi."

Shlomit did not refer to Palestinians by name in this story, and, in
fact, she rarely mentioned Palestinians at all. In the law office where she
worked as a paralegal, Shlomit shared work space with Palestinian Israeli
lawyers and sometimes had as clients Palestinian Israelis from neighborhoods around Jerusalem or Palestinian residents of East Jerusalem. But
when I asked her one day whether she has friends who are Palestinian,
she described a remorseful absence. "There isn't anyone with whom I
would have coffee, and there's no one who would come visit me. Of
course, in the past, before the whole intifada began, there were some
people who visited us. I used to have a good friend who worked with
me and lived near Ramat Rachel—how do you call the place? I forget. I
haven't been there in a long time. I used to go to her home. But today I
really don't have friends [who are Palestinian]." With coffee symbolizing
the quintessential casual contact, Shlomit explained that she does not
have this kind of contact with Palestinians, and that it is mutual: "I don't
go to them; they don't come to me." In our conversation, Shlomit used
words such as *etsleinu* (by us; among us) and *etslam* (by them; among
them), *shelanu* (ours) and *shelahem* (theirs), sedimenting distance between herself and Palestinians. Shlomit recalled with longing a coworker
who was a friend in the 1980s and into the 1990s, yet there were many
details of this relationship that Shlomit had already forgotten. She did
not mention the woman's name and did not recall the name of her town.
Shlomit's nostalgic but vague recollections echoed Daniel Lefkowitz's
depiction of Israeli Jews' narratives of encounter with Palestinian Israelis:

"the oft-repeated formula 'good relations with Arabs' referred to lack of contact, interaction, and knowledge" (2004: 104).

Palestinians did not have a tangible presence in Shlomit's life, but suspicion did. As she flipped the chicken and I arranged the fried pieces on paper towels to drain, she used the adjective suspicious as if it were a self-evident social category, as if it were clear what suspicion looked like, as if it were a physical description in itself. She tapped into circulating understandings of the term, but she experienced suspicion as something with a personal, bodily response: *she* should disembark, *she* should calm herself down. In her narrative, the suspicious person faded into the background while her own physical experience of alertness came to the fore: she twists her head, gets off the bus, hails a taxi. On buses, Shlomit enacted a state-like panopticism but she experienced her alertness, as she disembarked from the bus, as a form of personal agency.

Embodying the State

At this time of heightened anxiety in Jerusalem, suspicion was so proudly shared by Israeli Jews that, even when overtly and mistakenly turned against someone else, the response was often one of approval. Dvir, a graduate student in Jerusalem, explained that there is "a game Israelis play called 'spot the terrorist.'" It was something I had heard of several times before, always spoken about with a tense, uncertain humor, as if the speaker were aware of both its irony and its frank reality. Dvir laid out the deceptively simple rules: you look out for people with dark skin or wearing clothing that might possibly be a disguise. He told me with a combination of amusement and compunction that he himself plays this game. "Sometimes when there's a crowded, stuffed line to get on the bus, I feel the back of the guy in front of me, to make sure he's not wearing an explosive belt." Other times, Dvir investigated by engaging in conversation.

Once Dvir tried to speak to a fellow bus passenger who he imagined from the look of him "may be suspicious." Dvir was determined to hear the man speak to deduce his ethnicity from his intonation. He recounted the exchange: "I asked the guy what bus number it was. It was an excuse to get him to talk. 'What?' the guy said, 'you got on the bus and you don't know what number it is?' I answered: 'Well, I didn't know if it was the 32 or the 33.' The man replied: 'No, you thought I was a terrorist!' I said, 'Well, actually, yes.' The guy on the bus said back to me, 'That's okay. It's good you're alert. Keep up the good work!'" The two men first seemed to ridicule a national practice that could turn Israeli Jew against Israeli Jew, but very quickly they returned to applaud their shared suspicion. Stances of suspicion were esteemed as a national responsibility.

Dvir and his fellow passenger (whom Dvir concluded was an Arab Jew, or Mizrahi) shared in their imaginaries of violence: Dvir feared a bus bombing, envisioned an explosive belt, saw himself preempting an explosion. The other passenger quickly grasped Dvir's vision, and at that moment, an imaginary of Palestinian violence was captured in a fleeting encounter between Israeli strangers, all without an explicit utterance about Palestinians or bombs. Arab Jews were often stared at by fellow Israelis or stopped by police for their ID cards because of their skin color, much to their ire and affront, but, sometimes, as in this story, they found themselves scrutinized with suspicious stares as they themselves stared suspiciously in return.[10]

I found Dvir's suspicion at odds with sentiments he had expressed in earlier conversations about the recent Israeli-Palestinian violence. Dvir had told me he supported a two-state solution to the conflict and advocated Israel's disengagement from Gaza; he condemned Israel's occupation of the West Bank and the Israeli settlers who lived there. In these ways, Dvir considered himself politically left-wing. His enactment of suspicion, then, with its barely veiled racism, revealed a disjuncture between his stated and practiced perceptions of Palestinians. It was as Dan Rabinowitz observed in his ethnography of Arab-Israeli relations in Nazareth, where mainstream liberalism was not only unable to "engender fair and rational action" but also could "easily produce predatory discrimination" (1997: 10). I asked Dvir how his attention to bodily signs as expressions of identity melded with his liberal politics. His explanation was pragmatic: "I am alert because there is danger," he said to me.[11] Dvir's suspicion was perhaps so ingrained that it existed alongside, and even overrode, his conscious statements of liberalism. Dvir acted less like Shlomit with her self-protective sidestepping and more like Tomer with his state-sponsored guarding. Dvir was momentarily a policeman, a border guard, a soldier. He not only internalized the gaze of Israel's state and military system but also projected state surveillance back outward and even literally encroached on another person's body. Here, Dvir was not consciously applying government discourses of suspicion to the street; he had already internalized them and made state notions of threat indistinguishable from his own.

The Efficacy of Suspicion's Failure

As alert as those I have described in this chapter were to suspicion, none of the signs and markers they witnessed actually portended danger. No one reported that the person they suspected ultimately perpetrated a bombing. For these individuals, narratives of suspicion were tales of alertness, not threat. In their minds and experience, just sensing something suspicious somehow corroborated that suspicious signs and people were everywhere. The threadbare fellow who boarded the Jerusalem bus never turned out to be more than unkempt. Shlomit's "suspicious person" did not appear to rouse the concern of any other passengers. Dvir's "suspicious person" was an Israeli Jew as wary and alert as he. Not even Tomer confronted anyone malicious or even without a blue ID card. By the same token, no one actually reacted to their sense of suspicion as if they had truly seen a "terrorist." The red-haired woman on the Jerusalem bus moved to a different seat and Dvir engaged in conversation with the man in line in front of him. Shlomit disembarked to take a taxi. No one pounced, yelled, called the police, or ran away, having seemingly sensed that the person was not suspicious "enough" to warrant a public announcement. It was as if they were acknowledging that something was almost suspicious but not quite.[12]

There were, it is true, suicide bombings preempted by vigilant Israeli civilians or diligent security guards. In December 2005, for example, after a Palestinian suicide bomber detonated himself at the entrance to a shopping mall in Netanya, newspapers reported that a pedestrian had spotted a man walking "like a robot" toward the shopping center and shouted, "Suicide bomber! Suicide bomber!" to the security guards at the mall entrance. As the guards pushed the man against the wall to stop him, the bomber detonated the explosives, killing one of the guards. Israel Police Commander Moshe Karadi commended the guards for having identified the bomber and "prevented a major disaster" (*Forward* 2005). Still, the media more commonly reported on bombings not anticipated, on suspicious signs not foreseen, that is, on the nondetection of "suspicious people" at bomb scenes. The media viewed the absence of suspicion as newsworthy in itself. Following a Palestinian bombing of a crowded rush hour Jerusalem bus in January 2004, nearly every major Israeli newspaper reported that no one on the bus had detected the presence of a particularly suspicious person. "The driver did not notice any suspicious person board at any of the stops en route," said one report (*Ma'ariv* 2004). "The guard inspected the bus and cast his eyes over its various passengers, but did not view the bomber as suspicious," reported another (*Ha'aretz* 2004). Even in its absence, suspicion had presence and power.

The nature of Israelis' suspicions suggested that the "game Israelis play" was less straightforward than "spot the terrorist." The "game" of suspicion worked through the questioning and the ultimate failure to detect suspicion. Even when, time and again, a bombing was not preceded by the visible presence of codified suspicion signs, even when the suspicious signs people saw did not culminate in calamity, Israelis continued to expect seemingly "suspicious" people to be Palestinian suicide bombers, the media continued to imagine bombers to be emotionally and physically incongruous in scenes of Jewish Israeli life, and Israeli society continued to embrace alertness. A discourse of suspicion endured and imagery of the potential terrorists continued to circulate even when it was not predictive or did not "work" as colloquial wisdom said it would.

Israeli practices of suspicion were ultimately more a mode of controlling the idea of threat than a process of receiving information (Said 1978: 58). They were performative, practices that instantiate the effects they name, shape the categories and practices of those who draw on them, and constitute what people see around them. In their study of the conspiratorial thinking of contemporary power, Harry West and Todd Sanders analyze the "age of transparency" that ostensibly rests on notions of accountability and responsibility that would, in theory, generate trust, openness, and good governance. In fact, West and Sanders argue, transparency propagates mistrust and the very opacities and blindnesses it purports to obviate (2003: 5). Discourses of Israeli suspicion similarly promised intelligibility, visibility, and safety and yet created the very fears they claimed to temper, generating exceptional states of alertness and feelings of vulnerability. They reaffirmed for Israelis that Palestinians were threatening and that bombers were lurking everywhere. Suspicious surveillance was a practice of legibility that "produces more opacity," a reality in which individuals see nothing but signs (Aretxaga 2003: 404).

It was actually Israeli civilians' perpetual "failure" to interrogate bombers on the street that enabled the discourse to comfortably persist as part of everyday life and to be habitually reproduced at the level of embodied practice. Vigilance "worked" in the civilian domain when suspicion remained a hypothesis, a question about reality—Is it suspicious? Did that seem suspicious?—rather than a confident depiction of reality. Through lists and Web sites of suspicious signs, public announcements soliciting the public's vigilance, and civil guard training, the state made terrorist vigilance accessible and palatable to the public. As we saw for Dvir, suspicion generated fantasies of civilian apprehension and interrogation, fantasies of the state's efficacy and vigor, even when the object of his suspicion turned out to be a similarly alert Israeli Jew, even as he and his suspicious object transiently and tacitly acknowledged the ways the discourse can break down.

Israeli Jews' frequent failure to spot suicide bombers reminded civilians that their alertness was decoupled from military strategies of surveillance and intelligence and reinforced that the "state," and not they as individuals, was ultimately responsible for their protection. Israeli Jews were content to propagate fictions of the power of surveillance and the omnipresence of threat because alertness gave them some assurance that they would be able to avert the danger they anticipated. The valence of emergency that overlay everyday routines of walking, looking, and bus riding may have generated apprehensive pedestrians, but it also produced active citizens and fostered Israeli Jews' confidence in a protective state. Fleeting and failing as it was, however, suspicion still bred violence in multiple sites of daily life.

Chapter 5

Projecting Security in the City

Shimon: At night we do not drive on Route 6, because there was shooting there.

Esther: We go around it instead. Through Tel Aviv, and through the old roads. Through the usual road. And we never drive there at night. Only during the daytime. And also, one never goes to the Old City [of Jerusalem].

Shimon: Well, seldom.

Esther: And we try to avoid crowded places as much as possible. Which is very difficult, because if you want to go to the mall, for instance, and it's very crowded—

Shimon: Sometimes we do go there.

Esther: But sometimes an isolated place is the dangerous place and not a crowded place. For example, Armon Hanatziv. You don't know whom you're going to meet there.

Shimon: And we don't go by buses.

Esther: We do not go by buses. A crowded place is more dangerous than a deserted place. We think—we feel.

In this dinnertime exchange, Esther and Shimon Shenhav, whom we met in Chapter 3, shared perceptions of safe and dangerous spaces in Israel. They had devised and internalized schemas to ascertain what spaces to circumvent and what spaces to use, where they would feel safe and where unsafe. They cut into and completed each other's sentences with the synchronized diction and harmonized thinking of a long-married couple. There was a sureness in their speech that seemed to reflect considerable time spent discussing and exercising these concerns. Esther and Shimon agreed to circumvent Route 6, the Trans-Israel Highway located in some places along the Green Line. Because of a shooting on this road of an Israeli girl near the West Bank town of Qalqilyah, they favored smaller roads in the Tel Aviv region. They avoided Jerusalem's Old City because of its Palestinian population and saw the Malha Mall in Jerusalem as a likely target for a Palestinian suicide bombing. They steered clear of the Armon Hanatziv (literally Commissioner's Palace, after the headquarters of the British High Commissioner located on the hilltop) promenade, or *ha-Tayelet*, a space shared by Israeli Jews and Palestinians.[1] ("You don't know whom you're going to meet there.") They agreed that buses were to be avoided altogether. Together, they used a logic of safety and danger that depended on mutually established perspectives, on cause-and-effect, time-sensitive shifts in strategy, and emotion.

Esther and Shimon tapped into euphemistic shorthand in which "shootings" referred to Palestinian shootings of Israelis, "crowded" meant areas dense with Israeli Jews and thus susceptible to a Palestinian bombing, and "isolated" indicated places devoid of Jews although possibly filled with Palestinians. Palestinian space, in the couple's parlance, was nonspace, and their conversation was peppered with slippages from depictions of empty space to that of Palestinian space. They imagined much of Jerusalem as an abandoned urban landscape, a trope that typified media depictions of Israel as a nation in crisis during the early years of the second intifada (Stein 2002). Contemporary images of a vacant city also echoed early twentieth-century nationalist discourses of Jewish settlers of Palestine that used the notion of *kibbush hashmama*, meaning conquering the wilderness or the wasteland, to depict Palestine as an empty land that needed to be cultivated and converted into a hospitable environment (Yiftachel 1998).

Although public spaces were seldom the desolate landscapes depicted, the collective cadence of public movement had indeed changed by the second year of the second intifada. In describing the Jerusalem *midraḥov*, or "pedestrian mall," two months before the beginning of the second intifada, anthropologists Tamar El-Or and Eran Neria invoked Baudelaire's flaneur: "What an easy place for observation, what a classic place to walk after the walkers, to gaze at those who gaze. Walking decisively is difficult; the *midraḥov* acquires its own unhurried pace by the strolling masses . . . Be seen and watch the passing parade" (2004: 80). By contrast, when I arrived in Jerusalem three years after El-Or and Neria's observation, the downtown mall was a different place. The pathways of city walkers did not wander, weave, or meander, as Michel de Certeau (1988) described quotidian perambulation. With increasing fortification and amplified alertness, the city had become a place of decisive movement and strained rather than easy observation. Israeli Jews' fears of Palestinians and suicide bombings led them to avoid or minimize the time they spent in public urban areas. When they did not circumvent city centers entirely, they made their trips into town more efficient. On weekends, city police often bounded the *midraḥov* with barricades, and armed security guards inspected passing pedestrians. Pedestrians' glances, no longer easy or casual, appeared rigid and alert.[2]

Travel was negotiated and calculated, and the stories people told about their movement were strewn with references to safety and security. At the beginning of the second intifada, Tal, the grown daughter of Shlomit and Ilan Maimon, lived with her husband and first child not far from her parents in Jerusalem's French Hill. French Hill is part of the Jerusalem municipality but is located on the East Jerusalem side of the Green Line on territory Israel captured from Jordan during the 1967 war. Prior to 1967, the area was populated by Palestinians from Lifta who were displaced during the 1948 war (Khalidi and Elmusa 1992). The state annexed the area to provide territorial contiguity between the Hebrew University campus of Mount Scopus, which had been an Israeli enclave in Jordanian territory before the war, and the rest of West Jerusalem. During the second intifada, a large number of Palestinian attacks in and near French Hill decreased property values and made the neighborhood affordable for students such as Tal.[3] "It was a difficult time for a year until after the Ḥomat Magen," she said, referring to Operation Defensive Shield of 2002 (literally "Defense Wall"), the largest Israeli military operation in the West Bank since the 1967 war. Tal's movement became perfunctory, a posture she says she adopted following two Palestinian suicide bombings in 2001 at the French Hill Junction that connects northern Jerusalem to the sprawling Israeli settlement Ma'aleh Adumim via Highway 1, bypassing the Palestinian towns of Azariya and Abu Dis. Tal's depiction of vigilant movement in daily life was filled with images of obligation and curtailed enjoyment. "If I had to get money out of the bank, I would do the errand walking quickly, not at leisure, and without the kids. Just to get it over with. Even a medical appointment that Adin [her son] had in the city center, I put off for a few weeks until it got calmer . . . For two years, the only thing I would go into town for was my hairdresser. But I would choose a route on foot that would be less obvious."

Tal's spatial rigor had eased somewhat by the time we spoke in 2004, but as she said, "I still ask myself if I really need to do [an errand], or if I could make it shorter. And at road crossings, I still prefer not to be with other people around me. Every time I walk to the town center, I think twice about it if there is a [security] alert." Even when Israelis' use of city space was hyperattentive and constricted, people manipulated their imaginaries of space to enable them to travel without being overwhelmed by anxieties. Esther and Shimon's strategies of movement were punctuated with intermittent qualifications or exceptions that let them balance their fear of bombings and Palestinians with their desires for a normal life. They imagined patterns of safe and dangerous space that they could, with sufficient effort, discern and perhaps offset, a discernment that managed to coexist with popular perceptions of Palestinian suicide bombings as arbitrary and unsystematic.

Anthropologists have used a variety of spatial and psychological tropes to describe the ways political events, social constraints, and beliefs impress themselves on people's minds and condition not only their perceptions of place and space but also their modes of thinking. In his theorization of Micronesian navigation, Alfred Gell (1985) used the notion of mental maps to describe noncodified assemblages of mental images that situate people in a landscape.[4] To Gell, mental maps are not products of embodied familiarity, as Bourdieu (1977) saw them, but rather mediators between subjective perception and context-specific navigation. Not dissimilarly, Joel Migdal (2004) offers the term "mental maps" to describe how people construct social and symbolic boundaries in ways that maintain connections while signaling separation. "Mental maps incorporate elements of the meaning people attach to spatial configurations, the loyalties they hold, the emotions and passions that groupings evoke, and their cognitive ideas about how the world is constructed" (7). Focusing specifically on an East German border village, Daphne Berdahl uses the phrase "wall in our heads" to describe how political discourses of citizenship, foreignness, and surveillance imprinted figurative borders on villagers' imaginaries. Even after reunification, "walls in our heads" functioned as a cultural border constantly maintained through practices of self-identification and differentiation (1999: 167). In Yael Navaro-Yashin's study of the quasi-state of Northern Cyprus, the border region is not only a legal space but also one of the "psychic-political effects" of the penetration of the Turkish regime into psyches of subjected Turkish-Cypriot citizens (2005: 111). Her metaphor of "borders on the imagination" refers to the effects of sovereign power on people's unconscious lives (119).

Drawing on the spatial sensitivity and political potency of these phrases while highlighting the dynamic relationship that develops between people and spaces they traverse, I use the idea of security projection to describe the subjective, self-protective spatial imaginaries that people hold in their minds and carry with them as they move through their days.[5] In precise yet malleable ways, Israelis projected circulating imaginaries of suicide bombings and personalized perceptions of safety and danger onto the urban landscape. They filtered state discourses of security and national tropes about space through their minds and experiences and weighed these against desires for normalization, leisure, and taste. Projection occurs in two senses of the term. On the one hand, there is a calculation: the likelihood of a future suicide bombing is plotted and gauged. On the other hand, projection is a process of imagination: the visualization of a prospective bombing as well as bombings that have occurred in the past, creating a mental image of the bombing as an object, idea, emotion, or event. Security projections are emotive and intimate, yet they still worked like more tangible practices of everyday security in enacting militarized thinking and embodying Israeli notions of power and otherness. As in Gell's notion of mental maps, security projections overlay defined spaces and particular events with subjective beliefs about that space. It is as Esther Shenhav suggested when she said at the end of her conversation with her husband, "We think—we feel"; security projections were a simultaneously intellectual and perceptual process, an assemblage of bits and pieces of data, stories, and senses of place, woven into a protective map.

During the second intifada, Jewish Jerusalemites experienced their commutes to work as complex journeys they could embark on only after filtering security warnings they heard on the radio, on television broadcasts, via news feeds on Web sites such as *Ma'ariv*'s nrg.co.il or *Yediot Aharonot*'s ynet.co.il, from friends, or deduced from the siting of an impromptu city roadblock. This chapter describes the security projections that four individuals—Noa, Liora, Alon, and Sheri—conveyed to me though tales of daily transport. Michel de Certeau has used the term "spatial stories" to refer to "stories in the form of places put in linear or interlaced series," accounts of movement or "narratives of adventure" that functioned to "traverse and organize places" (1988: 115–16). As they found their way to work, and as they told me about this journey, Noa, Liora, Alon, and Sheri made "sentences and itineraries" from the paths they took and the concerns they had about Palestinian bombings (115).[6] Their tales of security projection were as important as the movement itself, as de Certeau said: "They make the journey, before or during the time the feet perform it" (116).

Noa, Liora, Alon, and Sheri appear, at first glance, to have much in common. They were all in their late twenties or early thirties and were all born in Israel. They all worked in West Jerusalem and often frequented the same neighborhoods, stores, and roads. Yet, their senses of safety derived not only from a shared matrix of warnings but also from personal experience and from different sets of knowledge circulating among friends and family. Their gender, familial status, political leanings, religious observance, military experience, and previous incidents of trauma uniquely conditioned their perceptions and practices of space such that their spatial stories conveyed individual subjectivity and the personal nature of security's embodiment. Spatial stories of security convey the ways security infuses the interstices of daily life. However, if maps in one's mind facilitate feelings of safety and confidence in the ability to cope with conflict, as we will see below, they also project the institutions of power and exclusion that created them.

Noa: Projecting Memory

Noa lived with her husband and toddler in the quiet residential neighborhood of Motza and taught math at a secular state high school in downtown Jerusalem. Five days a week, she drove her sedan on the Jerusalem-Tel Aviv highway into town, a twenty-five minute trip east toward the city. Noa Shahar's urban movement sparked a sequence of tactical recollection. Depending on the precise route she took to work, Noa counted approximately seven places for which she had what she referred to as "pictures in my head" and "points on my map," sites that triggered remembrances of past bombings. Sitting on the grass in her backyard with her son playing nearby, Noa narrated her daily commute to me.

Noa's spatial story, rambling and digressive, began at Maḥane Yehuda, the open-air produce market in downtown Jerusalem. She described her thinking as she passes it: "So many bombings there, you cannot even count them. [The market's produce is] much cheaper and so much fresher [than a supermarket's], but I don't go there now. . . . My high school was next to the market and we would go in the break to buy an apple in the market. During one break, there was a bombing, and one of our teachers went there to try to help—" Noa cut herself off, lost in her memory of 1988, when a Palestinian bomb hidden in a loaf of challah and left inside a grocery store in Mea Shearim injured three young girls. Although Mea Shearim is not far from the market or from the location of Noa's old high school, I verified later that the bombing was not, in fact, at the market itself, as Noa recalled. Her memory misplaced the bombing, conflating the space she feared then with a space she fears now—Maḥane Yehuda was the site of two more recent bombings. Noa's narrative digressed from a linear description of her journey to bind herself intimately to the violence of place.

Resuming her narrated drive, Noa moved from the market to King George Street. This is one of Jerusalem's main pedestrian thoroughfares, lined on both sides with small shops: the Ne'eman bakery, the Pinati restaurant, a Steimatsky bookstore, and clothing boutiques selling long skirts for religious women. The road is always tightly packed with taxis and Egged city buses inching so slowly that buses stopped for passengers are indistinguishable from those en route. On the densely packed sidewalk, one might see teenage boys with slicked-back hair, soldiers on cell phones, mothers with double strollers, pairs of scarved Muslim women chatting, religious Jewish teenagers carrying backpacks, American Orthodox yeshiva students heading for a pizza parlor, old ladies asking for change, and robed priests. Noa, however, alluded only to the Ha-Mashbir department store. She mentioned the store's name and continued on without elaboration with her journey, the very naming divulging that it was a point on her map, the site of a bombing in March 2002. As she said, "I'm driving and thinking, here, here, here, here was a bomb. When I pass through places where I know a bombing occurred, I always remember." Particular spaces set off what Christopher Tilley calls "flashes of memory" in his phenomenology of landscape (1994: 28). As sites invoked memories of past suicide bombings or conjured images of disaster, Noa's trip became a journey of reimagined bombings.

Noa's security projection intertwined the details of communal tragedy with her memory of her own traumatic experience of that event. "On Shlomzion Street, I remember the couple that went to have an ultrasound for the baby, to see that everything was fine, and left the building together, and they both were killed in a bombing." What Noa "remembers" here derived from media reports in March 2002 of a Palestinian suicide bombing that killed a woman pregnant with twins and her husband as they were leaving a medical clinic after an ultrasound exam. The bombing actually occurred on King George Street, but Noa's own experience of that event eclipsed the precise details of the bombing. It was as Merleau-Ponty said: "I am not the spectator, I am involved" (2005 [1962]: 272). The news story of the couple's ruinous ultrasound accrued personal poignancy because Noa learned she was pregnant right after the bombing.[7] The bombing blurred with Noa's embodied experience of driving past this site as an expectant mother, a form of sensory memories, in Nadia Seremetakis's terms, where "the meditation on the historical substance of experience is not mere repetition but transformation which brings the past into the present as a natal event" (1994: 7). For Noa, media reports felt like her own private tragedy, and her intimate empathy and sadness surfaced as she drove by.

In Noa's spatial story, she soon approached the school where she taught, not far from the pedestrian mall on Ben Yehuda Street. As before, her description of a bombing preceded and dictated her reference to the location. "And then the bombing in the pedestrian mall, three years ago or four years ago," she began, recalling a Palestinian suicide bombing on the Ben Yehuda pedestrian mall in 2001. "My friend, the one that I just talked with on the phone, was the teacher of one of the kids that was there [in the bombing], and his father tried to protect him from the explosion, and the father got killed because the fire caught him, and he died because of the fire. Just terrible stories that I cannot forget!" Noa culled from the news and from her friend's account, dwelling on sparse but personally poignant details. What was particularly striking about her narration was its cadence. When Noa described the experience of her close friend, she spoke with a sadness and intimacy that threatened to trap her and pull her too tightly into the upsetting memory. But then, almost abruptly, she moved on. She dwelled only long enough to visualize this site and to attach personal meaning to it. Her narrative, perhaps mimicking the cadence of her memory-filled commute, contained digressions and imaginaries but then pushed forward. "And when I went from Gaza Street to the university, there was one next to the Hilton Hotel, the new Hilton. And if you go through Eshkol Street, where Bus #26, with all the students from Boyer—" Noa's narrative wandered as she recalled a Hamas suicide attack in 1995 that killed many summer students en route to the Boyer Building at the Rothberg International School of Hebrew University on Mount Scopus.

Noa blurred distinctions between remembrance and projection. Although she was melancholic and rueful about bombings past, more than that, she was afraid that Palestinians would bomb these or nearby areas again. Her imagination of Jerusalem space was prognostic as much as remembered, anxious as much as mournful. The two phases of spatial imagination—recollection and prediction—were linked, such that information about past bombings became inseparable from premonitions of future danger. Noa saw her mnemonic movement as itself something that gave her a feeling of control over these bombings. "I know it's not logical, not rational," she told me, "but I have this idea in my head that if I'm thinking about a bomb, then maybe it won't happen." Thus, her memory-filled movement was not a form of memorialization but a physical and an emotional tactic to get through the day. She referred to it as her technique, and she felt that by maintaining a heightened state of consciousness as she drove she put herself in command over her safety. (When Noa's husband, Gil, overheard her using the word *tekhniqa*, he told me that his own technique was *hadhaqa*, meaning to repress, suppress, or push off. Presumably Noa's conversation with me amplified somewhat the extent to which she did focus on bombings and danger.) Noa made clear that she did not expect her technique would "work," that is, keep her and her family safe. She candidly acknowledged the likely futility of her efforts to avoid violence and the psychological role that her self-protective practices played. In this sense, she experienced her apotropaic strategy as akin to a protective ritual that contains within it the recognition that, beyond the concrete precautions taken in daily life, individuals themselves remain powerless to haphazard danger and bad fortune and must resort to alternative measures. Magical rituals, as functionalist anthropologist Bronisław Malinowski (1948) argued long ago, have the social function of alleviating anxiety, distress, and fear. The ability of Noa's security projection to confer on her a feeling of safety remained unmarred, as in a ritual system, even when she knew it would not operate in clear, tangible ways. As she overlay places with subjective beliefs about those spaces, Noa embodied circulating narratives of danger and threat and made them her own.

Liora: Schedules for Safety

Liora, a graduate student at Hebrew University in German literature in her early thirties, told me once, laughing, "I'm the only out-of-the-closet right-winger in my department." Liora's family had moved to Israel from the United States in the late 1980s when she was twelve. They settled in Zichron Ya'acov, where her parents still live, a picturesque Israeli town south of Haifa on the Mediterranean coast. A secular Jew and an Israeli American reared on her parents' patriotic commitment to Israel, Liora believed strongly in Jewish nationalism and Jews' right to the land of Israel, which to her comprises Jewish settlements in the West Bank and her own neighborhood of French Hill. She lived with her husband in an apartment in French Hill, a short bus ride from the university. In the 1990s, Liora traveled without hesitation on city buses between her apartment, the university, and her parents' house. But at the beginning of the second intifada, she began to structure her everyday travel according to a meticulous system of safety conditioned by publicly circulating notions of Palestinian bombings and private anxieties. If Noa's security projections accumulated memories, Liora's reflected a mental matrix of pliable calculations to help her strategically avoid times and places she felt were dangerous. Her constricted travel through the city gave bodily and material form to the data and discourse of security.

In the summer of 2004, as we sat in a noisy café at Hebrew University on Mount Scopus, Liora delineated her everyday techniques of travel in a way that intermingled anxiety, political belief, professional obligation, and familial relationships. Speaking in English, she described the paths she followed over the course of a typical day between 2001 and 2003. When taking the bus to school in the morning, Liora would wait until after 9:30, reckoning that the morning rush hour was a more common time for Palestinian bombings of Israeli sites. She told herself that the #4 bus through French Hill to Mount Scopus, even though it had been the target of Palestinian bombings in recent years, "felt safe at certain times." Her security projection relied on temporal and spatial calculations of danger. Spaces were familiar or usable at some times and off limits or inaccessible at others. Time itself could create an enclave of safety. When Liora was visiting her parents in Zichron Ya'acov, she would wait until 10 P.M. to take the bus back to French Hill, reasoning that Palestinian suicide bombers have rarely struck so late at night. In October 2002, a bombing by Islamic Jihad took place on the route she takes to her parents' house, but, because it was in the afternoon, Liora concluded that late-night bus rides were still "relatively safe."[8] As quickly as Liora reacted to her fears, she was also eager to latch onto even ephemeral signs of stability.

Liora delineated periodic amendments to her security projection, albeit shifts more in psyche than in schedule. If she needed to go to the university earlier than 9:30 in the morning, Liora would still take the bus but would tell herself, "It's just that small part. I still feel it's safe." After a politically motivated Palestinian shooting in her neighborhood in March 2004 killed George Khoury, a twenty-year-old Israeli Arab university student, Liora continued riding buses to campus. As she explained, the violent event did not interfere with the bus- and time-based mental map that she had established in her head. In her reasoning, it was a shooting not a bombing, and it had occurred in the evening when she does not take buses anyhow. For the sake of maintaining a "normal" work schedule, Liora temporarily suspended, but did not discredit, the system of safety. Eventually, however, Liora became too frightened to walk from the bus stop to her apartment, so she would ask her husband to meet her at the bus stop to walk her home. "It was *k'ilu* [as if] it would protect me or, if not that, at least I wouldn't die alone." Her husband became one of her apparatuses of protection, although Liora acknowledged that his power lay in enabling her to push frightening thoughts from her mind during that walk home. Her fastidious calculations of bus-schedule safety coexisted with a security sought through relationality.

Liora's spatial story was filled with abbreviations and euphemisms. Referring to "avoiding buses," "safer times," and "dangerous bus lines," her narrative steered clear of most references to Palestinians or bombings. She spoke of her efforts to elude bombings with hardly any mention of the word bombings and structured her travel around the imagined geographic and temporal strategies of Palestinian bombers without express reference to Palestinian agency. Her omissions were not uncommon. Israeli Jews often said that they "don't go to" a particular restaurant or that they are "afraid of" a particular street, assuming I knew that fear and avoidance connoted that a Palestinian has bombed the site in the past or that people perceive the site as a likely future bombing target. Like the discourse of empty space that connoted Palestinian spaces, discussion of violence was often emptied of reference to Palestinians, whether as individuals or as agents of violence. By focusing on buses as if bombings come from buses rather than from Palestinians, Liora turned buses into metonyms of previous bombings.

Scheduling safety and danger gave Liora the feeling of knowing even when she really did not. "We forget the uncertainties involved," Jenny Edkins says in her study of national memories of trauma, referring to Slavoj Žižek's notion of social fantasy, and "adopt an ontology . . . that depends on a progressive linear notion of time" (2003: 13–14). The fantasy involved in Liora's sense of safety was not wholly lost on her. As she said to me several times throughout her narration, "I know this is not rational." Liora told me that our conversation was the first time she had articulated her system to another person and she may have wanted to show her own awareness of its inconsistencies. A psychological approach might describe Liora's attempt to spatially and temporally isolate danger as a sort of compartmentalization, a form of dissociation that organizes thoughts and feelings about the self or knowledge about the world into separate categories in a way that minimizes a person's access to negative information (Showers 1992) even as that information still influences his or her emotion, cognition, and behavior (Spitzer et al. 2006). A number of psychological studies of Israelis' responses to suicide bombings have argued that emotional dissociation helps Israelis respond to trauma. According to one study conducted among social workers at a hospital in Haifa in 2002: "Our data reveal that peritraumatic dissociation played an important role in our respondents' adjustment to the traumatizing conditions" (Somer et al. 2004: 1089), where adjustment, according to the authors of the study, means the ability to "carry on with their 'normal' personal lives."

Although psychologists consider dissociation a sometimes necessary means of distancing oneself from experiences that are too much for the psyche to process (Binks 2000), the confinement of fear or danger through dissociation is also a political discourse, a recurring and politically charged way in which Israeli Jews talked about Palestinian violence. An illustration of this can be seen in a comical text titled "Where Is It *Really* Dangerous?" that circulated among Israeli Jews on the Internet and over e-mail beginning in 2001. Written by Uri Orbach, a right-wing news commentator and satirist, it isolated Gilo, a Jewish settlement in the southwest corner of the Jerusalem municipality, as the most dangerous location for Israeli Jews during the second intifada (see Chapter 7). I received an English version of the text in a mass e-mail sent by an American-born Israeli friend. It read:

> In Israel everyone knows that it is dangerous primarily in the territories and in a little bit of Jerusalem. In Jerusalem everyone knows there is shooting going on, but only in the neighborhood of Gilo. In Gilo everyone knows

that it is dangerous, but only on Ha'anafa Street. The rest of Gilo is pretty safe. On Ha'anafa Street everyone knows that it is dangerous, but not all along the entire street, just in the houses that face [the West Bank Palestinian town of] Beit Jalla.

The piece continued to segregate danger to a single street, to a set of apartments, to particular rooms within those apartments, and then only to the kitchen, because "in the bedrooms and bathrooms, it is totally safe." The text concluded:

> Those near the refrigerator know that where it is *really* dangerous is in the freezer, which is located directly in the sights of the sniper from Beit Jalla . . . And in the freezer above the refrigerator on one section of Ha'anafa Street at the edge of Gilo in Jerusalem in Israel? Aha! That is really a bit dangerous. If you stand there and get some frozen schnitzel out of the freezer, you are taking your life in your hands.

This humor worked because so many people recognized that they, too, engaged in such magical thinking. This thinking also engaged ideological discourses of Jewish strength and persistence. Like Liora's security projection, the satire turned the violence of the Israeli-Palestinian conflict into something with invisible agency yet clearly bounded confines. It created an image of very real yet isolated and controllable violence, suggesting that Palestinian violence is predictable and that Israeli Jews, if only they could learn its patterns, can compartmentalize that violence and persist with a normal life. If only chicken schnitzel is dangerous, then Israeli sovereignty is steadfast.

Disruptions to Liora's classification of what was safe and what was dangerous ultimately became disabling to her. In August 2003, Hamas perpetrated a suicide bombing at night on a bus line Liora had not considered particularly susceptible. "The *pigu'a* [suicide bombing] on Line 1 [near] the Old City threw me off. I felt I couldn't escape. I was trapped. I had a crisis." Liora lost the sense that she could forecast or avert bombings. "That was real terror, because real terror can get you at any time," she said. By the time of our conversation in 2004, Liora was exasperated with the constant scheming and calculating, which she found draining and potentially futile. She purchased a used car, which let her avoid buses altogether. Finances played an important role because it was not only the August 2003 bombing but also Liora's ability to finally afford a used vehicle that enabled her to allow the intensity of her daily computations to fade. "But I still take certain buses at certain times," she added in the end. Even as a driver, Liora continued to hold onto her earlier systematization, not wanting to discredit the system she had devised and relied on for so long. Security projections continued to be part and parcel of her subjectivity as daughter, wife, student, and Israeli.

Alon: A Military Mentality

Alon Cohen, twenty-seven years old, was a law student and about to start a prestigious clerkship. He lived with his Israeli-born parents in the same upper-middle-class apartment where he grew up in Rehavia, a garden neighborhood built for German Jews in the late 1920s. Alon had spent several years in the United States as a child when his father, a successful surgeon, took up various medical fellowships. He returned to Israel in time for high school, and matriculated into the IDF in 1996. Alon had always wanted to be a pilot, he said, but did not pass the requisite vision test and so served in the equally elite paratrooper unit, where he became an officer. On a daily basis, Alon's decisions about self-protective movement through the city used military modes of thinking.[9]

Sitting at his dining room table in October 2003 and snacking on pita, hummus, and grapes, Alon mentioned that he had read in *Ma'ariv* that morning about the events of the day before, when Israeli warplanes and helicopters launched five strikes against targets in Gaza, its heaviest air strikes in months, killing at least ten Palestinians, including two senior members of Hamas, and wounding over a hundred. Alon's morning read shaped his movement that day. "You expect retaliation [from Palestinians] soon after. So, like, today I avoided going out altogether." Alon hypothesized that Palestinian desires for retaliation might lead to suicide bombings in Jerusalem city spaces. Alon did not actually stay home all day—he left to go to a class—but he did return home afterward, and, more than that, he spoke about a curtailed agenda for the day. Alon also used cause-and-effect reasoning to make decisions about the paths his girlfriend Sarah should or should not take. The day of the strikes in Gaza, Sarah had planned to go produce shopping in Maḥane Yehuda. "After I read the paper, I told her that it wasn't a good idea to go today. There's no need to go." Alon tried to caringly protect, or perhaps controllingly regiment, his girlfriend's daily movement. Sarah did not heed Alon's advice, she told me later (she went to the market anyhow), but she did not mind his concern. And Alon was proud of his protective role. His self-image as rational protector was clearly more bravado than reality, and his idea of staying home was more a way of speaking than a reflection of his day, but Alon's security projection remained an important part of how he described his day, himself, and his relationships.

I asked Alon how he developed his practice of drawing correlations between fighting in the West Bank and Gaza and the safety of a given day. "It's just intuitive," he told me. I pushed, and he elaborated. "Usually, I can just see the connection. Like the bomb [dropped by the IDF] in Gaza to try to kill [Sheikh Ahmed] Yassin. There was retaliation the next day. They [Palestinians] usually stand by their threats. You can usually see the cause-and-effect factor. I am not saying it is our [Israel's] fault that we get bombed, but you can usually predict it." Alon was referring to the IDF bombing in September 2003 of a building in Gaza City in an attempted assassination of Palestinian leader Sheikh Ahmed Yassin. This wounded but did not kill Yassin. In the days after the attempted assassination, mainstream Israeli newspapers filled with conjectures as to the likelihood and scale of Palestinian retaliation, and so while Alon was not unique in his speculation, he attributed his own suppositions of retaliation to his army experience. "I had a little black book in the army." As a paratrooper and an officer, Alon carried a small black calendar, an unclassified military document prepared by military intelligence and distributed to soldiers. As Alon explained, it listed Palestinian commemoration dates on which, the IDF warns, "Palestinians are more likely to react. We got an updated [calendar] every year." Alon described one particular entry. "I remember the 29th or 30th of March was Land Day. There was tension [on that day] every year, sometimes rioting, because that's the day the [Israeli] government took some of their [Palestinian] land." Known as Yawm al-Ard in Arabic, Land Day commemorates the March 30, 1976, killing of six Arab Israelis in the Galilee by Israeli soldiers during peaceful protests over Israel's confiscation of Palestinian land. Since then, this has become a day for Palestinians and peace activists to protest the illegality of Israeli occupation.[10]

The intersection of the military and civilian spheres in Israel has been the implicit or explicit focus of a large body of Israeli social science scholarship since the 1960s. In their study of what they describe as three generations of this work, political scientists Oren Barak and Gabriel Sheffer (2007) argue that as scholars became more critical of the IDF hegemony and the militarization of Israeli society, they came to depict the military and civilian sectors as increasingly interdependent or even indistinguishable. The mutual penetration of the two sectors is generally studied in the context of military departments or policy networks, but sociologists such as Edna Lomsky-Feder (1995) have shown that military mentalities are also adopted in civilian lives and integrated into the stories people tell of themselves. Indeed, Alon's subjective assimilation of a military mentality in his civilian life conditioned him to use publicly available information (instead of intelligence material) in his own home (not an army base) to determine movement in familiar urban space (not in battle zones) for himself and his girlfriend (rather than for an army unit or large civilian population). He transferred, if not actual military information, then styles of specialized military thinking to his life. In security projections such as his, private affect and state discourse become almost indistinguishable. Military sensibilities become the private consciousness of daily life.

If Israel is a chronically "interrupted system," a country so habituated to war that the society moves dexterously between war and peace, as if the two modes were complementary rather than binary (Kimmerling 1985), Alon saw his projection of security as a strategy for living normally in a state of interruption. Alon presented his security projection more as a means to facilitate normalized sociality than as a way to manage fear. He portrayed his daily techniques as a way of being Israeli. "We Israelis," Alon concluded his explanation, "wouldn't be able to plan our lives if we didn't have a system." Reflecting on why he relied on this kind of system in his life, he said to me, "You try to find some kind of order in these things. Because life would be very boring if we didn't go out at all. This is exactly Kant or Hume," he added. "We need to have some kind of cause and effect." Alon referred the philosophical debate over whether causal conceptions can be inferred from experience and the roles through which one determines objective causal relations between things. He implied that Western Enlightenment thought combined with security thinking could enable Israelis to evade or even counter Palestinian violence.

Sheri: Projecting Faith

When I first met Sheri Kashani, she was mourning the death of her mother, killed in a bombing at a market in Jerusalem by al-Aqsa Martyrs' Brigades. Her mother's death, her father's subsequent illness, and her newfound responsibility for her two younger siblings, eleven and sixteen (in addition to her own young daughters, aged two and four) made for high levels of stress and pressure. Given the nature of her mother's death, I anticipated that Sheri would be particularly consumed with attention to safety and danger. In conversations with her over the course of a year, however, she never described calculated travel or places she avoids. Religious belief, more than security warnings, seemed to permeate her perceptions of space. Sheri considered herself a religiously observant Jew: she covered her hair with a scarf or hat and wore skirts in modesty, ate only kosher-certified food, observed the Sabbath, sent her children to religious schools, and prayed every morning.

Her theology made her particularly critical of rationalized evasions of danger. On a spring afternoon in 2004, soon after Sheri returned home from the ophthalmology office where she worked, we sat at her Formica kitchen table over Nescafé and chocolate tea biscuits. As her young daughters played, nibbling on the biscuits, I asked Sheri how she got to work that morning. She explained that she drove every morning in the car she shared with her husband to her work as a receptionist in Talpiot. Her husband rode the bus to the opposite side of town. Did she worry about her husband's safety on the bus, I asked her. She shook her head and answered:

> I don't have these kinds of thoughts. There are people who say, 'I'm not going on buses anymore or around the city or to the mall.' But I think it's an issue of trust in God (*emuna*). . . . To my regret, not everyone has faith, so he has to instead be rational, with acumen (*sekhel*). Because to say "I'm not going on buses any more"—if you need to die, if your fate is to die, you'll die another way, you'll die in a road accident, you'll die in an accident at work.

Sheri argued that those who try to control their own safety by avoiding particular areas are resorting to *sekhel*, reason, to the detriment of *emuna*. With the term *emuna*, she referred not just to belief in God but to trust in and reliance on God. She spoke of fate, of the idea of divine providence, to assert that death, whether in a suicide bombing or a car accident, is preordained. From her perspective, to be truly "rational" means to travel freely and accept that God, not individuals, has control over life and death.

This is not to say Sheri was unafraid when she traveled. On her way to work that morning, Sheri had noticed that the streets were still filled with police and roadblocks and that individual Israelis were more vigilant than usual. Several days before, the IDF had assassinated the founder and main spiritual leader of Hamas, Sheikh Ahmed Yassin.

> Look, I'll tell you the truth, today I was going through the city on King George Street. It was after the assassination. The roads were filled with soldiers and police. So I said to myself, "*Oy*, how scary this is." Like, all of a sudden, I had this sort of "wow" feeling, thinking, if all of a sudden I die, what will happen to my daughters? All of a sudden you have a thought like this! And then I . . . saw how [a soldier] was armed and all of a sudden I had a thought that everyone else has, that I'm not going to the city, to the bus, to the mall. But then I woke up. So today I had fear and said, "No, it won't happen to me." I also have faith. I know that everyone has fear, but you also have to believe.

Sheri "woke up," determined not to get caught up in self-protective avoidance of particular places, determined to take control of her flashes of fear. "I don't think all the time, maybe tomorrow I'll die, maybe next week I'll die. A person has to live in reality," a reality, she explained, "where you can die of a bombing or of cancer any day."

Sheri's sense of providence may have had much to do with the shock and trauma of her mother's death, which disrupted the stability of her family and her sense of control. Perhaps, by believing her mother's death was not only unavoidable but also God's will, Sheri could retain a semblance of meaning and order. But she was also a religious person and these are concepts familiar to observant Jews. I once visited a small, densely packed Judaica bookstore in Mea Shearim, Jerusalem's ultra-Orthodox neighborhood. Near the counter and next to a doll named "Sarahleh" who at the touch of a button could sing the morning blessing "modeh ani," was a display shelf filled with dozens of business card-sized laminated cards containing various blessings: for a safe trip, for a blessed home, for success in life, for good business, for safe military service. They were forms of amulets called *segulot*. I asked the bookstore owner, a middle-aged man with a velvet yarmulke and side locks, whether sales of these blessing cards have increased since the beginning of the intifada. He said yes but quickly reminded me that the best *segula*, or assurance for good fortune, is to pray. As he climbed a ladder to fetch a book for me titled *Wars of Ishmael* (subtitled, *The words of the sages about what the Ishmaelites will do to the Jews and the rest of the world at the end of days*), he said to me:

> God doesn't tell me to sit at home all day. If it [a bombing] is going to happen to me, it'll happen to me at home. There are two ways of conceptualizing this. A man can say "if I deserve it" (*im magi'a li*) then it'll come to me wherever I am, so I can go anywhere, even to dangerous places. But this isn't right. The second man can refer to God's attribute of strict justice (*midat ha-din*). If a man has committed sins, and they accumulate in him, even if he is in a place where he wouldn't have otherwise been hurt, he could find himself in a place where *midat ha-din* touches him. It's a thing of faith. But you still need a strong heart.

The bookseller referred to *midat ha-din*, the divine quality of justice and judgment and the idea that God exacts punishment for sin. He suggested that being struck by a suicide bombing may be a punishment from God, or at least fated.

Sheri, like this bookseller, trusted more in God than in calculated self-protection, but she still directed her hopes and prayers toward safety. Reflecting her Iranian heritage as much as her religious practice, her home was filled with *ḥamsa* amulets, house blessings, and a large photograph of Ovadia Yosef, the former Sephardic chief rabbi of Israel and spiritual leader of the Shas party. [11] Through private prayers seeking the well-being of her family, or *segulot* she hung throughout her home, Sheri focused on means other than tactical avoidance to play an active role in her own protection. I knew that Sheri did engage in certain patterns of avoidance. Whenever she and her husband went on a date, they would go to the Malha Mall in Jerusalem, a place Israeli Jews often described during the second intifada as a *maqom sagur*, a "closed place," with its implicit connotations of safety from Palestinian bombings. But as they drove their car to the mall, a small plastic card dangled from the rearview mirror. It was *Tfilat ha-Derech*, The Traveler's Prayer, the traditional Jewish prayer for a safe journey recited at the outset of a trip:

> May it be Your will, Lord, our God and the God of our ancestors, that You lead us toward peace, guide our footsteps toward peace, and make us reach our desired destination for life, gladness, and peace. May You rescue us from the hand of every foe, ambush, bandits and wild animals along the way, and from all manner of punishments that assemble in the world. May You send blessing in our every handiwork, and grant us grace, kindness, and mercy in your eyes and in the eyes of all who see us. May You hear the sound of our supplication, because You are the God who hears prayer and supplications. Blessed are You, Eternal One, who hears prayer.

Even those who did navigate the city by calculating risk relied on belief and prayer. Tal Maimon began during the second intifada to "add an additional blessing. I pray to God to keep us all safe." Every Friday night when lighting the traditional Sabbath candles, she offered a personal supplication for safety and concluded with a traditional prayer for peace: *Oseh shalom bimromav*, May God who makes peace in the high places make peace for us and for all the people of Israel. Amen.

Conclusion: The Complexity of Self-Protection

Everyday projections of security are a domain in which individual, idiosyncratic affect and "rationalized" public discourses of safety and danger become nearly indistinguishable, where personal creativity and military logic coalesce. Noa, Liora, Alon, and Sheri did not simply transpose national discourses of security and threat onto their daily trajectories. Their imaginaries of danger were unique products of family histories, relationships, places of residence, religious sensibilities, and political beliefs. Noa's Jerusalem was strewn with remembered bombings, projected dangers, and personalized experiences of violence. Liora's visualization was highly calculated according to her premonition of bombings at particular times and places. Alon turned media information into military data that shaped his sense of daily safety and danger while Sheri's imagined route through Jerusalem held more strongly to faith than to fear. Their security projections displayed an "interweaving of different scales (spatial, economic, political, temporal, social)," as Sarah Green has described the process of making sense of space (Green 2005: 90). In each spatial story, places were variable in their safety: dangerous, then safe, then threatening again, in a flexible and fickle system where spatial meanings were constantly renewed following new events and new experiences. Individuals located movement within a delimited and routinized system and held firmly and emotionally onto an understanding of their schemes for self-protection as systematic, even when their techniques, to use Noa's term, allowed appraisals of safety to be revised. Different "modes of ordering" came together to create a complex system for movement that nonetheless had an aura of coherence, something Annemarie Mol and John Law lay out in their anthropological perspective on complexity theory (2002: 11). "In being reduced to a probability and framed as a risk they are turned into something that, however erratic, is also calculable" (3). Israelis' security projections were adaptable and even volatile, but still experienced as reliable and consistent.

The fixation on the calculation and interpretation of danger was itself a reassuring process. Many studies of post-traumatic stress disorder (PTSD) and anxiety-related depression in Israel affirm that Israelis relied on social networks and the routine of daily life to cope with anxiety and stress related to violence. Psychologists at the Center for Traumatic Stress at Hadassah Hospital in Jerusalem, studying the development of narratives of trauma among Israelis shot at by Palestinians in 2001 outside Kiryat Arbaʿ, cited "continuity and coherence" as crucial components of "effective coping" (Tuval-Mashiach et al. 2004: 282). Some studies, often those that use terms such as "resilience" and "defensive coping," pass subtle political judgment on the relative merit of the Palestinian versus Israeli cause. A study by psychologists from the United States and Israel, for example, attributed the higher levels of PTSD among Palestinian citizens of Israel, as compared with Jewish citizens of Israel to "greater authoritarianism and greater support for political violence" among Palestinians (Hobfoll, Canetti-Nisim, and Johnson 2006: 213).

Although one might describe the creation of security projections as a form of coping during conflict, strategies of coping and the very language with which Israeli Jews talk about what it means to cope can function like other practices of security to proliferate exclusive notions of us and them, inside and outside. The expectation that one can control uncertainty and contingencies is itself a position of political power, as Peter Marris argued in *The Politics of Uncertainty*. Like access to other resources, the ability to master contingencies is an effect of freedom and authority (Marris 1996: 66). Indeed, the trust that Noa, Liora, and Alon had in the ability of violence to be compartmentalized, predicted, or projected, and their construal of Palestinian resistance as a patterned phenomenon that, with proper rationalization and planning, could be avoided, were at least partial products of a confidence in Israel's authority and impregnability. Fixations on personal strategies for coping can make people blind to the structural conditions and political relations their self-protection entails.

If spatial stories were a form of "coping" with the precariousness of life during the second intifada, the fact that the narratives often elided mention of Palestinian bombings, omitted reference to Palestinians, or referred euphemistically to empty spaces reflected the power and bias inherent in strategies for "getting by" in daily life. Spatial circumnavigation of Palestinian spaces went hand in hand with rhetorical evasion of Palestinians. Often, Israelis' avoidance of Palestinian neighborhoods was so routine that it did not even warrant mention in their narratives of movement. In this sense, security projections are part of a history of Israeli erasures of Palestinian presence, from the Hebraicization of the Israeli map after 1948 to the ways Jewish settlement harnessed Palestinian cultural forms while concealing Palestinian origins; from the prioritizing of Jewish archaeological sites over Palestinian ones to the erasure in Israeli schoolbooks of evidence of the *Naqba* and memories of Palestinian life.[12] Israeli Jews may have experienced security projections as attempts to manage emotion and violence, but the projection—that is, the visualizing of suicide bombings and the hypervigilance for Palestinians— also precluded awareness of Palestinians and Palestinian spaces. Israelis' modes of deliberate movement were echoed in the home in the form of calculated inhabitation, or staying home as a carefully planned decision, the subject of the next chapter.

Chapter 6

On IKEA and Army Boots: The Domestication of Security

The Israeli market for Swedish massages and bed-and-breakfast retreats swelled soon after the start of the second intifada. As both diversions from and antidotes to the tension wrought by conflict, people sought out herbal relaxants, yoga classes, and psychotherapy sessions. Israeli terror victims' funds coordinated with kibbutz guesthouses to offer free rooms to terror victims during certain days of the week. At a time when foreign tourism to Israel diminished dramatically, Israelis reportedly spent 17 percent more nights in local hotels in 2003 than they did in 2000 (Steinberg 2003). People saw their own homes, with new resolve, as places of escape where they could lay down their fear and vigilance and live as if threat was elsewhere. Particularly during the second year of the second intifada, Israeli Jews turned their sociality inward, replacing trips to cafés, bars, and restaurants with visits to friends in their homes. Israelis stayed home for a range of interrelated economic and emotional reasons. In the days after a suicide bombing, people tended not to leave their homes because of a sense of civic respect to those killed and wounded, wanting to imbue life and interactions with a subdued, respectful tone. Re'ut, a journalist who lived in a small *moshav* outside Tel Aviv, recalled, "With the first bombing of the first restaurant, people just sat inside. No one was in the mood to go out, or felt they could at a time like that." Economics was also a factor in the turn homeward. As a result of the intifada, the slowing of Israel's high-tech industry, and the wane in international trade worldwide, the country's gross domestic product (GDP) fell by 6 percent in 2001 and 2002 (Ram 2008: 73), and the most severe recession since 1966 set in (Strasler 2003). With both unemployment and credit card purchases on the rise, staying home let people be more economical, although prevailing attributions of domestic enclaving to fear and terror often obscured this fact.

As much as Israelis avoided public spaces, they spoke more about staying home than they actually did, and even after Israelis began to regain confidence in public space in 2003, the idea of staying home remained strong in its discursive form. A discourse of staying home conditioned social experience at least as much as did the physical practice. Talking about the need to stay home was a means to mourn the devastation of public spaces of leisure (Stein 2002), which was itself a way to direct blame toward Palestinians. Discourses and material practices of staying home were an arena in which national notions of security and threat were simultaneously avoided and generated. This chapter studies the political signification of domestic escape. Anthropologists of material culture have shown how domestic materiality and individuals' identity are mutually constitutive, meaning that the ways people decorate their home, the appliances they use, and the guests they entertain reflect individual taste even as these aspects of the home constitute individual subjectivity.[1] Political conflict inserts new variables into domestic materiality, new tactics and vocabularies of dwelling. Violence that enters homes in times of conflict, as ethnographies of war have shown, resignifies the spatial and symbolic protection that this space normally provides.[2] In describing this phenomenon in Israel, I use the term domestication of security to encapsulate how domesticity contained, evaded, and produced experiences and objects of national conflict, specifically of state security. Domestic practices and paraphernalia that Israeli Jews turned to as antidotes to anxiety themselves became artifacts of national security.

Palestinians could not easily experience their homes as retreats. As Julie Peteet explains, "The continuous violation of the [Palestinian] home—the violent entries, searches, and demolitions . . . quickly cast aside notions of home as a space distant from conflict" (1997: 108). From the Palestinian revolt of 1936–39 and the wars of 1948–49 and 1967, Palestinians' homes were the military front. More recently, Israel's policy of demolishing houses in the West Bank and Gaza Strip as a punitive measure against the Palestinian population and restrictions on movement imposed by Israel through checkpoints and the separation wall have denied Palestinians the ability to go home in the literal as well as the metaphorical sense. The loss of personal homes is tantamount to the absence of a Palestinian national homeland, both central to Palestinian experience (Feldman 2000: 16). "For the Palestinian exiled," Rabab Abdulhadi writes, "*going home* brings back memories of one's worst nightmares at international borders: interrogation and harassment, suspicion of malintent, and rejection of one's chosen self-identification" (2003: 89).[3]

The homes of Israeli Jews have not been threatened to the same extent, but their inhabitants similarly equate personal domicile with a national homeland.[4] "Home" was never simply a residential structure. Discourses of staying at home during the second intifada were bound with the nationalist concept of a Jewish homeland (*moledet*), the view of Israel as a place of refuge for a persecuted people after a two-thousand-year exile (Almog 2000: 44). The terms homeland and home (*bayyit*) similarly connoted belonging and security, and sometimes the two ideas blurred. When Sheri Kashani, the mother of two young girls who lived in Pisgat Ze'ev, criticized Israel's separation wall, her grievance was that seeing the wall outside her family's apartment made her feel not at home in the country. "I don't want the fence near my house. It's my home," she said, first pointing to her apartment and then gesturing with her hands open wide to refer to Israel more broadly. The wall constricted her family's home as well as her national home. Political campaigns harnessed the political resonance of "home." In the 2003 election for prime minister, for instance, the National Religious Party (NRP) used as its central slogan, "Guarding your home, NRP." Promising to protect people's homes conveyed the party's devotion to a Jewish nation and its promise of robust defensive actions against Palestinians. Here, the idea of home functioned the way it does in the case of the U.S. Office of Homeland Security, where, as Amy Kaplan (2003) contends, the very name of the institution creates a sense of the nation as home while, at the same time, propagating intense fear of lurking threat: "a sense of the foreign is necessary to erect the boundaries that enclose the nation as home" (59).[5] As a space and a political discourse, "homeland" provided security while proliferating deep insecurity.

To study domesticity as a phenomenon of conflict is not to suggest that Israelis could always find comfort at home, for the tensions of conflict often turned the home into a space of palpable violence. Simona Sharoni has pointed to the direct correlation during the first intifada between Israel's violence in the occupied territories and domestic violence in Israeli homes (1994b: 126). During the period of the second intifada, 47 percent of the women killed in domestic violence were reportedly killed by soldiers, security guards, and police officers carrying licensed guns that they turned on partners or relatives (Sinai 2005). Nor when I study domestic comfort do I imply that it was a phenomenon unique to the second intifada[6] or that it was the sole mode of solace during periods of tension, for indeed Israelis also found comfort in relationships, religion, and medicine (Bleich, Gelkopf, and Solomon 2003). Nonetheless, envelopment in the domestic was a pervasive means through which

Israeli Jews sought feelings of safety and achieved fantasies of escape, not only from Palestinians but also from Israel. This chapter begins with a discussion of the ways Israeli homes are already shaped by explicit state directives and by the more informal circulation of army artifacts. The spaces in which Israelis "stayed home" during the second intifada already contained material traces of the military and state strategies of civilian protection. I then examine the rhetorical, economic, and material expressions of the Israeli discourse of home, suggesting that fantasies of the home as a retreat reinforced a politics of normalization and the belief that conflict is sustainable.

The State at Home

Homes have been conscripted into Israel's quest for territory. Since Israelis began establishing settlements in the West Bank and Gaza, rows of small homes functioned like tanks or troops, "deployed in formation," as Eyal Weizman puts it, inanimate civilian soldiers that claimed Jewish space and displaced Palestinian villages and agricultural livelihood (2007: 84). On hilltops overlooking Palestinian homes, buttressed by electronic surveillance, the terraced, red-roofed homes have been integral to Israeli geopolitical strategy. My focus here, however, is on the ways interior domestic spaces have been configured by the state in the name of national security. Throughout the country, on the stone walls of apartment buildings or fences around community centers, one can still spot orange and black stenciled signs with the word *miqlat* (shelter), pointing local residents to the nearest communal bomb shelter. These signs have been present for decades, some dating from the 1960s, when the government began requiring new apartment buildings to contain communal bomb shelters. During the Gulf War in 1991, when Israel was faced with Iraqi SCUD missile attacks and feared chemical attack, government directives for protection at home became more explicit and meticulous. The Ministry of Defense instructed civilians to transform a bedroom or bathroom in their home into a "sealed room" (*heder atum*) with windows sealed with duct tape and plastic tarpaulin. In the name of national security, Israelis bought tape and tarp and revamped a portion of their homes according to state instruction. During air raid warnings, civilians heeded government directives to don gas masks, enter the sealed room, and place a wet cloth along the bottom of the closed door and masking tape along the top.[7]

After the war, Israel's newly created Home Front Command (Pikud ha-Oref) formalized and elaborated these directions under the Doctrine for the Protection of the Civilian Population. Every new building was required to contain a sealed, ventilated, and easy-to-reach space that could provide several hours of "protection" against both conventional and chemical weapons without the need to wear gas masks. It was called a *merhav mugan dirati* (residential protected space) or by the acronym *mamad*, but people more commonly referred to these rooms as their *heder bitahon* (literally, security room). The Home Front Command's instructions for this "do-it-yourself security" (Lichtman 2006) were exhaustive. As outlined on the Home Front Command Web site, "The *mamad* is five square meters per residential unit, and it includes no more than two external walls. The *mamad* contains a shock-resistant, outwards-opening door, located on an internal wall." Shock-resistant windows were to be sealed by attaching polypropylene adhesive tape 30 microns thick and 50 wide around the window and over hinges and locks. Through sealed rooms and security rooms, the state not only entered into but also shaped the organization of domestic space to protect citizens, as well as to engender civilian trust in the state.

In the spring of 2003, when the impending American invasion of Iraq triggered fear in Israel of Iraqi reprisal reminiscent of the Scud missile attacks in 1991, the Home Front Command again directed civilians to prepare sealed rooms and acquire supplies for the protected space. Israeli newspapers filled with government directives for civilian protection at home. In anticipation of a chemical attack, Israelis were to prepare a small room in the home hermetically sealed with plastic sheeting and duct tape and supplied with food, water, emergency lighting, and a transistor radio. All civilians and foreign workers were instructed to assemble their "protective kit," a box containing a gas mask, an air filter, and an atropine shot (an antidote for poison gas). In contrast to diligent compliance in 1991, however, most Israelis brazenly disregarded these directives, choosing to maintain their regular routines rather than engage in preemptive defense. "I bought plastic because they told us to," one longtime resident of Arad told me, "but I ended up using the plastic to cover the table!" Israelis became more eager to conceal than to fortify sealed rooms. The "materiality of dwelling" (Humphrey 2005: 39) has a powerful ability to instill ideology and produce new social forms but not always in the straightforward way the state intends. In Caroline Humphrey's study of Soviet communal dwellings, she argues that prefabricated communal hostels did not so much generate socialist ideology as deflect it: "ideology was embedded-released-diverted in and by material life" (Humphrey 2005: 50). In Israel, sealed rooms became a domain for the creative reformulation of government dogma, as Shlomit Maimon attested in her description of home renovation.

In 1999, an extensive remodeling of the Maimon family's attached stone house in Ramat Eshkol converted the home built in the early 1970s into a three-story, open-plan space. When Shlomit first moved into the house, the basement contained a room that, with its below-ground walls and blast-resistant door, could function as a bomb shelter. Shlomit, however, wanted this space to serve as a bedroom for one of her sons and she removed the thick door, a shelter's fundamental feature, to make the room more welcoming and to create more space for book storage.[8] The decision was partly one of design, but Shlomit also expressly wanted to do away with the shelter. "We came to this house with the feeling that in a new home you don't want to install defense." Shlomit used the phrase *la'asot haganot* (to do defense). "When you come to a new house," she continued, "you don't want to think about how to be afraid in it. We said that we would not keep that space as a *miqlat* (shelter). We do not need a *miqlat*. We all thought that way. Although if you think about it, it is not very logical to be in this country and not have a *miqlat*! We have lived through a number of wars in this country. It's not like we're in Peace Now or something." Shlomit explained that her disinclination to retain the shelter was not a sanguine hope for peace but rather a desire to suspend thoughts of fear and danger. She felt that a shelter would remind her of the potential for danger, thus creating rather than allaying fear. Yet even as she spoke to me, Shlomit questioned the logic of her decision to do away with the door. "I don't know what made me think we don't need a *miqlat*, as if we're academics that think only about our books!" In the spring of 2004, at least, bookshelves more so than blast-proof walls facilitated her fantasy of safety. Still, Shlomit's home never truly evaded state visions for defense, for even without the shelter's heavy door, she continued to sense the shelter's absent presence whenever she passed her son's basement room.

Uniforms in Reserves

The boundary between military and social spheres in many Israeli contexts is permeable and intermingled,[9] and the home is no exception. The military is materially and relationally integrated into many Israeli homes, quietly permeating space and daily life in ways that constantly transpose the comfortable and uncomfortable quality of objects. With two to three years of national military service mandatory for all Israeli citizens over the age of eighteen (the state exempts or excludes Israeli Arabs who are not Bedouin or Druze), it is not surprising that military objects pile up at home. Shai, the Bergmann family's younger son, was in the final year of his military service when I lived with the family in Arad in 2004. Shai's IDF-issued possessions were in constant circulation throughout his parents' home. On alternate Fridays, when he arrived home for the weekend, as many soldiers do, his long green army duffel

Figure 9. Shai's parents' living room. His army uniform hangs over a chair in the foreground.

bag sat by the front door until he returned late from the bar with his friends. Throughout the weekend, his army boots stood by the stairs and his camouflage officer's shirt seemed permanently hung over a living-room chair. During the week, while Shai was stationed at checkpoints in the West Bank, his mother and father cycled his IDF-issued undershirts and socks in and out of the washing machine. Israeli washers and dryers were also drafted to serve the country. "This is what it meant to be part of Am Yisrael (People of Israel) during that period," Shlomit Maimon once told me as she recalled hanging her own son's laundry out to dry when he was stationed in Lebanon. Ever present and in constant motion, the cycles of clothing gave military service a palpable presence at home.

The bedroom that became mine while I lived with the Bergmann family belonged to Shai's twenty-six-year-old brother Itai. A mound of olive-green t-shirts and long underwear were piled in his wardrobe. Army uniforms hung from metal hangers and a green duffel bag lay in the corner. A framed photograph of Itai with his family at his army discharge ceremony hung on the wall over his bed, and a casual snapshot of him as a young soldier sat on the corner of his desk. Wearing dark sunglasses, he is smiling with a gun slung across his shoulder. The array of camouflage suggested active duty, but Itai had been out of the army for four years and was currently spending the year traveling in Thailand with his girlfriend. His childhood bedroom was frozen in time, the military objects waiting until, once a year, they would be called up for Itai's annual military reserve duty.

Figure 10. Itai's dusty army boots tucked in the corner of his attic bedroom, together with the gas mask kit distributed by the government to civilians in 2003.

The circulation of Shai and Itai's military objects through the home not only mingled military and civilian aspects of life but also blurred the boundaries between them. They hovered inexplicably between the familial and the martial, filling domestic spaces with, if not discomfort, then uncertainty. "As these seemingly mundane objects circulate," Linda Green says of camouflage cloth turned into small market trinkets in Guatemala's Highlands, "they normalize the extent to which civilian and the military life have commingled" (1999: 63). Army objects also overlay mundane domestic artifacts such as sheets and washing machines with military overtones: an "insidious militarization of daily life" (63). Yolanda Gampel (2000) uses the notion of the uncanny in her psychoanalytic study of Holocaust survivors in Israel to describe experiences of terror that confound all that is familiar and soothing, experiences that can never be fully articulated. When memories of the uncanny, she argues, are layered over with what she calls backgrounds of safety, following psychoanalyst Joseph Sandler (1960), the result is ambiguity and confusion. Senses of safety exist but always alongside feelings of fragmentation. A similar process was at play in Israel during the second intifada, when domestic spaces strewn with military materiality became contexts for a discourse of "staying home." When comfort was pursued in already fraught domestic spaces, domestic artifacts and practices intending to protect body, space, and consciousness contained within them strains of violence. But even if army objects militarized intimate space, families such as the Bergmanns did not see their own home as in any way uncanny or inhospitable. Shai and Itai's mother Naomi realized her home was filled with army gear, and, I sensed, experienced those artifacts now and again as quiet reminders of her family's duty to the state. Still, her home did not feel any less intimate to her. In fact, the wash cycles appeared to have the opposite effect: domesticating military life and rendering the military familiar.

A Discourse of Staying Home

Staying home and narratives of staying home were fundamental components of Israeli Jews' experience during the intifada, particularly among urbanites in their twenties and thirties. The emotional intensity and elaborate detail of people's stories of staying home reflected their sense of the political significance of domestic retreat. For Ori Maimon, Shlomit and Ilan's twenty-eight-year-old son who grew up in Jerusalem and lived with his wife in Haifa, a discourse of staying home overlay his narrative of this period of Israeli-Palestinian violence. In the fall of 2003, he looked back to 2002 as a distinct phase of the intifada. "That was a time when we met in apartments," he recalled. "It was the same as going out, but less exciting. But we didn't need to get dressed up, and it was cozier." By glossing the reasons for staying home and talking about coziness and convenience, Ori accentuated the effects of the intifada on his daily life while normalizing the process. He described the time spent at home with a degree of acceptance and even contentment; he highlighted the advantages of staying home rather than bemoaning the interruption posed by the intifada. By November 2003, Ori and his friends continued to meet in people's homes: "We don't go out for a burger. If it's just to get food, we'll get takeout and then eat at home. If we just want to talk, there is no reason we should go out, so we just sit in someone's house. If it's a beer we want, you can't achieve that atmosphere if you stay at home, so we *would* meet in a bar." Ori presented a carefully considered scheme according to which he would eat at home if it did not infringe on the overall social experience, but he would be willing to venture to a restaurant if he sought a particular cuisine, did not want to cook, or was feeling claustrophobic. Tellingly, Ori's description of the turn homeward during the height of the intifada was peppered with references to eating out. Staying home was not merely an assessment of danger; it was also a valuation of aesthetics and ambiance. "We really did spend a lot of time at home then," he concluded his narrative, as if he knew that the discourse of staying home was more politically potent than any effort to go out.

Gil Shahar, the husband of Noa who lived in Motza outside Jerusalem, also spoke expressively about his experience of staying home during the second intifada, even as he later mocked the very way Israelis dramatized their experience of staying home. Gil told me his story of staying home to illustrate how he lost what he called "a post-Zionist ideal of freedom, of living your life." The winter of 2002 was the first time he amended his plans because of the fear of Palestinian violence. Gil and Noa, then his girlfriend, went with two friends to a bar in downtown Jerusalem:

> We went to a place called Focaccia Bar. The guard checked our bags very carefully and everyone was, well, there was some kind of tension. Then I heard someone say that they announced in the news that there is a terrorist in the center of Jerusalem, right at that moment! Maybe he was heading to one of the cafés! So, we decided to go home, because how could we sit there knowing he might come to the bar? We all decided to go. It was the first time I remember thinking to myself, "Wow, we changed our plans, we want to go home." And so we hung out at home, not in the bar.

Gil's voice was low and glum as he finished his story. For him, the return home represented a difficult adjustment in his social environment. Gil was not so much lamenting Palestinian violence or the danger of public space as much as bemoaning the loss of a social space that represented normal life. Although some people returned to cafés after bombings to demonstrate their resilience in the face of conflict and to assert their defiance of Palestinians, others like Gil returned, in his words, "to make the world know that I'm not changing my normal life!" Like his wife, Gil considered himself a post-Zionist, which he described as "an ideal of keeping your life, your normal life."

On an earlier occasion, Gil had actually ridiculed the way fellow Israelis told dramatic narratives of staying home, seemingly like his own. "It's just that it sounds good to say in the newspapers, the *Jerusalem Post* or *Yediot*, 'Oh, we are all staying home because of the situation.'" Gil was cynical about the ways people spoke about staying home as if they needed to take cover from violence, whereas really, he claimed, the reasons were more mundane. "If [Israelis] don't go out it's usually because we are tired or busy or studying. Or the places are full." Staying home "sounds good," he said, suggesting that it conveys suffering or lays blame for the

Israeli-Palestinian conflict on Palestinians. Clearly, however, Gil himself did not fully escape the hold of the discourse of staying home.

Staying Home Economics

The discourse of staying at home may have exceeded actual practice, but the turn homeward nonetheless generated new modes of domestic consumption. Food was particularly significant for the culture and economy of home. In large part, food served those physiological and social functions it often does in contexts of stress, acting not only as a soothing and distracting indulgence but also as a conduit for feelings of family, togetherness, and tradition. Food provided reassurance and warmth and mediated people's connections to their family and their community (Counihan 1999: 37). During the second intifada, Israelis overlaid food practices with nationalist valences of suffering and, equally, of perseverance. As a woman in Arad said to me, "Food is a source of comfort, especially now, when the family just caves in. Life is really concentrating more on home. Because it's scary out there."

Around the country, restaurants quickly found ways to cater to those afraid of dining out who nonetheless wanted the feeling of eating out. Cooking classes, newly popular, tried to appeal to people who wanted to avoid restaurants but still socialize through food (Rousso 2003). Restaurants and cafés, particularly in large cities, began to offer takeout food for the first time, to counteract the decline in dining-in sales and to allow people to transfer feelings of public sociality to the home. In the fall of 2003, leaflets began to appear under apartment doors. A popular café on Ben Yehuda Street in Jerusalem advertised an extensive menu with "Take Away" written in English in large letters at the top. A flier for "Café Filter" advertised "Delivery" available between 12:00 and 23:00. Rebecca Stein (2002) argues in her analysis of the politics of consumption during the second intifada that the transition to takeout threatened Israeli Jews' desires for an open and cosmopolitan public sphere. Although coffee in paper mugs impinged on fantasies of Jerusalem as Paris, the fear and violence that spurred this new mode of consumption were often swept aside, replaced by the novelty and possibility it afforded.

Indeed, Israelis focused more on the ingenuity of intifada substitutions than on the political conditions of their emergence. New routines of domestication included small adjustments people made to their dining habits so as to feel safe without sacrificing scheduled plans. On Fridays, a weekend day for most Israelis, Ilan and Shlomit Maimon's favorite place for a leisurely lunch of *me'orav yerushalmi* (a mixed grill of organ meats with onion, garlic, and spices served in pita bread) was a small stand in

Jerusalem's downtown Maḥane Yehuda market. For years, they parked one street over and walked to the small food stand, where they ate their mixed grill on bar stools. Beginning in 2002, the couple modified this practice. Ilan drove to the restaurant to pick up two sandwiches and then brought them home, where he and Shlomit reconstructed their Friday routine at their kitchen table. When Ilan and Shlomit described this to me, their focus was only parenthetically about the effects of the second intifada; their real focus was the challenge of eating their delicacy while it was still warm and the pleasure of a dual delight in home and in *meʿorav*.

In addition to literal forms of consumption, the media reinforced the role television could play in turning the home into a site of safe sociality. Israelis have long zealously watched the evening news, and, during the second intifada, stations appealed specifically to peoples' desire to engage with the nation from the comfort of their home. A marketing campaign of Arutz 2 (Channel 2), Israel's most popular television station, relied on domestic iconography to depict the home as a domain of national unity and diversion.[10] One of Channel 2's 2004 ad campaigns used the slogan, *Shtayim ze tamid bi-yahad!*, or "Two is always together." The motto proposed that television viewers stay together—that is, with the station and with each other—at home. In the winter, the ads featured steaming cups of coffee and rainy day scenes presented as viewed from a cozy interior, appealing to familial and national camaraderie at home. And watch television Israelis did. In 2001, according to the Central Bureau of Statistics, Israelis purchased 25,930 more televisions and over 78,000 more videocassette recorders (VCRs) than they did in 2000 (Israel Central Bureau of Statistics 2007). Video rentals, according to the CEO of Blockbuster in Israel, peaked immediately following suicide bombings in 2002 and 2003. Following a series of bombings in 2002, rentals increased by 50 to 60 percent, while during periods of calm, the CEO reported, sales were only 10 percent above average (Lori 2002). Anecdotally, people told me that they and their friends were watching more television than usual during the intifada (particularly new Israeli reality shows), rented more DVDs on the weekends, and downloaded more movies from www.kazaa.com, a peer-to-peer file-sharing Web site first introduced in the Netherlands but very popular in Israel. Fear and a national discourse of staying home generated an intensely media-filled retreat into the home.

Intifada Decorating

Domestic retreat during the second intifada heightened interest in home aesthetics, and purchases of furniture and home-decorating items increased by 20 percent in 2001 (Israel Central Bureau of Statistics 2009b).

In sometimes dramatic but generally unassuming ways, and often more in daydreams than in reality, Israelis physically redesigned and socially reconceived their homes as sites for comfortable sociality. People sought ways, as Naomi Bergmann put it while sitting in her Arad living room, "to arrange your environment so you don't feel you're in a difficult situation." With a new coat of paint or a re-angled sofa, domestic space could become a refuge. The process of redecorating could itself serve as a distraction from political violence, a means, in Mary Douglas's terms, to impose "system on an inherently untidy experience," to purify and demarcate one's interior life as separate from the national reality (1966: 4). The materiality and the process of home decorating were apparatuses for the security of everyday life.

Children were often the impetus for decorated spaces. This was the case for Vered, whose drive to Jerusalem opened this book and who lived in a working-class neighborhood of Holon in a multigenerational apartment she shared with her son and his girlfriend, her older daughter and her two children, and her youngest daughter and her boyfriend. Vered's dimly lit home was filled with comfortable but worn furniture packed into tight spaces, but her granddaughters' bedroom was a world apart from the rest of the home. In the room the two sisters shared, a frilly canopy matching the purple-and-white flowered wallpaper hung over two bright pink bedspreads. In the corner of the room, a computer with Internet access allowed the seven- and nine-year-old girls to take turns chatting on instant messenger. Decorating the room in this way, Vered explained to me, was a priority for her and her daughter, despite the fact that the two salaries that supported the household rarely allowed for comparable lifestyle indulgences. Vered hoped their room would lure her daughters to play indoors rather than on the street, where she feared Palestinians could place bombs. "It's because, especially now, we want the girls to enjoy playing at home. You know, there's no such thing as a safe place now. I don't understand Arabs, I just don't understand them. Houses are safe, *barukh Hashem* (praise God), but our country is not good now, not at all." The pink room, in Vered's mind, would envelop her grandchildren in a calm and consoling environment, a sanctuary that would enable the granddaughters' life to feel ordered and unimpinged by the extraordinary conditions of conflict, or by "Arabs." The room may have been pink and lacy had there not been an Israeli-Palestinian conflict, but Vered justified its décor by tapping into notions of pervasive danger and Palestinians' unreasonableness. Even when it took the form of interior decorating, self-protection was infused with the binaries of safety and danger, Jew and Arab.

Israeli discourses of national security were also projected onto transnational companies specializing in home décor. IKEA Israel, the Israeli branch of the Swedish chain selling hip, affordable home furniture and accessories, was politically fraught even before it opened. The Israeli media carped that the company opened branches in Kuwait, Saudi Arabia, and the United Arab Emirates before opening in Israel and accused IKEA's Swedish founder and chairman, Ingvar Kamprad, of de facto complicity in the Arab boycott of Israel. This may have been what spurred the marketing manager for IKEA Israel to boast when it did open in Netanya in the spring of 2001 that the store would be "two times the size of any existing retail store in Israel and bigger than any other IKEA store in the Middle East" (Berger 2000). Jewish communal leaders hailed the opening of IKEA as a boon to Zionism, "another chink in the attempts that are still out there to boycott Israel" (Altman-Ohr 2000).

Whether it was patriotism or the thrill of BILLY bookcases, as soon as the Israeli branch opened, IKEA became immensely popular. Marveling at Scandinavian flatware and testing minimalist settees was an affordable imagined escape that also had political resonance. One woman from Arad in her fifties, about to make the over two-hour trip to buy shelves at IKEA, explained that making such a long journey all the way to Netanya to buy ornamental objects was a way of assuring herself that "things are normal enough that I can treat myself to this." Walking through IKEA's homey showrooms was an opportunity to immerse herself in the imagined life of another person or another place. She would make the trip even though she was afraid to drive on Route 6. In the pursuit of comfort, normalcy became synonymous with escape.

IKEA was aware of the fantasies it provided for Israelis. Romi Gil, IKEA Israel's director of design, noticed in 2004, "Many people can sit for hours. They chat, move furniture, mothers change diapers, couples lie on the bed, get under the blanket" (Hadar 2004). Not unlike IKEA customers in other countries, Israelis benefitted not just from imagining the items as their own but by immersing themselves in a consumptive, comfortable environment that belonged to another world. IKEA's popularity in Israel was invigorated, according to Aryeh Sivan, head of the Interior Design department at the College of Administration, by "our [Israeli Jews'] thirst for imitating the way things are abroad, in order to be equals among equals" (Shilo 2005). IKEA's Scandinavian fantasy afforded feelings of Israel's normalcy as a nation and Israelis saw IKEA as a way to normalize their lives during the intifada. KARLSTAD loveseats and birch veneer beds became proof that Israel is "a member with equal rights in the community of nations," as A. B. Yehoshua wrote in 1980.[11]

Textual retreats into dwelling publications, as well as the physical reorganization of the home, turned decorative domesticity into a component of Israel's fortified homefront. The media indulged and proliferated the idea that Israelis needed feelings of escape in order to cope with the political situation. Israel's Channel 2 launched a new home improvement show called *Avodat Bayyit* (*Housework*) and, in August 2004, a new Israeli cable television channel called *Kol Eḥad Yakhol* (*Anyone Can*) focusing on do-it-yourself (DIY) home design was launched. *Ḥadarim* (*Rooms*) by Orly Robinson was a best-selling book of interior design in 2003, featuring photographs of cozy, rustic living rooms, glowing fireplaces, and kitchen windows looking out onto wooded backyards, domiciles hardly Middle Eastern. Interior decorating television shows blossomed in the United States, United Kingdom, and elsewhere beginning in the late 1990s, but the parallel development in Israel assumed resonances of the Israeli-Palestinian conflict. In 2002, Israeli daily newspapers began to devote more space and attention to stories about cooking, fashion, and foreign travel. One food writer for *Haʾaretz* was told by the paper not to discuss current events in her column. "My editors say that *Haʾaretz* is so heavily political that people resort to my column to relax a little. So why bother them again with everything they just run away from?" Her own perspective was more complicated, and she took it upon herself to find a middle ground "between comfort and complete escapism," as she put it. But around the country, newspaper articles with titles such as "Journey to Inner Space" (Hadar 2004) and "The Age of Anxiety" (Lori 2002) proliferated and showed how Israelis were "pampering [themselves] with new appliances and binging on sweets—these are all ways in which Israelis are coping with the trauma of the home-front war."

Between 2002 and 2004, the number of design magazines published in Israel increased by 40 percent while bookstore sales of design magazines increased by 15 percent in 2003 (Hadar 2004). In June 2004, I perused the section of home decorating, design, and architecture magazines at the Steimatsky bookstore on Jaffa Road in Jerusalem. There were six habitat magazines published in Israel in Hebrew, including *Binyan Vi-diyyur* (*Building and Housing*) and *Architecture and Design Quarterly*; and over ten international publications in Russian, French, Spanish, and English. The Israeli magazines were often self-conscious about, or at least aware of, the diversion they offered from the Israeli-Palestinian conflict and made explicit reference to the intifada. The June 2004 edition of *AKOKA: Architecture and Interior Design*, a glossy magazine published in Tel Aviv, opened with the following letter from the editors:

Dear Readers,

   During these difficult times of instability in our country and in the world, we present *Akoka* No. 18 (the symbol of Life) to bring a bit of sanity and culture into our lives, and to prove that it's still possible to enjoy quality in an environment that provides inspiration and hope for the continuance of creativity and technological development on behalf of mankind. Contrary to our previous editions, this time the magazine is mostly dedicated to the design of the private house, emphasizing a subject that is so important to us all.[12]

This letter had overtones of holistic psychology—inspiration, hope, creativity—combined with a specifically Jewish form of reassurance based on the numerological system of *Gematria,* or Hebrew numerology. (The Hebrew word *chai,* meaning life, is composed of two letters that have a numerical value equivalent to the number eighteen, which is a lucky number and a symbol of life.) The language of the editorial may have been New Age, but its implication was political, namely, that readers should retreat from national politics and into the pages of the magazine. Perusing the magazine, the editors suggested, would provide the reader with a respite from the tension and instability of life in Israel. As promised, the issue contained stunning photographs of sunny homes with green lawns and airy home offices, all located in Israel but appearing to be elsewhere, or anywhere. The magazine implied that inhabiting these lush architectural spaces or, perhaps just as much, imagining oneself in them, would proffer a taste of normalcy and comfort to Israelis tense and despondent living through prolonged conflict. The Israeli home was configured as an alternative to conflict, a bourgeois space in which Israeli modernity, with its European and cosmopolitan air, could persist, but more safely and in isolation.

There is much that was not exclusively Israeli about the proliferation of home improvement in Israel in recent years. Furniture stores, architecture magazines, and the media of real estate provide a kind of retail therapy to consumers almost the world over. IKEA has, of course, generated fantasies far beyond Israel about artsy, minimalist alternative identities, as shown, for example, in a recent ethnography of "Ikeaization" in France (Hartman 2007). Israeli Jews' desires for home comfort exemplified bourgeois practices of fortification found elsewhere, such as in the world of the Saõ Paulo elite, described by Caldeira (2000), where middle-class communities turned their homes into "fortified enclaves" that proscribed an exterior presence and denied rapport with the rest of the city. Some aspects of Israeli enclaving were not unlike those of the middle-class American families Setha Low describes who encase themselves in gated and guarded communities to seek not only personal safety but also social purity and economic security (2003a). The surge of DIY projects and products (cement, wall paint, molding) in Britain, according to Alison Clarke, was bound with aspirations for taste, distinction, and social sameness. Through DIY, people engaged in "fantasy and action, projection and interiorization" (2001: 25). Decorating homes afforded Israelis similar diversion and aspiration, but domestic fantasies had particular consequences when bound with imaginaries of Palestinian bombings, and when home comforts acted in tandem with state discourses that juxtapose the familiar and the foreign, the safe and the threatening, the Jewish and the Arab. IKEA, home magazines, and new coffee machines enabled Israelis to feel as if they were not in conflict, as if they had nothing to do with the Israeli occupation of Palestinian territory. As much as security was about keeping Palestinian "terror" out of Israel, in its everyday domestic form, it was also about keeping Israel out of the Middle East. Domestic materiality offered Israelis imagined escape, not just out of conflict but also out of Israel.

Conclusion: The Politics of Comfort

Homes seem, at first glance, to defy the dogma and strain of the public sphere, as Lauren Berlant argues: "Domestic privacy can feel like a controllable space, a world of potential unconflictedness (even for five minutes a day): a world built for you. It may seem of a manageable scale and pacing; at best, it makes visible the effects of one's agency, consciousness, and intention" (2000: 6). Even as the domestic domain into which Israelis retreated was already permeated with state directives and with militarized artifacts, homes still felt like havens to their inhabitants. With pink canopies and takeout *me'orav yerushalmi*, forms of material sociality imbued with feelings of ease and escape during this period, Israeli Jews could "live *as if* threatening contexts are merely elsewhere" (5) and shield themselves from the public spaces they saw as perilous and bleak. They could protect their minds and bodies from an overwhelming reality. Creating a pleasing interior and swathing family members offered not only feelings of escape or respite from a disordered outside world but also a sense of control, at least over one's immediate environment. And yet, as Israeli Jews enveloped themselves at home, objects and practices of domestic comfort carried with them ideas intrinsic to Israeli political discourses of security, including notions of defense, fantasies of normalization, and binaries of safety versus danger. Rhetoric of "staying home" implied that Palestinian violence had instilled danger and desolation in the Israeli landscape and that Israelis were not able to go about their normal routines. "Staying home" did not diverge from conflict but operated within its confines.

This is not to say that Israelis were unaware of the uncanny juxtaposition of conflict and comfort. Staying home was sometimes bound up with people's misgivings about their presence in Israel and even their reservations about their identity as Israelis. In the winter of 2004, Noa Shahar described a clash between intimacy and violence she had experienced that morning as she watched television while nursing her son:

I got up at ten in the morning. I sat to nurse [my son] Adin. On Channel 2 the news was already over, but on Channel 10 there was a cooking
and traveling show about international cuisine, with views, wonderful views
and everything, and running underneath were the headlines of the recent
news: a suicide bombing on [bus] line 19. And [the headlines] ran and
ran: those hurt, those killed, telephone numbers [of local hospitals]. The
suicide bomber, the driver, the rescue workers. And I am looking at this:
on top they are cooking gourmet food, and on the bottom these headlines.
And I am breastfeeding Adin. And I had this feeling of how could I possibly
bring a baby into the world when we live in such a reality? This feeling that
I'm irresponsible for raising him here, that it's an egoistic thing to bring a
child into the world in Israel.

Noa was incensed by the way the media tried to control violence by over-
laying bombing with gourmet food. She wanted to distance herself from
the television's apparent mockery of tragedy and from this country that
seemed to her in this moment to aestheticize and routinize suffering.

As Noa breastfed Adin in front of the streaming news on television, two
disparate fantasies intermingled. There was the fantasy of normalization,
perpetuated by the Israeli media and undergirded by an Israeli ethic
of perseverance, one where cooking shows and suicide bombings could
not only coexist but could regulate each other. Even as she criticized this
fantasy, Noa did not exclude herself from it. Her synchronized breastfeeding and news-watching embodied it, and she was ashamed of this. "I
look at Adin" she said, "and I try not to think about it. But I don't really
succeed in finding comfort because I don't see things going to a good
place." With the intrusion of the news into her living room, Noa could
not experience her home as a space of escape or safe closeness with her
son, and she blamed herself for getting into this situation. As much as
Noa enclaved herself, she remained uncomfortable at home and in her
homeland. She questioned her commitment to living in Israel both for
her complicity in Israeli military violence and for the inevitable violence
that would become a part of her son's life. And yet, despite Noa's wish
to separate herself from "the world where we live," from the national
uncanny, she maintained her own fantasy of escape from Israeli politics.
She had recently cancelled her subscription to *Ha'aretz* so that she would
not have to be reminded of Palestinians' suffering at Israeli hands. She
refused to engage in debate about Israel's separation wall. Noa's fantasy
regenerated the politics of comfort she so detested.

Fantasies of home during the second intifada were a form of everyday security, a way of shielding oneself from violence and the fear of
violence that effectively placed a blinder on the reality of life. Retreat
during conflict inevitably relies on fantasies of escape and imaginaries of
normalization. It seeks an idea of the normal with such intensity that it
surpasses the imagined target and creates a hypernormal, a normal that

exists only within people's minds. In a culture of security where alertness can be endlessly amplified and enclaves further fortified, the hypernormal becomes the new reality. But hypernormal interiors, seemingly well-intended parental protection, and self-protective pursuits of comfort create a setting in which it is possible not to cope with the situation but to ignore it in a way that enables a resignation to it. In one's home as in one's homeland, acting as if it is possible to escape conflict encumbers the ability to imagine alternatives to "national security."

Chapter 7

Seeing, Walking, Securing: Tours of Israel's Separation Wall

On a hot, dusty Saturday afternoon in July, a man in his late forties wearing a navy-blue polo shirt, khaki pants, and a blue baseball cap stood in front of a cement barrier in Gilo. Gilo seems like a suburb on the southern edge of Jerusalem, although it is a city-sized Jewish settlement beyond the Green Line in the occupied territories, built in the 1970s on a hilltop overlooking Bethlehem and the Palestinian refugee camps that surround it. A deep gorge separates Gilo from Beit Jala, a Palestinian town that is part of the Bethlehem municipality. In the fall of 2000, Fatah's Tanzim militants used Beit Jala as a base to fire into Gilo to protest the Israeli occupation of the Balata refugee camp. The IDF subsequently bombarded Beit Jala with tank shells and helicopter gunships. Gilo became the neighborhood that, as described in Chapter 5, is "*really* dangerous." After months of gunfire and mortar attacks, the Israeli government constructed a two-meter concrete wall, much publicized by the Likud Party, that ran the length of Gilo's border with Beit Jala.[1] The Jerusalem Municipality commissioned Russian Israeli immigrants to cover the concrete slabs with a mural. The painted pastoral scenes concealed the wall that concealed Beit Jala, replacing the Palestinian town with an imaginary one with green hills, lush agricultural terraces, and white cement houses, but with none of its Palestinian residents. The wall became a nostalgic hypersimulation of a real that never was, a substitution for a Palestinian landscape that had been quite unknown to Gilo residents. "They brought an artist that gave the residents a very nice view, a peaceful view of the area behind the wall," as one Israeli tour guide put it. The man

Figure 11. Man from Tel Aviv in front of the wall in Gilo.

standing in front of the Gilo wall smiled as his wife photographed him standing in front of Beit Jala in front of an idyllic likeness of Beit Jala.

The Gilo wall is only one segment of a roughly 400–mile barrier Israel has been building to separate Israeli cities and Jewish settlements from Palestinian towns and villages in the West Bank. The barrier has become the largest and most costly single construction project in Israeli history (Weizman 2005: 225), a state scheme that is turning the perimeter of the land Israel seized in 1967, a border unrecognized by the international community, into a physical reality.[2] In 1995, soon after Rabin's government began to construct a fence around Gaza (to little media attention) with the slogan "get Gaza out of Tel Aviv,"[3] Rabin appointed Moshe Shahal as head of a commission to probe the idea of building a barrier along the Green Line. In this early phase, support for the wall was couched in a discourse of unilateral separation, the idea that Israel would not be able to agree with the Palestinians regarding a future Palestinian state and must act alone (Rabinowitz 2004). After Rabin's assassination in November 1995, the new Likud government did not espouse the idea of a wall, in part out of fear that the barrier would demarcate a border between Israel and Palestine that would leave Jewish settlements on the Palestinian side.[4] Indeed, early advocates for separation were predominantly from the left-wing Labor party, which saw the fence as compatible with and in fact facilitating a future Palestinian state. Into 2000, the proposed barrier was often advocated to impede the transfer of stolen vehicles from Israel into the territories, but it was nonetheless clear at this date that the fence would demarcate a border. In fact, the government was informally calling this plan Metzodim, or Fortresses. When Prime Minister Ehud Barak revived the campaign for the wall in July 2000 following the collapse of the Camp David talks, he stated, "It is my assessment that we need to separate from the Palestinians. Simply separate ourselves, physically—us here and them there" (Selwyn 2001: 225).

Not until 2002 did support for the wall became almost exclusively enveloped in notions of "security needs." According to Israel's Ministry of Defense, "The Security Fence is a manifestation of Israel's basic commitment to defend its citizens, and once completed, it will improve the ability of the IDF to prevent the infiltration of terrorists and criminal elements into Israel" (Israel Ministry of Defense 2003). The government presented the wall as a temporary form of "defense" against "terrorists," a provisional protective filter to reduce the ability of suicide bombers to enter Israel by obstructing and screening all Palestinians. "To provide security, Israel must control the high ground in order to dominate the area and not have others dominate us," said Colonel Dan Tirza, the IDF's chief planner of the route of the barrier and Sharon's chief adviser on the wall. The wall was built to govern through surveillance, through seeing and being seen, what Weizman calls "visual domination" (2007: 81). Many Israeli politicians supported building the wall on the grounds that it solved the "demographic threat," as Finance Minister Benjamin Netanyahu often called it, by keeping a Jewish voting majority in Israel, particularly in Jerusalem.

In June 2002, seven years after the Labor government had first proposed the idea for a barrier along the Green Line, Sharon's Likud government officially announced its plans to erect a wall between Israel and the West Bank. The Israeli Ministry of Defense under Shaul Mofaz presided over the wall while its construction and technology were outsourced to private contractors, high-tech firms, and security companies.[5] By 2003, portions of the wall were sixty meters wide and eight meters high, a complex of electric and barbed-wire fences, cement-slab walls, trenches, dirt roads, observation towers, cameras, ditches up to five meters wide, and trace paths that disclosed the footprints of anyone crossing. Notionally, the barrier ran along the Green Line, but it diverged in many places to embrace Jewish settlements in the West Bank on the Israeli side of the wall.

Just as the wall itself twisted and interwove, so too did its political justification, international adjudication, and military mobilization. Critics of the wall contended that the government was using the wall to determine state borders ahead of a final diplomatic agreement, to perpetuate Israeli occupation of Palestinian land, and to make a Palestinian state impossible (Ben-Eliezer and Feinstein 2007). Far from being temporary, they argued, the state wants the wall to function like Jewish settlements in attaining so-called facts on the ground so that returning territory to Palestinians later would be deemed more difficult.[6] Israeli activist organizations protested and Palestinian villages filed petitions to the Israeli Supreme Court contesting the route of the barrier, arguing that the wall was not built along the Green Line but rather around Jewish settlements.[7] They maintained that the wall penetrates into Palestinian territory, fragments the West Bank into enclaves, and cuts through Palestinian neighborhoods, separating Palestinians not only from urban centers but also from their own land, workplaces, and families. Indeed, Palestinian passage into and out of these enclaves entailed a complex system of resident permits, requests for which were often denied.[8] In July 2004, the International Court of Justice at the Hague declared the specific course of the wall not necessary to attain Israel's stated national security objectives and, in its infringement of Palestinian rights, a breach of international law (International Court of Justice 2004).

Soon after this verdict, Israel reapproved a path closer to Israel's pre-1967 boundary with the West Bank, but construction almost simultaneously began on a new segment of the wall between Jerusalem and Ma'aleh Adumim. Thus it continued that the construction and contestation of the wall progressed, back and forth, and indeed ultimately forth. In April 2006, intent on accelerating completion of the wall, Prime Minister-elect Ehud Olmert ordered all existing gaps in the barrier to be plugged with temporary fences and then permanently closed.

If the separation wall, with its sensors, trace paths, and panoptic watchtowers, purported to survey Palestinians on the "other" side, Israeli tours of the wall set out to survey the wall itself, offering tour participants privileged perspectives on the controversial construction. In June 2004, tourism Minister Gideon Ezra urged foreign tourists to visit the wall. "The security fence needs to be added to tour routes for incoming tourists." Visitors, he insisted, need "every tool to understand the nation's security problems" (News24.com 2004). Tours of the wall were seen as a way to support the undertaking and to boost tourism at a time when violence was keeping visitors away.[9] The wall attracted busloads of Jewish North American tourists, many who came on "solidarity missions" to show their support for Israel through whirlwind visits.[10] The wall was also an object of fascination for Israelis themselves. Journalist and historian Tom Segev (2005) called the wall "one of the most fascinating tour sites that one can go see today in Israel." Guided tours of the wall, the focus of this chapter, enticed Israeli Jews with fantasies of safe encounter with Palestinians and with the Israeli military.[11] The tours were an opportunity to indulge curiosity, reify a state project, and flirt with controversy.[12] As the state created the wall through steel and cement, tours of the separation wall buttressed the motives of the structure by seeing, moving, and walking around it (de Certeau 1988: 130).

Tours of the separation wall might be considered a form of "disaster tourism" or "dark tourism," as scholars use the terms, a type of political tourism that turns sites of death and distress into commercialized spectacles through voyeuristic visits.[13] Tours of the separation wall shared perhaps deeper qualities, however, with local traditions of exploring the Israeli landscape. The *tiyyul* (hike) has long been considered central to Israeli civic life. Hikes are a form of secular pilgrimage, as Tamar Katriel studies them (1995), a means to display and strengthen connections to a Jewish landscape (as opposed to a Palestinian one), a way to lay political, social, and emotional claim to the land. Israeli Jewish society has long seen *tiyyulim* as a form of *yedi'at ha'aretz*, literally "knowledge of the land," suggesting both an intellectual knowledge and a physical intimacy (Ben-David 1997: 140). Tours of the separation wall might also be placed in the tradition of the highly ceremonial yet commercial pilgrimages to Masada that have functioned for Israeli youth and tourists, in Yael Zerubavel's analysis, to solidify a patriotic narrative of collective sacrifice and well as national heroism (Zerubavel 1995). Like these civic treks, tours of the separation wall generated an emotional connection to the Israeli landscape while, as in "disaster tourism," creating a spectacle of conflict.

The man standing in front of the Gilo wall was a participant in one of the daylong tours of the wall I joined in 2003 and 2004. The three tours I describe in this chapter were organized by Israeli groups for Israeli and North American Jews. All concentrated on the Jerusalem Envelope (*'Otef Yerushalayim*), a particularly controversial stretch of the wall because of its division of Palestinians' homes from Palestinian land and Palestinian towns from each other. The first tour I describe, offered by a commercial touring outfit based in Tel Aviv, was attended by secular Israeli Jews and conducted in Hebrew. Professors from Hebrew University led the second tour I describe and an Israeli human rights organization I will call Tzedek organized the third. I was a paying or otherwise integrated participant on each tour. Although I mentioned to each tour's guide that I would be taking notes for my research, I did not pose my own questions during the trip itself. My analysis is based on the tours' itineraries, on the guides' narratives, and on participants' questions and dispositions.

Participants on all the tours, equipped with rudimentary knowledge gleaned from newspapers and television and carrying digital cameras, water bottles, and sun visors, were eager to receive in-person views of the barrier. Each tour offered views of the wall from a similar set of vantage points, moving from the city center, where the wall was indiscernible, to manicured lookout points in East Talpiot, through checkpoints and over the Green Line, to Jewish settlements such as Gilo. Each tour transported participants by bus between sites, which were encircled on foot. But if the tours had comparable moods and routes, they engaged in different modes of seeing (or not seeing) the wall itself and Palestinians on the other side. Each tour displayed disparate forms of analysis, whether historical, social, or economic, and its own political perspective. By preserving Jerusalem as a "view," the tour from Tel Aviv depoliticized the Jerusalem landscape and, with it, the complexities of the tensions between Palestinians and Israelis. The Hebrew University tour appeared to present the wall as an object of critical scrutiny but ultimately echoed state support for the wall as a necessary reaction to civilian fear. Tzedek's tour was the only one to interrogate government claims and allow participants to see and hear Palestinians.

This chapter suggests that, beyond simply scrutinizing a political structure, tours of the wall reproduced qualities of the wall and in doing so themselves functioned as artifacts of security. Like the other everyday practices of security studied in this book, tours of the wall surveilled Palestinians, overlooked Palestinian life and experience, and offered comfort to Israeli Jews. By tantalizing participants with imaginaries of terrorists and infiltration, yet, at the same time, maintaining distance from Palestinian space, the tours made security seem tangible, something that Israelis could achieve through construction. Unlike religious pilgrimages to Israel that are about "transforming quotidian reality" (Feldman 2007: 354), tours of the separation wall did not set out to create a revelatory experience. These tours were always implicitly about what could not be seen, what was concealed, what was kept out.[14] By classifying the landscape and creating feelings of fortification, wall tours tended to confirm participants' views and securitize rather than sacralize national space.

The Tour from Tel Aviv

In a glossy promotional brochure that circulated inside the Hebrew edition of *National Geographic Traveler* in spring 2004, a small Tel Aviv-based company advertised a host of daylong tours for Israelis. One could sign up for a day in the old city of Beersheba, a visit to rustic cafés in the pastoral Sharon area, or a daylong tour of the Jerusalem Envelope. Described as a tour of *ha-matsav* (the situation), as Israelis referred to the Palestinian-Israeli conflict, it would examine the wall and the Jewish areas within the Jerusalem segments of the separation wall. The company promised that participants would see the seam zone (the land between the separation wall and the Green Line),[15] would view housing developments around Jerusalem, would see "examples of security," and would have views of many different neighborhoods. The tour was geared specifically to Israelis from Tel Aviv, for whom details of the Jerusalem landscape and glimpses of ultra-Orthodox Jews were unfamiliar and alluring. Late morning on a Saturday in July 2004, an air-conditioned coach departed Tel Aviv for Jerusalem. Most of the seventeen participants, who had paid 75 NIS, roughly $20 for the day, were secular Jewish married couples in their fifties and sixties.[16] The mood on the bus was relaxed, animated, and eager.

Our guide, Amnon, was a retired engineer who lived in the Jewish Quarter of Jerusalem's Old City, a self-educated expert on Jerusalem geography, archaeology, and urban development. This was his first time leading a tour of the wall (the case for all the tours I attended) and his narratives seemed less rote and more tentative than they might become. In a casual conversation I had with Amnon and another participant before the bus arrived, he admitted that he was not even aware before that morning that the tour would expressly analyze the wall. He had intended to lead a tour of Jerusalem geography that would look at "the land that we [Israel] captured in the 1967 war," but the company had marketed the tour as a tour of the wall to have more current appeal. With slight adjustment, Amnon thought he would easily accommodate a focus on "security and defense." He emphasized, however, "I don't want politics," by which he meant that he did not want to draw attention to the recent legal battles surrounding the wall and was not eager to encourage discord among the tour participants about the wall. Of course, the guide's very sense that the wall could be explored without debate was itself an acutely political stance. The tour depicted the wall as if it were an organic component of the Jerusalem landscape, one among many unavoidable ways that Israel has claimed space to establish a nation and enable Jewish life. A particular perspective on security was thus conveyed, one in which fortification and territorial claims were an inevitable part of creating a Jewish nation.

At noon, the tour's first stop was Mevasseret Zion, a city-sized, upper-middle-class Jewish settlement in the West Bank, northwest of Jerusalem. The bus drove us to the base of a water tower at the highest hill in the settlement so that we could see, as Amnon put it, a *nof* (a view). Amnon described the panorama of mountaintops before us: The ruins of the Castel Fortress, the site of a 1948 battle; the Jewish settlement Neve Samuel, built in 1996; and the red-roofed houses of the Jewish settlement of Har Adar that was founded in 1982 and underwent considerable expansion since 2000 on land belonging to the Palestinian villages of Bidu and Qat-taneh. Already, the guide's desire for what he hoped would be an apoliti-cal perspective on the wall was palpable. As he spoke beneath the water tower, and continuing throughout the six-hour outing, Amnon described Israel's military defeat of Palestinians and neighboring Arab countries, settlement of the Jerusalem landscape in areas Israel captured in 1967, and construction of the wall as the proud triumphs of a vulnerable state rather than the contested maneuvers of nation-building.

We looked out past his pointed finger toward a snaking cement wall and Amnon offered his first introduction to the separation wall, initiat-ing us into the language of his framing: "If you look to the right you'll see our problem. You see Har Adar, which stands on the Green Line. But next to it are two Arab villages that you've heard in the news: Beit Surik and Bidu." Several participants unfamiliar with the villages asked him to repeat the names, and, when he did, knowing nods suggested that they had just made the connection between an actual place and a name they recognized from the newspaper. By referring to the proximity of Har Adar to Beit Surik and Bidu, Amnon broached the dilemmas of a wall that divides Palestinian and Jewish residential areas so close to one another. And yet he spoke about the location of the Palestinian towns as "our problem," suggesting that it was Bidu's closeness to Har Adar that was the problem, not vice versa, that is, not Israel's construction of the wall on Bidu's land. The guide explained that residents of several Pales-tinian villages northwest of Jerusalem, including Bidu, petitioned Israel's High Court of Justice to oppose the route of the wall planned for their area. This fact engaged the participants, who acted as eager as journalists to see and comprehend the fence's route. Hands shot up and questions were asked, but Amnon hardly entertained their desires for detail and debate. "We don't know yet what will happen," he said regarding the Pal-estinian petitions and the wall's final route. As eager as the participants were to scrutinize the wall's placement, Amnon was keen to return to a discussion of Jewish settlement and post-1967 Jerusalem expansion. Returning from the wall to the "view," Amnon continued: "And there you see Mount Scopus . . ." and so forth. Only fleetingly was the wall's contestation presented.

We settled again into our bus seats and Amnon prepared us for the next stop, the Jewish settlement Gilo. There, he said, we will really have "a view for our eyes," for we would see both the cement barrier of Gilo and also, in the distance, the separation wall. His reference to the ce-ment barrier as a delightful vista was only partly sarcastic, for his more common invocation of the wall as a "view" naturalized and neutralized the wall as an inexorable part of Israeli history. By turning everything in the Jerusalem landscape into something meaningful and interesting,

Amnon obscured the wall's controversy. The bus deposited us in a parking lot hemmed in by the painted barrier. With an air of boldness and excitement, Amnon beckoned us to climb a steep dirt mound on which the cement wall had been erected and then to swing around the end of the wall to the opposite side so that we could look at Beit Jala. We followed him with the rogue feeling that walls are not supposed to end or that we should not be on the other side. Amnon soon directed our gaze downward toward a single house in the Palestinian village: "That is where most of the shooting came from." Our attention was quickly directed away from the site of Palestinian resistance to a holy site, only to learn that it was itself a site of conflict. "That is Rachel's Tomb," Amnon said, pointing to the place believed by Jews to be the gravesite of the biblical matriarch and by some Palestinians to be the Bilal ibn Rabah mosque. It is a traditional Jewish pilgrimage site for pregnant women and for those trying to conceive, although it was also a site of fierce contestation and violence. In 1996, Israel spent two million dollars to encase the small domed tomb in a sheath of reinforced concrete with firing holes, defensive trenches, camouflage netting, and an adjacent military post. The separation wall further separated the tomb from Bethlehem, and IDF soldiers were stationed to monitor the entry of pilgrims and tourists from Israel.

Rachel's Tomb sat on the outskirts of Bethlehem, where our attention was directed next. The guide's concern was not the city itself but a "bypass road" that ran southward on cement supports above the valley. The road provided passageway, in the words of the guide, from southern Jerusalem to Jewish settlements in the northwest West Bank, circumventing Bethlehem. Throughout the West Bank, roads and tunnels under Israel's control serve as infrastructure evasion of Palestinian space, letting Jewish Israeli traffic travel over or under land that is under Palestinian control. The guide's speech was peppered with words that emphasized Israeli contiguity and connectivity, with terms such as *ḥotseh* (bisect; cross), *mitḥaber* (join; unite), *ḥibur* (connection), *ʿoqef* (bypass), *maʿavar* (passage), and the English-derived *bypassim*. Amnon's description of the Bethlehem bypass presented all aspects of the landscape as a network of Jewish spatial continuity. Walls and fences were, to him, not enclaving and constraining, but rather enabling Jewish movement and life.

For our final gaze from Gilo, Amnon pointed toward a segment of the wall visible in the distance. "The *ḥoma* (wall) will pass from—" The guide was cut off by a man on the tour who corrected him: "No, *gader* (fence)." Two middle-aged women next to me argued noisily over whether the barrier is a wall or a fence, all but drowning out the remainder of Amnon's description. The terms used for the barrier were, of course, politically

Figure 12. View from Gilo of the Israeli "bypass road" that runs over Bethlehem to connect Jewish settlements in the West Bank to Jerusalem.

charged. Israeli government ministries tended to emphasize its protective function and temporary construction by referring to it as the *gader bitaḥon*, or "security fence." The Ministry of Defense called the wall by several names, including *merḥav ha-tefer*, which it translates as "security fence" but is literally translated as "seam zone". Palestinian activist organizations refer to the barrier as *jidar al-fasl al-ʿunṣuri*, a racial segregation wall, or an "apartheid wall." Most Israeli Jews called it *ha-gader ha-hafrada* (separation fence) or just *ha-gader* (the fence). What Amnon referred to as a wall, the interrupting participant wanted to call a fence to make the structure seem impermanent and devoted to the specific task of keeping potential Palestinian bombers from Israel. Amnon, careful not to inflame debate, nodded and used the term *gader* the next time he referred to the barrier. His intent and that of the for-profit guide outfit was not to transform perceptions of the wall but, if anything, to bolster existing viewpoints. When participants were critical of the wall, it was generally because they doubted its efficacy for Israelis and not because they were concerned about its effects on Palestinians. As one man said to me, "[The wall] worked in Gaza, but they [Palestinian bombers] will always find a way in."

Although Amnon reveled in Israel's ongoing history of settlement, he presented the Israeli landscape and with it Israeli sovereignty as a fait accompli: undeniable and irreversible. As a participant on this tour, I often felt that Amnon turned wherever we were standing into a static and homogenous place from which "other" (Palestinian) places were simply spaces to be bounded. Amnon offered the majority of his explanations from within the moving bus. In one exemplary comment, he gestured to the Jewish and Palestinian neighborhoods then in our field of vision, and our eyes followed his finger as it moved across an arc: "Ma'ale Ad-umim, 'Isawiya, 'Anata, al-Tur, Al Azaria, and then we see the wall again. You see how the wall divides the Mount of Olives from Al Azaria? The wall here stops on purpose. Drive more [he said to the driver]. Here. There's an opening in the wall. . . . Now you can enjoy the desert view." At eight other times that day, Amnon pointed to the wall and identified the Palestinian cities flanking it, and participants themselves persistently asked him to show them locations of Palestinian towns they had heard about in the media. If naming and distinction were privileged forms of knowledge on this tour, classification was generally an end unto itself. "Now, enjoy the view," Amnon often concluded, as if a break in the separation wall existed for the sake of our aesthetic pleasure. Palestinian towns and villages, unified and obscured into the so-called scenery, were present only as spaces that did not conform, spaces that needed to be managed and constricted.

Over the course of the day, the tour made several stops unrelated to Jerusalem geography. We stopped once for an early lunch, once more for ice cream and toilets at the Haas Promenade, and yet again for a leisurely coffee at a café right outside the walls of Hebrew University on Mount Scopus. After 6 P.M. the tour culminated at one of the most picturesque scenes in Jerusalem, the ancient wall of the Old City by Jaffa Gate illuminated from below with dramatic theatrical lighting and from above by a setting sun. As the pink orb descended over the stone wall, I wondered if Amnon saw the Old City wall as simply an older and perhaps more romantic variant on the separation wall. To Amnon, the two walls, built centuries apart, intermeshed in a harmonious vista of Jerusalem history and geography. Both, the tour seemed to suggest, are constituent parts of the Jerusalem landscape; both are complicated but inevitable parts of Israeli history. Both were objects of curiosity but not of debate. By embedding a study of the wall within a broader examination of Jewish settlement, the wall, and with it Israeli security more generally, became a way of organizing the landscape so as to preserve Jewish history.

The Hebrew University Tour

After lunch at the Faculty Club of the Mount Scopus campus of Hebrew University in July 2004, thirty-three Israeli and visiting North American social scientists gathered to begin a tour titled "Jerusalem Under Stress."

As the culminating event of a conference on the ways societies "cope with crisis," the tour was thematically pertinent but also intended to be a social and an enjoyable afternoon excursion, a diversion after three days of formal papers. The tour's two guides were both professors of Israel geography, one originally from North America and the other born in Israel. The conference brochure explained that the tour would examine the wall in the broader context of the occupied territories and human rights. Before we boarded the bus, the two guides described a more specifically political objective: "to show the effects of terrorism on Jerusalem's landscape since 2000." The tour would analyze how Israelis' "stress and attempts to cope with the situation" manifest themselves spatially and how a range of architectural formations, from fences to neighborhoods to walls, function as forms of "security." While the tour would analyze the materiality of Israeli security, it ultimately presented the Jewish Israeli landscape as an innocent victim of Palestinian terror.

As we boarded the bus, each participant received a set of stapled papers containing two maps and two aerial images of Jerusalem. Finely printed in color and carefully labeled, the maps were produced in the cartographic laboratory of the Hebrew University Geography Department. The apparent professionalism of the maps lent the tour an air of authority from its outset and introduced the wall, even before we could see it, as a discrete and coherent object of study. It was as Nadia Abu El-Haj showed in her study of Jewish archeology in Palestine: "Cartography presented Palestine as a concrete, coherent, and visibly historic place, a sustained object of scientific inquiry, charted and recognizable on modern maps" (2001: 23). With aerial maps in hand, jackets removed from suits, high-heels switched to sneakers, and sociological jargon replaced with relaxed conversation, participants were curious and ready for the tour. Throughout the afternoon, the guides took seriously that the wall was an attempt to unilaterally define borders and assert Israeli sovereignty, but they also sympathetically suggested that Israel constructed this architecture out of fear. Although they upheld the wall as an object of analytic scrutiny, they also echoed state discourses of the wall as a necessary reaction to Palestinian violence.

Downtown Jerusalem was the tour's first stop, where we were to detect "signs of stress" in the urban landscape. The English-speaking geography professor spoke broadly about recent urban development and its tensions with historic preservation. He accentuated the hardship of Israeli life in conflict while underscoring the ability of Israeli Jews to persevere by drawing our attention to the sparse pedestrian traffic on King George Road, to stores on Ben Yehuda Street that had closed "because of the situation," and to "the resilience of Israeli businesses" remaining open on Jaffa Road. The North American participants nodded in agreement while the Israelis chattered audibly, perhaps inured to such observations. Our attention was then drawn to other marks of the conflict in the commercial landscape: dents in a gift shop doorpost from shrapnel from a suicide bombing, a plaque in memory of those killed in a nearby bombing, and fences enclosing the restaurants we passed. The Israelis continued to talk among themselves; this segment of the tour was clearly geared toward foreign visitors. Referring to the landscape of gates and guards, the guide explained: "These are ways [Israelis] try to live with the situation and provide the best security possible." Before returning to the bus, one guide pointed to the preparations underway for a summer street fair that would begin that evening, another sign, he avowed, of Israeli strength and persistence.

After a short drive, we found ourselves clustered together on the edge of a paved lookout point in East Talpiot's Promenade. Battling the wind, we turned as instructed to the map we held in our hands, titled "Jewish Neighborhoods in Jerusalem after 1967." A color-coded key identified "Arab residences," "pre-1967 Jewish residences," "post-1967 Jewish residences," "Unbuilt areas," "Main roads," "Roads," "Cease-fire lines after 1949," and "Municipal boundaries after 1967." None of the purple "Arab residence" areas were named and so Jewish settlements bordered what appeared to be unnamed Palestinian spaces. Spaces designated "Unbuilt areas" were also unlabeled and thus appeared, to a lay map-reader such as myself, to be ownerless and empty spaces, almost a moral mapping of land for the taking. The map seemed to diagram an imaginary wherein Jewish neighborhoods existed as separate entities unaffected by and oblivious to neighboring Arabs. The view the guides plotted for us mirrored the map we held in our hands. Our gaze was directed to the snaking grey cement slabs of the separation wall before us, which the guides pointed to without discussion of the Palestinian towns of Silwan, Abu Tor, Shaykh Sa'ad, and Sur Baher also in our field of vision. The tour from Tel Aviv had identified Palestinian towns almost like a game of bingo, but now they were not named at all. As Sarah Green has written, "Ambiguity can be as hegemonic and subject to disciplinary regimes as clarity; confusion, lack of means to pin things down, can be as actively generated as positive assertions and constructions of truth" (2005: 12). The tour's vision and its map created a palpable politics of ambiguity, where lack of specificity was not a lack of data but rather an intentional obfuscation of the other.

The two professors suggested we take thirty minutes to amble around the promenade. A child-oriented Renaissance festival happened to be taking place, and the social scientists adopted its festive mood, standing in line together at a kiosk to buy chocolate and watermelon *artikim* (ice cream Popsicles) and sitting on benches to watch jugglers, knights on horses, and Jerusalem police patrolling the area. I couldn't help but wonder whether our comfortable vantage point itself precluded a thorough understanding of the wall's effects on Palestinian life. Like the tour from Tel Aviv, this tour had an ambiance of leisure that created an obvious incommensurability with its supposed object. Was it, as Roland Barthes described the effects of the *Blue Guide* on tourist experiences of Spain, "a nice neat commedia dell'arte, whose improbable typology serves to mask the real spectacle of conditions, classes and professions" (1972: 75)? Tourists of the separation wall certainly took conscious steps toward understanding, but with a Popsicle in one hand and a camera in the other, the embodied stance of their survey did temper empathy with those the wall confined.

Har Homa was our next stop. Translated as "walled mountain," Har Homa is a highly controversial Jewish settlement built in part on forested land that had been owned by Palestinians in Beit Sahour before it was captured by Israel in 1967. As the Israel-born professor explained, the announcement in March 1997 that the Israeli government would build homes in Har Homa to accommodate 30,000–40,000 Israelis sparked Palestinian riots in the West Bank and Gaza and, many say, precipitated a nineteen-month breakdown in the peace process. Construction was frozen provisionally in response, but by the time of our tour, the walled mountain was already dense with thousands of government-subsidized housing units. "The quality of what people get here for a relatively low price," the guide told is, "is very nice, a very good deal." He described the development as if he were a real estate agent giving us a tip on a bargain property rather than an Israeli endorsing a settlement.[17] Paradoxically, this analytical stance seemed to convince the academic members of the Hebrew University tour to accept the guide's comments without question.

As we stood on a dusty hill on the edge of Har Homa with the separation wall's concrete slabs visible in the distance, the guide spoke at length about the context and construction of the wall. His stance seemed defensive, perhaps because he was presenting the separation wall to North Americans only days before the highly publicized ruling at the International Court of Justice.

> The IDF wanted to stop people who make attacks, to deter them from coming into Israel. And, as you can see, the distance between Bethlehem and Jerusalem is 600–700 meters. So all you need to do is walk, it's a nice 7–10–minute walk, and then you're in Jerusalem. In Jerusalem alone more than 380 people were killed by suicide attacks. More than one third of the casualties happened in Jerusalem. So the Defense Minister began to plan this barrier around Jerusalem. It's the biggest ever public project in Israel, about 3 billion U.S. dollars. . . . But nobody's building a temporary fence that costs 3 billion dollars. Okay? You can move parts of it here and there, but this is, in fact, unilateral separation of Israel from the [Palestinian] territories.

The guide wavered between sanction and critique of the wall. On the one hand, he justified the wall as a necessary reaction to the ease, in his mind, with which a Palestinian suicide bomber could walk from Bethlehem to West Jerusalem. On the other hand, he joined critics of the state claims that the wall is temporary and implied that the discourse of temporariness masks the unremitting occupation and the wall's role in permanently defining borders. The guide's monologue continued:

> It's hard to see it from here, but it's a very sophisticated fence. The best of the Israeli high tech is invested in the fence. That's why it's so expensive. You have sensors that help track digging below the fence. If somebody's touching or cutting or jumping over, in the command centers, you can know what's going on. It's a smart fence. . . . In fact, it's proven very efficient. Since the fence [has been] active in the northern part of Israel, no suicide attack, not even infiltration, has managed to pass the fence. Besides that, it has reduced the crime rate. It gives Israelis a sense of security. It's not a magic solution for all the problems, but, in the meantime, it has proved itself very efficient. It's not a one hundred percent solution, but this is something positive.

The guide spoke of the wall with patriotic pride in its "high tech" sophistication; he depicted the wall as a military technology that should be assessed based on whether it prevents "infiltration," rather than on the effects it has on Palestinian-Israeli diplomacy.

Despite the guide's periodically critical perspective, his sympathetic defense of the wall was most patent. He qualified and mitigated the wall's presence to portray it as a judicious and restrained construction. Speaking of the segment of the wall that ran alongside Har Homa, he explained, "They're only putting the wall where the houses are very near," suggesting that the looming concrete slabs are placed only where they are necessary to protect civilian spaces. When the guide attested to the wall's effects on Palestinians, he presented hindrance to Palestinians as a necessary sacrifice: "It's creating a lot of problems, as you well know, for the Palestinian people, especially near the wall. But the Israel government decided that in order to keep the lives of Israelis, this is something that should be done, despite problems it causes to Palestinians." With casual language that belied the starkness of his viewpoint, the guide approved of the wall as "efficient" and "positive." As he said, persuaded by state justification for the wall, "Every country wants to have some kind of control over what's happening."

The Hebrew University tour fashioned an epistemology of the wall intended for international scrutiny. The pretense of this tour was that the wall needs to be questioned and dissected and the tour indeed scrutinized microscopic marks of shrapnel as well as immense barbed-wire fences as physical manifestations of fear and conflict. The guides offered an intellectual analysis of the wall as an emotional and economic border. And yet, the tour still substantiated state protection and reproduced government propaganda about the visual appeal and economic incentive of living in Jewish settlements. The tour did not just sanction Israelis' stress but reified their fear, turning these emotions into concrete realities that materially demanded the containment of Palestinians. From the perspective of this tour, the landscape and people of Israel are easily scarred and the country must protect itself even if it impinges upon Palestinian lives. It was as if scholarly analysis itself authorized fences, trace paths, and confinement.

The Tzedek Tour

If the tour from Tel Aviv billed itself as a sightseeing expedition and the Hebrew University tour as an analytical field trip, the tour offered by the human-rights organization Tzedek presented itself as an activist exploration. Committed to conceptions of human rights and international law, Tzedek aims to bring Israeli and international attention to Israeli military violence in Gaza, military abuses of Palestinians in the West Bank, expropriation of Palestinian land in building in East Jerusalem, and, more recently, the de facto annexation of Palestinian land and impairment of Palestinian movement through the separation wall. In November 2003, Tzedek organized a daylong tour of the wall for rabbinical students from Hebrew Union College, a Reform rabbinical school with campuses in Jerusalem, New York, Cincinnati, and Los Angeles. The participants, primarily American but also Jewish Israeli students in their mid-twenties and thirties in their first year of rabbinical school, saw the tour as an important part of their immersion in Israel and of their rabbinical training, which encompassed knowing how to present Israel to synagogue congregations abroad. They were sentient political tourists, persistently asking questions about the wall's form and location within a broader context of conflict. Acutely aware that they were seeing "exceptional space" (Agamben 1998: 168–71), they listened eagerly, often nodding in amazement or agreement, seemingly poised to take in new understandings. The tour's itinerary and narratives, as well as the informants it consulted along the way, set it apart from the other tours and also from the state's delineation of the wall. It challenged participants to scrutinize the government claims about security and to consider that the wall works more through punishment and devastation of Palestinian life than through hermetic separation. In particular, the tour supported the argument that the wall exists more to maintain and to protect Jewish settlements in the West Bank than it does to prevent Palestinian suicide bombers from entering Israeli cities. And yet, in other ways, the tour still reaffirmed that security is something that can be achieved in tangible and material ways.

The day began at 8:30 on a Friday morning in an auditorium at Hebrew Union College in Jerusalem filled with twenty-five still-sleepy students. Two Tzedek researchers gave a PowerPoint presentation to illustrate the route of the barrier, diagram its configuration (patrol road, trace road, electronic fence, etc.), and detail the illegality of its route according to international law. In contrast to the Tel Aviv tour's depiction of the wall as an already established component of the Israeli landscape, Tzedek's digital slides dissected the construction of the wall into a host of deliberate, ongoing decisions. The focus of the presentation was a four-stage chronology of the state's construction of the wall beginning in June 2002, with each phase designated by additions to the barrier and concomitant legal violations. For instance, Stage 1, we learned, was completed in October 2003 and covered 125 kilometers from the Palestinian village Sallem to the Jewish settlement Elqana in the northern West Bank. The presentation referred to the wall as the "separation barrier," avoiding the ideologically laden terms "apartheid wall" and "fence," but using the term "regime" to refer to the role of the wall in Israel's governance of Palestinians. Despite its informed criticisms, the PowerPoint presentation lent the state project a coherence that the wall's construction and legal contestation largely lacked in reality. Relying on quantified space and enumerated populations, the polished and linear slides depicted the construction of the barrier as an organized state scheme. Like the schematic diagrams that Annelise Riles studied in a Fijian activist organization that lent "an impression of maplike completeness" in ways that other documents of the organization did not (2000: 122), Tzedek's PowerPoint presentation was a stark visual aid that masked the political and spatial messiness we would discern over the course of the day. Similar contrasts between the human-rights organization's political critique and its lingering alignments with state discourse surfaced throughout the tour.

As the group left the auditorium, a Tzedek staff member announced that the small bus we were about to board would be marked with the word "Tzedek" in Arabic only. They did not want Palestinians to see the bus as "Israeli" or hostile. She also explained that the group was pointedly not going to be accompanied by an armed guard, as the other tours were and as nearly all Jewish Israeli tours of this size are. "The organization thinks it's better—safer—this way," she suggested with similar reasoning. For Tzedek, the absence of signs of Israeli security was a strategy for ensuring their peaceful travel in the West Bank.

Our first stop was a rocky, brush-strewn hill outside East Talpiot, a Jewish settlement (or, from the Israeli government's perspective, a Jewish suburb of Jerusalem) southeast of Jerusalem, outside the Green Line but on the Israeli side of the separation wall. The guides directed our attention to the valley below, where a barbed wire fence and trace path comprised a segment of the wall. One guide held up a poster-sized map titled "Jerusalem's Changing Borders," while the second guide described the fickle nature of the wall's physical form and legal status. If the tour from Tel Aviv was fixated on connectivity, this tour emphasized the wall's nonlinearity and the ambiguous nature of national space more generally. We learned that the wall already encircled most of the northwestern and western edges of the West Bank while secondary barriers were cutting Palestinian villages in the West Bank off from each other. The noncontiguous wall twists and turns, the guide told us, folds in and out, straddling the Green Line and bisecting neighborhoods and families. Lacking physical solidity, it is strewn with gaps, fissures, and cracks, as if the physical form of the wall embodied the inconsistency of government opinion and the doubling back of state policy. The wall's route had not yet been reviewed in Israeli or international courts at the time of the tour, but the guide predicted (correctly) that some segments might be torn down in a few months and others further buttressed. At times, Tzedek's focus on the capricious nature of the wall and its route blurred with state discourses on the wall's temporariness, but ultimately highlighted the wall's contentiousness as well as opportunities for activist influence.

We drove next to Abu Dis, a Palestinian town in East Jerusalem administered by the Palestinian National Authority. At the time of our visit, an eight-foot concrete wall composed of three-foot-wide panels ran down the middle of the town. The rabbinical students watched, engrossed, as Palestinian children wearing backpacks, women in long skirts, and men walking home from Friday prayers squeezed through cracks between the panels or climbed over the wall, assisted by a chair placed on the other side. We observed this not from a distance but at eye-level, and the students' questions about the intentions of the wall and its partition of schoolchildren from their schools reflected this proximity. Tzedek's object of scrutiny was not a line in the landscape or a distant object but a colossal, ominous barrier: flagrant and tangible, even to the tour participants.

In January 2004, only two months after our visit, Israel would begin to construct a wall more than twenty feet high through Abu Dis that could not be circumvented. Tzedek had arranged for a Palestinian woman, a resident of Abu Dis, to speak to us about the impending construction. She was an Israeli citizen, but she had married a Palestinian from Abu Dis who was not. Speaking in English, she told us that she grew up in the Old City of Jerusalem, where much of her family still lives and where her family has lived for 400 years. In September 2002, IDF roadblocks began to impede residents' movement, but the wall would soon make her family's regular trips to Jerusalem for family visits, ballet classes, and music lessons unviable. Speaking with intensity, she compared the Israeli government to the medieval Christian Crusaders intent on capturing Jerusalem from Muslim rule; and she compared the separation wall to ethnic cleansing. "The Crusaders used to say, 'In the name of God.' Now they say, 'In the name of security.' . . . The wall is a total incursion of West Bank lands. Sharon is lying. He is changing the borders. . . . Is building walls the only way to keep your Jewish purity?" Immediately, a Tzedek guide interrupted to argue that the state only wants to build walls to prevent suicide bombers. The woman countered that suicide bombers are not terrorists and that killing an IDF soldier is not terrorism. The guide appeared frustrated and the rabbinical students shifted uncomfortably. Although a Palestinian voice was an essential element in the Tzedek tour, the guide did not tolerate the woman's vilification of Israel. The Tzedek tour was willing to hold the wall up to the scrutiny of international law but not, it appeared at this moment, to the scrutiny of an individual Palestinian.

In a conversation several weeks later with this Tzedek guide, who was also a full-time researcher for the organization, I asked him to reflect on the exchange in Abu Dis. He said to me, "I completely reject her views, especially this speech about Jewish purity. It's completely hatred. [She was] changing and falsifying the real motivation for the construction of these walls. I don't agree with her interpretation. It has nothing to do with Jewish purity, it has to do with fear, with basic and very human fear." Although the researcher did not speak formally on behalf of the organization, he did embody a sentiment expressed throughout the tour, namely that while Tzedek challenges the wall's route and its imposition on Palestinian life, it retains a fundamental sympathy for Israel's protection of its citizens. By taking Israeli fear seriously as a legitimate justification for constructing the wall, he echoed national discourses that model Israelis' emotion as a reasonable impetus for state intervention.

A halting drive through dusty roads brought the tour bus to Jabel Mukaber, a Palestinian neighborhood in East Jerusalem. We stood on a narrow dirt road hemmed in by a huge mound of earth, cement blocks, and trash. On the other side of the littered rampart stood Sheikh Sa'ad, a Palestinian village in the West Bank accessible to East Jerusalem only by crossing the earthen wall into and through Jabel Mukaber on foot. Not content for the guides or the visual landscape to speak for themselves, Tzedek had arranged for a resident of Sheikh Sa'ad in his forties to offer his own sense of the meaning and daily experience of the space. He walked toward our group by climbing over the mound from the Sheikh Sa'ad side. Although some Sheikh Sa'ad residents have the legal status of permanent residents in Israel, this man, like most residents, held a Palestinian identity card and could not enter East Jerusalem without a

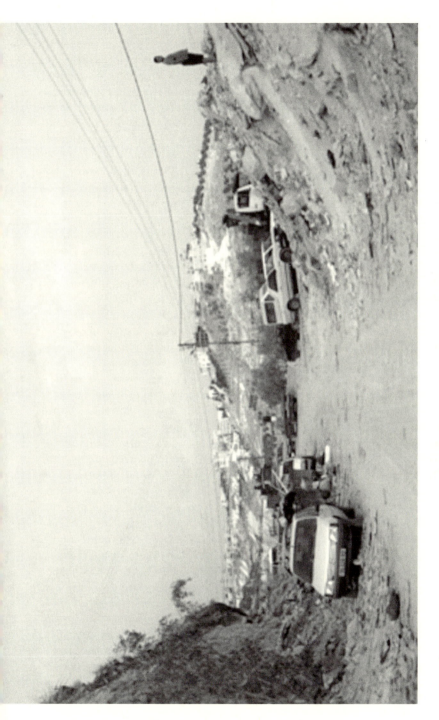

Figure 13. A large mound of dirt created by the Israeli government separates the East Jerusalem village of Jabel Mukaber from Sheikh Sa'ad.

special permit from Israel's Civil Administration of the occupied territories.[18] He explained that daily life would soon become even more encumbered: the planned route of the separation barrier in the area would block the only road leading to the village with an eight-meter wall. He also underscored the political symbolism of the seemingly simple mound of dirt itself. The IDF had isolated Sheikh Sa'ad from Jerusalem and the West Bank, and the heap of rubble, while not fully precluding movement from one side to the other, did impede travel and, moreover, symbolized Israel's power and presence.

The guides corroborated this argument throughout the tour, albeit informally. As we walked back to the bus, one guide said to several students near her, "the road block is clearly a punishment . . . and not a security consideration." Agreeing, the second guide portrayed the wall as violence against Palestinians in the name of security. A suicide bomber, he said, "could easily get through here, but it makes life difficult for everyone else. . . . The goal of the government is politics and not security." The guides suggested that Israeli constructions (such as the mound) with pretenses of separation are "ineffective" in that they do not actually prescribe Palestinian movement and thus exist less to deter Palestinian suicide bombers than to create unilateral borders and protect Israeli settlers. The guides repeatedly pointed to such pretenses of separation, such as gaping holes in ostensibly hermetic barriers and roadblocks with no personnel. In asides set apart from the official tour, the guides questioned the ability of fractured barriers to provide "real security" or even a semblance of security. What they were saying was not at odds with the organization's mission or with the rest of the tour, but in their private asides they were more likely to speak about security in a concrete way. Fundamentally, they objected to the route of the wall and its material reality but not to the desire for a wall to begin with. They denounced Israeli military violence but did not question the need for security. Rather than calling for an end to occupation, for example, a guide suggested how inspection at a particular checkpoint might proceed more humanely.

Tzedek exemplified an Israeli voice critical of occupation and the violence of security. By accentuating the materiality of the wall, the tour made an important distinction between acts of state security that intend to protect Israeli civilians and state projects of separation and exclusion that work more to disrupt Palestinian life. The immediacy of the wall to tour participants and their engagement with Palestinians allowed Palestinian experience to speak as its own case against the wall. In these ways, the tour modeled national security as something that should foster coexistence between Israelis and Palestinians. At the same time, the tour reconciled a stance of human rights for Palestinians with sympathy for Israeli desires for separation. By pointing to ways the wall might be positioned along a different route so as not to bisect Palestinian towns, the guides implied that the wall is serving a necessary purpose. Even as the tour problematized state discourse about the wall, it still reified Israeli security as a reasonable objective that could be materially achieved. By speaking of the ways in which security "works" and ways it does not, by suggesting that excluding an armed guard from the trip could in fact realize better security, and by contemplating how a wall within the Green Line could more humanely achieve security, the tour affirmed that legal and diplomatic amity could be achieved through variations on existing "security" strategies. The organization reaffirmed that security could truly be achieved through material investments in the landscape.

Conclusion

As IDF soldiers and security company guards patrolled the area of Israel's separation wall on foot, in armored cars, and from observation towers, wall tour participants engaged in an ambulatory surveillance of their own. More than simply providing tours of a political artifact, the tours of the wall themselves reproduced qualities of the wall and engaged tropes of everyday security that have been examined elsewhere in this book. As I elaborate below, the tours surveilled Palestinians without truly seeing Palestinian life and provided Israeli Jews with feelings of comfort.

Tours of the separation wall mimicked the wall's surveillance of Palestinians. Participants' attention was often directed to sites, not for their inherent historical, geographical, or even political interest, but for the "view" they offered of the wall, of Jerusalem neighborhoods, and of the "other" side, that is, of Palestinian villages that could be seen at a remove from the obstructing wall. Separation was made visible and knowable from lookout points. Like the wall's observation towers and cameras, the tours "saw" by making spatial distinctions between Israeli and Palestinian spaces and through an almost obsessive naming of Palestinian cities and villages. Designations of "inside" and "outside" the wall and the focus on Jewish contiguity gave a panoptic order to national space. The use of maps as vehicles of coherence made patterns of settlement and disputed land appear naturalized and clearly defined, while color-coding reified differences between Palestinian and Israeli. This reproduction by tour guides and participants of the surveillance and separation of the wall was not only a product of the internalization of state discourse but also a visceral and an emotion-filled rendering of security, a process where scopic engagement enacted and doubled state surveillance.

For all the naming and identifying of Palestinian villages, neither the Tel Aviv nor the Hebrew University tour entered Palestinian residential areas, spoke with Palestinian residents, or saw Palestinians' homes within a close range of vision. Although tours, in theory, purport to illuminate and clarify, tours of the separation wall were more likely to conceal and obscure by gazing from a distance from within space they defined as Jewish. The guides of the tours from Tel Aviv and Hebrew University favored macroscopic views, attending to topographical patterns rather than to the wall's everyday effects on Palestinian life. The pretense of legibility exacerbated the extent to which the tours obfuscated contestation. Lacking explicit self-consciousness about the ease with which they crossed checkpoints and moved from one side of the wall to the other, tours of the wall tended to conceal the privilege of movement that enabled their panoptic view. The very fluidity of their passage over the Green Line enacted the imaginary of Jewish contiguity that the tours were so keen to point out in the landscape.

Although participants may have returned from the tours feeling they had privileged access to behind-the-scenes views, the tours, with the exception of Tzedek's, offered rather limited perspectives on diplomatic intricacy. With controversy and ambiguity enveloped in pleasure, and with separation and distinction so clearly defined, tours appeared to ease participants' concern about the wall and about their safety, reassuring them that the wall was real, that it created and retained an inside and an outside. In this way, the tours were ultimately more about experiencing security than about ascertaining and understanding it. Tours of the wall, like the network of fences, trenches, and watchtowers snaking through the West Bank, and indeed like national security writ large, were a material and discursive assemblage characterized as much by what they contained as by what they obscured.

Tours of the separation wall, like other everyday practices of security, offered controlled fantasies of making the perceived terrorist visible but only perceptible enough to provide a safe "sense of the foreign" (Kaplan 2003: 59). By fluidly crossing borders and easily attaining sight, the tours constructed and performed the nation as a place that is bounded, safe, coherent, and controlled. As the Tzedek tour illustrated, there are, to be sure, significant Israeli voices of protest against state violence and occupation. However, even censures of state security accommodated checkpoints and walls as feasible means of attaining some form of reconciliation. Practices that questioned or mocked prescribed registers still held tightly onto discourses of national security and reproduced state notions of fear, threat, and defense at the level of everyday practice. When participants of separation-wall tours, like Israeli pedestrians more generally, reinforced separation by walking it, gazing at it, and embodying its blindnesses, security becomes as much about closing the self as it does about keeping the other out.

Epilogue: Real Fantasies of Security

National security permeates the practices of everyday life. During the second intifada, the ways people organized their homes, experienced their bodies, and took care of their children were conditioned by shared notions of danger and threat and state-mediated conceptions of what is safe and what risky. In homes and public spaces across the country, desires for comfort and protection shaped relationships and propelled economies. Imaginaries of Palestinian violence impinged on what Israeli Jews ate and where they ate it, the cities they visited, and the ways they moved between places. Pedestrians could not help but see the threatening signs they expected to see. Through a vigilant gaze, all objects appeared potentially perilous and all people suspicious. The result was a hyperalert and fearful populace increasingly concerned with its own well-being and ever more bound to the apparatus of state security.

Even in this environment of pervasive security, Israelis still assumed critical stances as they debated the value and efficacy of security. They probed whether a security guard with a metal detector wand could deter a suicide bomber, for example, or whether the cement walls bisecting Palestinian cities would really mitigate political violence. Publicly or privately, they questioned the intentions of state violence in the name of security and the state's ability to protect all Israeli civilians from physical harm.[1] Critical not just of the violence of security, but also of the ways violence and security are normalized in daily life, some Israelis shunned social practices such as watching the news after a Palestinian suicide bombing or returning to a café after a bombing. In a setting where people often felt exceptionally unsafe, there were outlets to express genuine bodily and existential fear as well as political frustration. Should we even live in Israel, there were Israelis who asked, and expose ourselves to this, and be complicit in this?

When Israeli Jews disparaged the inefficacies of security or criticized military brutalities, however, this did not always preclude their engagement with national security. It is not that Israeli Jews inevitably reproduced state security discourse, but rather that the desire for everyday ease tended to prevail over the commitment to analyze and amend. When individuals calculated the ways they would drive to work, decided that they would sit in the back of a café, or dissuaded their children from taking city buses, they did so out of a desire for control and comfort. The emotional, relational, and familial aspects of personal safety, combined with the yearnings of those living in intense conflict for even a veneer of normality in daily life, enabled Israelis to convince themselves that avoiding Palestinian neighborhoods or scanning for suspicious people were not political acts, to believe that facilitating personal safety was a sacrosanct and unassailable deed of self-preservation. Yet these thoughts and acts were themselves shaped by and part of a system of Israeli sovereignty that has overlooked Palestinian life and suffering and that has constantly delineated an "us" and a "them," a "here" and a "there."

These binaries were perpetuated by fantasies of life as normal and sustainable as it is. Efforts to escape danger, such as driving along the painted cement barrier of Highway 6, blurred with efforts to evade reality. Walls in the mind, like walls through the landscape, generate fantasies of Israel as elsewhere, as somehow outside the Middle East. They engendered illusions of Palestinians as invisible and of violence that could be kept at bay. In minute and routine but forceful ways, practices of everyday security constantly affirmed and re-entrenched fantasies of separation and threat without cultivating efforts to seek an end to conflict. So powerful are fantasies of security that they can become indistinguishable from and, indeed, can incite political conflict. In fact, when the Israeli government organized what it called the largest civil defense drill in Israeli history, the reactions of both Israeli civilians and neighboring rival governments suggested that simulations of security could prompt very real responses. I conclude this book with a description of a so-called security drill that makes us question the boundaries between fantasy and reality and between security and violence.

The 34–day war between Hezbollah and Israel in 2006, known alternately as the Second Lebanon War, the Israel-Hezbollah War, or the July War, resulted in more than one thousand civilian deaths, mostly Lebanese, as well as criticism of Israel's miscalculation of the strategic consequences of invading Lebanon.[2] Censure from within the Israeli government, which centered on the failure to respond to Hezbollah missile attacks and to prudently secure industrial areas,[3] led to the establishment in September 2007 of a new government branch, the National Emergency Authority, dubbed Raḥel, an acronym for Reshut Ḥerum Leumi. In the spring of 2008, the National Emergency Authority, together with the Home Front Command, organized a drill to test the readiness of civilian defense bodies to deal with missile attacks and biological and chemical weapons, as well as to convey to the Israeli public that the government had made progress with regard to preparedness. The drill, called Turning Point II (Nekudat Mifne 2), began on April 6, 2008.

Each morning for five days, Israelis awoke to radio announcements describing the scenarios being enacted that day: On Monday, there was a Katyusha missile strike from Gaza in Netivot and Ashkelon, an attack on Ben Gurion International Airport, and a hazardous material spill in the Haifa Bay. On Tuesday, a rocket landed on the Knesset and government employees were rushed to shelters. Later that day, the Home Front Command forces evacuated casualties from a building collapse in the Nazareth area, where ground-to-ground missiles equipped with chemical warheads had been fired. As part of the exercises, the Cabinet of Israel met to make decisions regarding the management of the war on the home front. This was the first time a Cabinet session was part of a security exercise. Prime Minister Ehud Olmert and Defense Minister Ehud Barak reviewed various situations, making decisions as the events unfolded (Azoulay 2008). In these hypothetical situations, the government played itself. On Wednesday, there was an explosion at a major chemical plant at the Haifa Port. On Thursday, a chemical-warfare missile struck Emek Medical Center in Afula and 300 wounded civilians were rushed to the emergency room. Newspaper articles used quotation marks to draw attention to the simulation of it all: "Military Drill Leaves 100 'Dead'," and "The 'war,' which has already claimed close to a 100 'casualties,' is expected to escalate Wednesday" (Greenberg 2008a, b); "Dozens of Israeli civilians were 'killed' on Sunday as Israel went to 'war' with Syria, Hezbollah and Hamas" (Katz and Lappin 2008).

The third day of the drill was dedicated to civilian preparedness. In the weeks leading up to the drill, Israel's Home Front Command sent mailings in Hebrew, Arabic, English, and Russian to homes throughout the country; the mailings contained instructions on how to prepare the home for war or emergency, multimedia CDs, refrigerator magnets, and color-coded maps. The maps, which divided Israel into twenty-seven regions and five belts according to the distance from Hezbollah's missile array, informed people how much time they would have to react in case of a missile attack. On the day of the civilian drill, the Home Front Command had hired an eminent senior news anchor from Channel 2, Gadi Sukenik, to serve as the face of civil defense. In a live broadcast on

Channel 33 from 10 to 11 A.M., Sukenik instructed the country on how to choose a protected space and how to behave during an alert. At 10 A.M., when 1,500 sirens wailed for a minute and a half throughout the country, schoolchildren and hospital patients dutifully headed to the nearest shelter.

In the thick of daily life, however, Sukenik's advice appeared to be largely disregarded. At 9:30 that morning at Café Hillel on Emek Refa'im Street in Jerusalem, the café that had been bombed and rebuilt in September 2003, a man in jeans sipped his latte as he penciled numbers into a Sudoku puzzle. A young woman on her cell phone sat with her laptop. Across the room, two people were having a business breakfast and two friends chatted about their weekends while a Beethoven violin sonata played overhead. At 10 A.M., the moment for the biggest civilian defense drill in Israel's history, sirens began to wail in the streets. Over the sonatas, however, it was barely audible. The Sudoku continued, as did the laptop typing and breakfast meeting. I stepped outside the café, where I saw that the cars had not stopped in their tracks and pedestrians continued to walk as usual. "Why has no one responded to the air-raid siren?" I asked the guard. He glanced at me while continuing to tap out a text message on his cell phone. He looked back down and shrugged, not interested in assuaging my concern. Obviously, he seemed to be telling me, everyone knew this was a drill but was making particular effort to disregard the siren. They were normalizing not just conflict but security itself.

The National Emergency Authority distinguished between this exercise drill and ongoing "real" alerts. Since January 2001 and more so since Israel's disengagement from the Gaza Strip in August 2005, Sderot and other Israeli areas near the Gaza border had been the target of thousands of Qassam rockets launched by Palestinian organizations based in Gaza, primarily Hamas and Islamic Jihad. The Israeli government installed a radar system or "red alert alarm" to warn Israelis about possible shellings. Once a rocket was fired and the siren sounded, residents had fifteen seconds to reach a bomb shelter. On the day of Turning Point II's nationwide civilian siren in 2008, residents of Sderot were excluded from participating in the drill because the government wanted them to continue to be on "real" alert for Qassam rockets.

In many ways, however, Turning Point II's simulation of security was no less "real" than other acts of Israeli security. During the drill, it was impossible to distinguish between the fantasy and the reality of security, whether at the level of embodied experience or of state practice. In fact, there was a sense of concern in Israel that the drill would heighten tensions with Lebanon and Syria.[4] An elementary school principal in Ma'alot, a city in Israel's Galilee region, expressed concern that the drill would somehow come true. "The whole world knew that at 10 A.M. there would be an exercise and I worried that someone would use this to make it a real emergency" (Hai et al. 2008). Out of concern or fascination, the Israeli media reported on the seriousness with which neighboring governments were taking Israel's drill. Israel's Army Radio (Galei Tsahal) announced that while the exercises were being held, "Hezbollah terrorists" were deployed for an all-out confrontation. *Yediot Aharonot* reported that Syria perceived Israel's drill as part of the country's plan for a comprehensive Israeli strike of Damascus. Syrian deputy foreign minister Faisal Mekdad, according to the *Jerusalem Post*, warned: "If Syria is the target of all of this, know that we are following the drill and are also developing our capabilities and our plans to face the Israeli maneuvers" (*Jerusalem Post* 2008). Syrian defense minister Hassan Turkmani announced plans to hold a nationwide emergency drill to prepare for natural disasters and other emergencies (Nahmia 2008). Lebanese Army commander General Michel Suleiman reportedly ordered his troops to raise levels of alert and preparation in all military units until the end of the Israeli military drill (Frykberg 2008).

It was a war of preparedness. Syria monitored Israel's drill, and Israel scrutinized Syria's simulated reactions to its own simulation. Governments appeared to take preparation as a threat in itself. How can one say where the drill ended and "real" security began? Over the course of the drill, the Israeli government asserted its authority, schoolchildren ran for cover, and foreign states felt threatened. News reports of simulated security threats sounded no different than regular reports of suspected security threats. Hezbollah and Syria may have been justified in their equation of Israeli security with Israeli violence, of Israeli readiness to protect with Israeli readiness to wage war. Fantasies of security and simulations of rescue had the power not only to instill trust and calm but also to incite antipathy and hostility. The fantasy of security generated by the drill was a veritable political reality.

Those sitting at Café Hillel during the drill may not have been consciously participating in the emergency activity, and indeed they appeared to carry on with their routines. Still, they were, in the ways I have analyzed in this book, engaging in everyday security. Playing Sudoku while shielded by an armed security guard, eating a sandwich while sitting in a café bombed several years earlier by a Palestinian Hamas militant, and hearing the clash of classical music and alert siren—these are all intense engagements with structures of state security. The kind of state the Sudoku-playing man was enacting may not have been the same state that the schoolchildren rushing to bomb shelters or the civilians volunteering in the Home Front Command's simulation of chemical-warhead attacks envisioned, but his seemingly apolitical concerns for comfort and normalization were themselves part and parcel of the Israeli discourse of security. The normalization of the drill was, indeed, the essence and power of security, whether in the form of government rhetoric or everyday practice: the ability to turn fantasy into grim reality and emotions into walls.

The blurring of fantasy and reality or violence and security transpires not only in Israel but also in other contexts of ongoing conflict where violence exists in either overt or more veiled forms. The Israeli context suggests that when state institutions of security join together in daily life with culturally resonant narratives of fear and threat, the result is a populace with heightened anxiety who seek ways to maintain fleeting feelings that life in conflict is sustainable, that a society suffused with military violence is tenable. Discourses of normalization and of threat become coeval, occurring at the same time and in the same spaces. Everything becomes more routine even as everything becomes more menacing. Belief that there is a homogeneous "other" that can or should be confined and a liberal cosmopolitanism that persists as if unaware of its logics of exclusion breed the desire for more security. Entrenched in daily life, discourses of security do not resolve tensions between safety and danger, order and disorder, peace and violence, but rather hold these in perpetual opposition.

Notes

Introduction: The Practice of Everyday Security

1. According to Dorit Beinisch, president of the Supreme Court of Israel, speaking at Princeton University's Woodrow Wilson School on April 16, 2009.

2. For a study of Israel's defense expenditure, see Shiffer 2007.

3. Sharon's address at the Herzliya Conference, "The Balance of Israel's National Security," December 18, 2002.

4. See Weber 1947: 78; and Agamben 2002.

5. For historiography of the field of security studies, see Baldwin 1995; Steven Miller 2001; Klare 2001; and Smith 2005.

6. In the mid-1990s, Barry Buzan, Ole Waever, and Jaap de Wilde shifted the traditional lens of security studies away from an exclusive focus on the state and political-military institutions to study security in its social context. They argued that security does not precede discourse, that it is not a priori, or "real," but rather that it is instantiated by its utterance (Buzan et al. 1998: 24–25). Scholars influenced by Michel Foucault, Jacques Derrida, and Judith Butler problematized this social constructionist approach, arguing that linguistic acts do not construct the social relations and political identities but rather perform them: security instantiates the subjects it also serves. See Campbell 1992 and Edkins 2003.

7. In this book, I refer to the first and second intifadas without italics or capitalization, following Khalidi 2006 and Lockman 1989.

8. For a comparison of the origins of the first and second intifadas, see Hammami and Tamari 2001.

9. For a discussion of the political resonances of these different strategies of self-identification, see Jean-Klein 2002. On the political and psychological motivations of Palestinian suicide bombings, see Hage 2003 and Moghadam 2003.

10. See, for example, Michael 2007.

11. See also Zulaika 2003.

12. See also Mansour 2002.

13. Begoñã Aretxaga (2003: 402) calls this a "paranoid dynamic." See also Leach 1977.

14. See Foucault 1998, 1994a.

15. See also Csordas 1994, 2002.

16. Psychological studies of Israeli responses to fear of Palestinian violence include Bleich, Gelkopf, and Solomon 2003; and Shalev et al. 2006.

17. The work of Rebecca Stein and Ted Swedenburg (2005) exemplifies a robust engagement with Israeli politics and history. Other work that attends to the mutual constitution of knowledge practices, intimacy, and politics includes Abu El-Haj 2001; Kahn 2000; Slyomovics 1998; Ben-Ari and Bilu 1997; Rabinowitz 1997; and Dominguez 1989.

18. For detailed ethnographic studies of Palestinians' daily encounters with the Israeli military, see Hammami 2004; Hajjar 2005; Bucaille 2004; Makdisi 2008; Bornstein 2002b; Rabinowitz and Khawla 2005; Peteet 1994; Jean-Klein 2001; Sa'di 2002; and Rosenfeld 2004.

19. Michel Foucault's suggestion that there is no position outside power-knowledge relations and the absence of a Foucaultian theory of resistance more generally have inspired a large body of literature, one that suggests that even if, in the case of this book, security is everywhere, there are still spaces and agents of resistance to it. Judith Butler 1993 has argued that the very reiterative and repetitive nature of norms carries with them their own possibility of reappropriation and resignification. From this perspective, even if Israeli subjectivity is an effect of the state power of security, security and other Israeli discourses of power are not entirely constitutive of it; see Butler 1997. Mahmood 2001 offers an alternative, culturally specific rendering of agency that derives not only from resistance to norms and power but also from processes of continuity and stasis.

Chapter 1. A Genealogy of Israeli Security

1. To put this in context, Israel's security services market in 2002 was estimated at $700 million, with 100,000 "security" workers employed throughout the country, according to Lagerquist 2002.

2. Defense expenditures in Israel increased 16 percent between 2000 and 2002. Expenditures declined in 2003 and 2004 as the intensity of the conflict abated, but Israel's disengagement from Gaza inflated expenditures in 2005. See Shiffer 2007: 196.

3. For more comprehensive histories of Israeli defense as an institution and an ideology, see Ben-Eliezer 1998 and Shlaim 2000. For a critical review of Israeli revisionism and its politics, see Lockman 1989 and Penslar 2001.

4. Compare to Gordon 2009, which studies the Israeli military as a "collaborative public space" for Israel's security industry.

5. On the British Mandate of Palestine, see Segev 1999 and Pappe 2004.

6. Information about Hashmira's history derived from the company Web site, www.hashmira.co.il, which since 2009 began to link directly to the Hebrew site of the security company G4S. Translation of Hashmira documents is my own.

7. The predecessor of Haganah was Hashomer (The Watchman), established by socialist Zionists in 1909, itself a successor of Bar-Giora, founded in 1907. Other splinter paramilitaries included the Irgun Tsva'i Leumi (National Military Organization), known as the Irgun, founded in 1931; and the Lehi, the Hebrew acronym of Lohamei Herut Yisrael (Fighters for the Freedom of Israel), founded in 1940. After the founding of the State of Israel in May 1948, the role and infrastructure of the Haganah were transferred to the army of the new state, the IDF. See Schiff 1985.

8. The controversial issue of whether Palestinian refugees fled of their own

accord or were expelled by Israeli forces has been examined closely by Benny Morris 1987. Morris paints a complex picture in which some sets of the Arab population were expelled while others fled before forces arrived, but in neither case did Israel, he argues, have a "grand design." Morris has been critiqued from Palestinian perspectives, such as Nur Masalha 1991, and from Israeli ones, such as Karsh 2003.

9. For a history of the Israeli military occupation of the West Bank and Gaza, see Gordon 2008; Pappe 2004; Bucaille 2004; and Weizman 2007. Feldman 2008 provides an archival ethnography of the Israeli occupation of Gaza.

10. For instance, this rhetoric permeates an article written by Israel's minister of foreign affairs, Yigal Allon (1976).

11. Israel's presence in this unratified zone expanded and formalized until its withdrawal in May 2000. See Sela 2007.

12. On the first intifada, see Lockman 1989.

13. On the link between economic liberalization and security in Israel, see Ram 2008: 66. For comparison to the commodification of private security elsewhere, see Loader 1999 and Newburn 2001.

14. Group 4 Securicor was founded as Group 4 in Belgium in the 1960s and has grown to include Falck, Wackenhut, Securicor, Rock Steady Group, and ArmorGroup International.

15. Recent literature on the privatization of security depicts the distinctions between public and private with regard to government outsourcing, mercenaries, private police forces, gated communities, and military weapons in the hands of private citizens as increasingly difficult to distinguish. On the privatization of security, see Huysmans, Dobson, and Prokhovnik 2006; Feigenbaum, Henig, and Hamnett 1999; and Newburn 2001.

16. In 1980, Israel's Jerusalem Law avowed that all of Jerusalem, including East Jerusalem, is the capital of Israel. Most countries, however, keep their embassies in Tel Aviv because Israel's annexation of East Jerusalem in 1949 was seen as unauthorized, given that the United Nations Partition Plan for Palestine of 1947 had called for the internationalization of the city. According to the United Nations, East Jerusalem is occupied territory and will be the land over which a future Palestinian state will exercise sovereignty. The Palestinian Authority ratified a law in 2002 that indicates Jerusalem as the future capital of a future Palestinian state.

17. On the role of renaming streets in the process of Israeli nation-building, see Azaryahu and Golan 2001.

18. The Civil Guard was established in response to the killing in Maʿalot of Israeli high school students by the Democratic Front for the Liberation of Palestine. It also emerged in the wake of the Yom Kippur War, which, according to Baruch Kimmerling, "reemphasized a feeling of individual responsibility" (1978: 113).

19. This is an example of Ulrich Beck's argument that solidarity derives more from insecurity than from need (1992: 49).

20. On the politics of relations between Mizrahi and Ashkenazi Israelis, see Shafir and Peled 2002 and Yiftachel and Meir 1996.

21. Founded in 1934, Aliyat ha-Noʿar brought Jewish children, many of them orphans, to Israel from Europe during and after World War II. It remains a department of the Jewish Agency.

22. There is considerable governmental and scholarly debate over whether the Fourth Geneva Convention, adopted in 1949, applies to or forbids the

establishment of Israeli settlements. Israel does not accept that the Fourth Geneva Convention applies de jure but has claimed to govern itself de facto by its provisions, vaguely defined.

23. The discontinuity between pre- and post-1977 settlement movements in Israel is reflected in the terms used for settlement. Beginning with Zionist agricultural settlements in the early twentieth century, the word *yishuv* referred broadly to Jewish settlement in the Land of Israel. The religious settlement movement used the term *hitnaḥlut,* from the biblical root n-ḥ-l, to refer to settlement outside the Green Line. This term implies a rightful inheritance, as in the land God allotted to the twelve tribes of Israel in the Land of Canaan, and Israeli settlers who use this term assert national and messianic entitlement to the land. For those critical of Israeli settlement in the Palestinian territories, *hitnaḥlut* carries a negative connotation, although many Israelis, left and right, still use the term *yishuv* to refer to Jewish settlements in the West Bank and Gaza.

24. Zachary Lockman (1996) has argued that interactions between Israelis and Palestinians have been characterized as much by cooperation as by conflict and as much by integration as by separation; that Israeli and Palestinian identities, tastes, and economies intersect and have been mutually formed. Nonetheless, in what Daniel Lefkowitz has called institutional forms of segregation, Israeli and Palestinian lives, livelihoods, economies, and spaces are to a large extent bifurcated, with separate school systems, social services, media broadcasting, and government ministries (2004: 88). See also Romann and Weingrod 1991.

Chapter 2. Senses of Security: Rebuilding Café Hillel

1. ZAKA, which stands for Zihui Korbanot Asson (Identification of Disaster Victims), was founded in 1995, but the organization crystallized and its activity increased and formalized during the second intifada. See Nurit Stadler, Ben-Ari, and Mesterman 2005 and Solomon and Berger 2005.

2. Don Handelman is describing the May 2001 collapse of the Versailles wedding-reception hall in West Jerusalem, a fatal calamity that was at first mistakenly treated as the result of a Palestinian bombing, with units of Israel's Home Front Command called in.

3. In Israel, damage to Israeli property from suicide bombings was generally repaired at government expense by the Property Tax Department. Physical injuries and deaths from Palestinian violence were generally covered by Bituaḥ Leumi (National Insurance Institute).

4. Daniel Monk's study (2002) of architecture and the Israeli-Palestinian conflict draws attention not to the role of architecture in conflict but to the historical logics and theories of representation that enable claims to be made in the first place about the relationship between built form and conflict.

5. I use the term artifact following its conceptualization by scholars of Actor Network Theory, which recognize things, people, technologies, and ideas as participants, or artifacts, that are shaped by and constitutive of a network. See Latour 2005.

6. Quoted from www.israeltrade.gov.il.

7. For comparison, see Allen 2006: 121. In this study of Palestinian martyrdom posters, Allen uses an experiential notion of aesthetics to analyze the paradoxical politics of martyr poster design, simultaneously repressive and sympathetic, factional and familial: "the personal memories and values of viewers survived and surpassed the sheer multiplication of posters and their nationalist messages."

8. In studying the state as produced through everyday practice, I follow anthropological studies of the state that analyze it as an unbounded, amorphous, and imagined entity constantly created and reified through localized institutions and practices. See Mitchell 1991; Gupta 1995; and Brown 1995.

9. On Israeli discourse of ethnicity and constitutions of self, see Dominguez 1989.

10. Vadim Volkov (2000) describes a similar practice in Russia, where KGB agents often entered the private security sector.

11. See also Lyon 2005.

Chapter 3. *Pahad:* Fear as Corporeal Politics

1. On Palestinian women's experiences of fear under Israeli occupation, see Abowd 2007.

2. Recent scholarship on the politics of fear includes Glassner 1999; Robin 2004; Altheide 2006; Bourke 2005; and Stearns 2006.

3. Fear as a political experience in Israel has been studied primarily by psychologists and has tended to focus on Jewish settlers in the occupied territories (Billig 2006) or on extremist or fundamentalist Israeli Jews (Neuman and Levi 2003). Studies of fear across the population as a whole are generally statistical (Arian 2002) or depict fear as a strategy of coping (Bar-Tal 2001: 609).

4. When residents of Tzur Hadassah, which lies within the Green Line, travel to Jerusalem or Tel Aviv, most opt to save thirty minutes by driving via the Gilo tunnel, a so-called bypass road that leads from southern Jerusalem to the Gush Etzion settlements, circumventing Bethlehem.

5. On the role of narratives of persecution in galvanizing Israeli nationalism, see Zerubavel 1995; Segev 1993; Shlaim 2000; Lentin 2002; and Young 1990.

6. On Israeli discourses of victimhood during the second intifada, see Ochs 2006.

7. The 3,000 percent increase in business reported in 2007 by Beit El Industries, the leading Israeli maker of nuclear, biological, and chemical warfare defense systems, was attributed to concern over the Iranian threat (Westervelt 2007).

8. So pervasive was this rhetoric of threat during the second intifada that the media used the same rhetoric to frame a host of other social concerns. The impending recession in 2003, for example, was presented as an "economic threat," organized crime was a "national threat," and a case of tainted baby formula was compared to the threat of terrorism.

9. *Ha'aretz* ran a critical response to Shavit's article in which Daniel Bar-Tal and Akiva Eldar 2005 agreed that collective memory of fear is a formative experience for Israeli Jews, but they questioned Shavit's claim that Israel is facing an existential threat as well as his assumption that the conflict is generated by the threat to Israel, and not by the occupation itself.

10. The title of the book is translated *Hear O Lord: Poems from the Disturbances of 2000–2006.* The word "disturbances" (*meora'ot*) references Palestinian violence against Israeli Jews in the 1920s and 1930s, an example of the cultural practice of using past violence to describe the present.

11. See also Abu-Lughod 1986; Lutz 1988; and Rosaldo 1980, 1984.

12. Other poststructuralist work on the embodiment of emotion includes Reddy 1997; Lyon 1995; and Beatty 2005.

13. On Israeli cultures of masculinity, see Ben-Ari and Dardashti 2001 and Sasson-Levy 2003.

14. We could speak similarly about the ways motherhood gives people particular confidence to talk about national security. A newspaper editorial about the separation wall, for example, cited a critic as follows: "As a mother of three small children living in Jerusalem no one is more concerned with Israel's security than I. But Israel cannot manipulate our legitimate security fears to advance a political goal" (Montel 2004).

15. For Israelis and Palestinians, motherhood is implicated in nationalism, state-building, and resistance. See Stoler-Liss 2003; Kanaaneh 2002; and Neuman 2004.

16. The broad spectrum of ultra-Orthodox Jews, Haredim, are so called because they tremble before God: "one who trembles in awe of God" (Isaiah 66:2, 5). The liturgy of the daily Jewish prayer book reinforces that fear (the words used are *paḥad* and also *yir'ah*, meaning both to fear and to see) is both positive and negative. Fear of God is seen as generative, productive, and necessary in order to complete religious commandments. At the same time, *yir'ah* or *yir'at shamayyim* (fear of heaven) refers to fear of divine punishment.

Chapter 4. Embodying Suspicion

1. Nostalgia for suspicious objects is expressed in the vignette "Suspicious Objects" in Shelach 2003.

2. Although one could argue that suspicious objects were already functioning for Israelis as metonyms for Palestinians.

3. www.oref.org.il, accessed in 2005, but since redesigned.

4. Scholars have studied many forms of Israeli erasures of Palestinian landscape and memory, a practice both spatial and discursive. See, for example, Morris 1987; Slyomovics 1998; Abu El-Haj 2001; and Campos 2007.

5. The strategies used to permanently settle Bedouin in villages are described in Falah 1989 and Fenster 1997. On Israeli Bedouins' conflicting identities as Israeli and Palestinian, see Dinero 2004.

6. Since 2005, intense legal battles over the validity of Reform conversions to Judaism led the Interior Ministry to drop the category *le'om* altogether, lest people be labeled Jews who are not Jewish according to some Orthodox definitions. As of 2010, only the presence or absence of a Hebrew birth date, in addition to a Gregorian date, indicated whether a citizen is Jewish or non-Jewish. Debate over these designations is ongoing.

7. On the codes of participation in Israel's political community, see Shafir and Peled 2002: 125.

8. Tens of thousands of Palestinians not in the Palestinian population registry are waiting for their ID cards to be approved by the Israeli Civil Administration.

9. For analysis of racial profiling of Muslims in the United States after September 11, see Rana and Rosas 2006 and Newman and Levine 2006.

10. On cleavages between Ashkenazi and Mizrahi Jews, see Massad 1996 and Peled 1998.

11. Dvir's argument resonated with that of Daniel Bar-Tal and Yona Teichman (2005: 14), in which they argue that Israelis' negative perceptions of Arabs are a cultural strategy that "prepares the young generation to . . . function in a threatening and stressful context."

12. One corollary to Israeli alertness for a particular matrix of bodily signs is that Palestinians sometimes navigated Israeli military checkpoints by tapping into Israelis' assumptions about Palestinian appearance and style. The Bayt Hajjar residents Tobias Kelly studies, for example, found ways to acquire cars with yellow Israeli license plates as opposed to green Palestinian National Authority ones, and also knew which make of car (Volvo) Israeli soldiers were likely to wave unquestionably through a checkpoint. Evading suspicion was a bodily performance. With tight jeans, certain styles of facial hair, and American hip-hop blasting on the car radio, Palestinians could, albeit to a small extent, play into and thus confound the expectations Israelis had of the correlation between appearance and identity, all without presenting a legal document (2006a: 97).

Chapter 5. Projecting Security in the City

1. After 1948, Armon Hanatziv became a demilitarized zone that served as the headquarters for UN observers. After the 1967 war, Israel captured this land. Esther and Shimon were most likely thinking of an act of violence that occurred in 2002, when a Palestinian stabbed a twenty-five-year-old resident of Kibbutz Kefar Hanasi in the Jerusalem Peace Forest, Ya'ar ha-Shalom, which is near the Promenade. The Haas Promenade, located on a ridge just inside the Green Line in East Talpiot, was a project of Teddy Kollek when he was the mayor of Jerusalem in the 1980s.

2. Urban anxiety is not, of course, unique to Israel. As Thomas Blom Hansen observes, referring to issues of citizenship and civil rights, "Unruliness, ambiguity, intensity, and anxiety are defining characteristics of the urban experience in most parts of the world" (2001: 6).

3. French Hill closely trailed the Jerusalem city center in the number of Palestinian attacks (Savitch and Garb 2006: 160).

4. On Mongolian mental maps as an abstract system of orientation, see Humphrey 2001.

5. The violence of Israeli military control had an acute effect not only on Palestinian imaginaries of safe and dangerous space but also on their very ability to travel. Reema Hammami (2006) offers an ethnographic analysis of Palestinian commutes across the Qalandiya military checkpoint, pointing to how Palestinians experience Israeli spatial control and inequality.

6. Deepak Mehta and Roma Chatterji study memories of a communal riot in Bombay both through "sitting narratives" and also by "walk[ing] the invisible spaces" of the city with informants who had experienced violence (2001: 108).

7. On the process of traumatic memory, see Kaplan 2005.

8. Ian Loader (1999) shows how individuals in Britain display comparable forms of idiosyncratic risk assessment when they purchase security hardware or private policing services.

9. For comparison, see Mehta and Bondi 1999, a gendered analysis of how university students experience and manage fears of violence in urban space.

10. Elizabeth Faier says about this event: "During the days before Land Day, the Jewish media forewarns pandemonium and danger, even though, in many ways, Palestinians carefully plan whatever chaos might ensue; it is bounded disorder" (2004: 171).

11. On the use of amulets in Israel, see Barr et al. 2000; Sered 1993; and Bilu and Ben-Ari 1992.

12. On the replacement of Arabic names with Hebrew ones, see Benvenisti 2000; Azaryahu and Golan 2001; Suleiman 2004: 1361; Peteet 2005: 1383. On Israeli settlements as a palimpsest of Palestinian life, see Slyomovics 1998. "From its establishment," Michelle Campos has argued, "the Israeli state has been actively involved in forgetting and making forgotten the non-Jewish past of the land of Israel-Palestine" (Campos 2007: 58).

Chapter 6. On IKEA and Army Boots: The Domestication of Security

1. Most notably, see Miller 2001: 119 and Carsten and Hugh-Jones 1995. An exemplary study of domestic organization as a domain of state change is Yan 2003.

2. Ethnographies of violence particularly attentive to the ways conflict resignifies the spatial and symbolic significance of the home include Nordstrom 1997; Aretxaga 1997; Green 1999; and Lawrence 1997.

3. On the impact of Palestinians' confinement to the home during Israel-imposed curfews, see Jamjoum 2002; Abdelhadi 2004; and Giacaman et al. 2004.

4. Despite widespread recognition of the political resonance of home and homeland to Israeli Jews, little work has been done on the actual material culture of Israeli homes. Susan Sered does attend to the routines of domestic life among elderly Jewish Kurdish and Yemenite women (Sered 1992).

5. See also Jackson 2005.

6. On staying home as a routine of the first intifada, see Kimmerling 1985: 99.

7. On Israeli experiences in sealed rooms during the Gulf War, see Werman 1993.

8. Because the family did not build the home as a new structure, they were able to circumvent building codes requiring all new homes to have shelters, although their removal of the door would not necessarily have been approved by the city.

9. Analysis of the intermingling of the military and civilian life in Israel has been central to Israeli social science scholarship on the state. While earlier work focused on the permeable boundaries between civilian and military spheres in Israel, a "partial militarization of civilian life and a partial civilianization of the military" (Horowitz and Lissak 1989: 197), later work studied how the military mediates the relationship between the Israeli state and civil society. See Horowitz and Lissak 1989: 197; Kimmerling 1993; Helman 1997, 1999; Ben-Eliezer 1997; Maman, Ben-Ari, and Rosenhek 2001; Azaryahu 1999; Handelman and Katz 1995; and Lomsky-Feder and Ben-Ari 2000. For a historiography of this scholarship, see Barak and Sheffer 2007.

10. In 1993, Channel 2 became Israel's first commercial television station.

11. A. B. Yehoshua 1980: 139, cited in Segev 2002: 5–6.

12. The translation is the magazine's. For this letter to the editor and several other articles, the magazine provided an English translation alongside the Hebrew.

Chapter 7. Seeing, Walking, Securing: Tours of Israel's Separation Wall

1. On the fortification of Gilo as a locus of national and personal struggle, see Kallus 2004.

2. For comprehensive studies of the wall, see Lochery 2005 and Jacoby 2007.

On the wall's political and legal intricacies, see Kershne 2005; Koury 2005; and Lynk 2005. For analysis of the wall as a form of Israeli exclusion of Palestinians, see Usher 2005; Lagerquist 2004; Weizman 2007; Trottier 2007; and Sorkin 2005. Uri Ben-Eliezer and Yuval Feinstein (2007: 179) examine the failure of activism against the wall in the context of Israeli sovereign practices. The effects of the wall on Palestinian real estate are examined in Savitch and Garb 2006. Other scholarship of note includes Bowman 2004; Rabinowitz 2004; and Ellis 2004.

3. Beginning in 2000 under Prime Minister Ehud Barak, the Gaza wall was buttressed with steel walls, buffer zones, and observation posts.

4. In July 1997, Likud Defense Minister Yitzhak Mordecai officially objected to the separation fence plan of the Rabin government and placed its construction on hold. In late 1999, in a resolute project that revived Moshe Shahal's plan, Prime Minister Ehud Barak proposed a fence along an approximation of the Green Line, which would enclave the West Bank as Gaza already had been. For analysis of the early left-wing support for separation, see Rabinowitz 2003 and Weizman 2005.

5. According to one report, a single private security company held 90 percent of the security contracts at the wall's construction sites in Jerusalem (Yamin-Wolvovitz 2004).

6. On the state discourse of temporariness that surrounded the wall, see Weizman 2004: 186–87.

7. There was not a sizeable Israeli protest movement against the wall, although art by activists on both sides of the wall functioned as a form of nonviolent resistance; Boullata 2005: 257. The work of Machsom Watch, a human rights organization of Israeli women who visit, monitor, and intervene when possible at the checkpoints in the West Bank, has productively protested other aspects of Israeli separation and control. See Hallward 2008 and Naaman 2006. On Beit Surik's petition to Israel's High Court of Justice, see Yoaz 2005 and B'Tselem 2004b.

8. Within the bureaucratic permit system imposed by Israeli authorities on residents of the West Bank in order to cross through checkpoints, permits were denied, supplied, or sometimes expired with seeming arbitrariness, according to Kelly 2004.

9. Tourism has long been an instrument for Israeli nationalism. Kobi Cohen-Hattab 2004 examines how Jews and Arabs used tourism and tourist maps as political propaganda in the first half of the twentieth century. Glen Bowman 1991 studies how Israeli tour guides for Christian pilgrims in the 1980s affirmed the "otherness" of "the Arab" and stressed the dangers of the Palestinian landscape. Richard Clarke 2000 contrasts Palestinian and Jewish tourism in the mixed Jewish-Palestinian city of Hebron, the latter focusing on the *suk*, checkpoints and refugee camps; and the former on religious sites and Jewish settlement. For comparison to tourism in other countries, see Heidi Dahles's (2002) study of tourism as a strategic extension of foreign policy in Indonesia.

10. Particularly since 1967, "solidarity missions" have been organized by a range of Jewish organizations around the world, from the Zionist Federation of Great Britain to the liberal Jewish magazine *Tikkun*. Through concise tours of Israeli sites and meetings with Israeli political officials, they aim to support the Israeli economy through their tourism, to educate Diaspora Jews about pressing political issues, and to captivate participants—socially and financially—with evocative feelings about the "holy land."

11. Tourism around walls embroiled in conflict has been studied in other contexts. Debbie Lisle 2007 examines the different forms of propaganda that

mediate tourist encounters with partition in Northern and Southern Cyprus. Simon Guy (2004: 88) studies the Berlin wall as "a tourist spectacle" and Duncan Light 2000 argues that Berlin Wall tourism appeals to people's curiosity without compromising post-communist identity. Stephen Boyd 2000 notes that tourism around the wall in Belfast began in the 1980s.

12. Beyond tours of the separation wall, security more generally has been turned into a profitable tourist industry in Israel. The "Ultimate Counter-Terrorism Mission," for example, was a seven-day tour organized in 2008 by the New York-based Shaneson Consulting Group, which calls itself a homeland security and counter-terrorism consulting firm. For $5,095 including airfare from New York, the tour went well beyond the visits to military bases and checkpoints often included in Jewish American tours of Israel. It included briefings with former Shin Bet and Mossad officials, discussion with "undercover Palestinian agents," observation of a "security trial of alleged Hamas terrorists," and a training session in the "Hisardut Israel Survival System" (whose motto is "Knowledge is power. Learn to live without fear!"). For all the expertise it offered, the tour appeared to convey what Jewish North American missions to Israel have for decades: Israel has much to teach Diaspora Jews but is itself vulnerable to threat.

13. On "dark" or "disaster" tourism, see Foley and Lennon 2000; Strangea and Kempab 2003; and Milesa 2002. Debbie Lisle 2006 problematizes critiques of dark tourism to battlefields and war zones, arguing that it plays a crucial political role in societies emerging from conflict.

14. In his study of walking tours of London, Adam Reed (2002: 132) highlights the appeal of "non-visibility"—attraction to things that cannot be seen or that are too fleeting to photograph.

15. The seam zone is designated a "closed military zone" by the IDF, which means that Israeli citizens, including those who live in the nearly 100 Jewish settlements in this area, can enter and exit but, with few exceptions, non-Israeli Palestinians who live in the zone cannot exit and other Palestinians cannot enter. Human rights groups in and out of Israel have declared the seam zone, together with the separation wall, illegal under international law.

16. Over 40 percent of the Jewish Israeli population identify themselves as secular, according to Israel Central Bureau of Statistics 2009a.

17. Gutwein 2006 has argued that Israeli settlements have become an alternate form of social welfare in the context of the linked conditions of occupation and privatization, "a mechanism which compensated the lower classes for the damages inflicted upon them by the privatization of welfare services in Israel."

18. When Israel seized and annexed stretches of the West Bank into the jurisdictional area of Jerusalem in 1967, the new municipal border divided Sheikh Sa'ad, making only some of its residents Israeli citizens. It was not until the early 1990s, when Israel placed a militarized closure on the occupied territories, that the "far-reaching consequences of the differentiation in status was realized" (B'Tselem 2004a). Avram Bornstein (2002a: 213) has argued that closure, functioning primarily to assure Israeli voters of their safety, did less to prevent Palestinians' entry from the West Bank than to oblige Palestinians to enter illegally.

Epilogue: Real Fantasies of Security

1. Recent studies of protest and critique within Israeli society include Helman 1999; Linn 2002; and Abu-Nimer 2006.

2. For assessments of military and diplomatic strategy during the 2006 war, see Harel and Issacharoff 2009 and Hovsepian 2008.

3. The Winograd Commission, established by Prime Minister Ehud Olmert to investigate Israel's military engagement in the 2006 Israel-Hezbollah War, attributed primary responsibility for Israel's "very serious failings" to Olmert, as well as to Defense Minister Amir Peretz and Chief of Staff Dan Halutz. The Commission has been criticized for ignoring Israel's war crimes, specifically its failure to discriminate between the Lebanese civilian population and Hezbollah combatants.

4. Israelis may have recalled a military exercise debacle in 1959, dubbed "Night of the Ducks" (*Leil ha-barvazim*). At a time of particular tension with Egypt and Syria, the IDF General Staff planned to test the readiness of its reserve troops by simulating an emergency, but the broadcast on Israel Radio (Kol Yisrael) calling up troops sounded to the country like a genuine emergency broadcast and incited panic. Syria, too, believed Israel was preparing a surprise attack and began to mobilize its army at the borders. The IDF officers responsible for the military drill were removed from their posts. See Royhman 2006.

Bibliography

Abdelhadi, Amer. 2004. "Surviving Siege, Closure, and Curfew: The Story of a Radio Station." *Journal of Palestine Studies* 34, 1: 51–67.

Abdulhadi, Rabab. 2003. "Where Is Home? Fragmented Lives, Border Crossings, and the Politics of Exile." *Radical History Review* 86: 89–101.

Abowd, Thomas. 2007. "National Boundaries, Colonized Spaces: The Gendered Politics of Residential Life in Contemporary Jerusalem." *Anthropological Quarterly* 80, 4: 997–1034.

Abu El-Haj, Nadia. 2001. *Facts on the Ground: Archaeological Practice and Territorial Self-Fashioning in Israeli Society*. Chicago: University of Chicago Press.

Abu-Lughod, Lila. 1986. *Veiled Sentiments: Honor and Poetry in a Bedouin Society*. Berkeley: University of California Press.

Abu-Lughod, Lila, and Catherine Lutz, eds. 1990. *Language and the Politics of Emotion*. Cambridge: Cambridge University Press.

Abu-Nimer, Mohammed. 2006. "Peace Building in Postsettlement: Challenges for Israeli and Palestinian Peace Educators." *Peace and Conflict: Journal of Peace Psychology* 6, 1: 1–21.

Agamben, Giorgio. 1998. *Homo Sacer: Sovereign Power and Bare Life*. Stanford, Calif.: Stanford University Press.

———. 2002. "Security and Terror." *Theory and Event* 5, 4: 1–2.

Allen, Lori. 2006. "The Polyvalent Politics of Martyr Commemorations in the Palestinian Intifada." *History & Memory* 18, 2: 107–38.

Allon, Yigal. 1976. "Israel: The Case for Defensible Borders." *Foreign Affairs* 55, 1: 38–53.

Almog, Oz. 2000. *The Sabra: The Creation of the New Jew*. Berkeley: University of California Press.

Altheide, David L. 2006. *Terrorism and the Politics of Fear*. Lanham, Md.: AltaMira Press.

Altman-Ohr, Andy. 2000. "Founder of IKEA Store Haunted by Nazi Past." *Jewish News Weekly of Northern California*, April 7.

Aretxaga, Begoña. 1997. *Shattering Silence: Women, Nationalism, and Political Subjectivity in Northern Ireland*. Princeton, N.J.: Princeton University Press.

———. 2003. "Maddening States." *Annual Review of Anthropology* 32: 393–410.

Arian, Asher. 1995. *Security Threatened: Surveying Israeli Opinion on Peace and War*. Cambridge: Cambridge University Press.

————. 2002. "Israeli Opinion on National Security." Tel Aviv: Jaffee Center for Strategic Studies, Tel Aviv University.

Augé, Marc. 1995. *Non-Places: Introduction to an Anthropology of Supermodernity.* London: Verso.

Azaryahu, Maoz. 1999. "The Independence Day Military Parade: A Political History of a Patriotic Ritual." In *The Military and Militarism in Israeli Society*, ed. Edna Lomsky-Feder and Eyal Ben-Ari, 89–116. Albany: State University of New York Press.

————. 2000. "Israeli Securityscapes." In *Landscapes of Defence*, ed. John R. Gold and George Revill. Harlow: Prentice-Hall.

Azaryahu, Maoz, and Arnon Golan. 2001. "(Re)Naming the Landscape: The Formation of the Hebrew Map of Israel 1949–1960." *Journal of Historical Geography* 27, 2: 178–95.

Azoulay, Yuval. 2008. "Civil Defense Drill Starts Sun." *Ha'aretz*, April 4.

Baldwin, David. 1995. "Security Studies and the End of the Cold War." *World Politics* 48, 1: 117–41.

Bar-Tal, Daniel. 2001. "Why Does Fear Override Hope in Societies Engulfed by Intractable Conflict, as It Does the Israeli Society?" *Political Psychology* 22: 601–27.

Bar-Tal, Daniel, and Akiva Eldar. 2005. "Right of Reply: The Meek and the Mighty (Response to Ari Shavit)." *Ha'aretz*, August 7.

Bar-Tal, Daniel, Dan Jacobson, and Tali Freund. 1995. "Security Feelings among Jewish Settlers in the Occupied Territories." *Journal of Conflict Resolution* 39, 2: 353–77.

Bar-Tal, Daniel, and Yona Teichman. 2005. *Stereotypes and Prejudice in Conflict: Representations of Arabs in Israeli Jewish Society.* Cambridge: Cambridge University Press.

Barak, Oren, and Gabriel Sheffer. 2007. "The Study of Civil-Military Relations in Israel: A New Perspective." *Israel Studies* 12, 1: 1–27.

Barr, Joseph, Matitiahu Berkovitch, Hagit Matras, et al. 2000. "Talismans and Amulets in the Pediatric Intensive Care Unit: Legendary Powers in Contemporary Medicine." *Israeli Medical Association Journal* 2, 4: 278–281

Barthes, Roland. 1972 [1957]. "The Blue Guide." In *Mythologies*, trans. Annette Lavers. London: Hill and Wang.

Barzilai, Amnon. 2004. "Post-Modern Terrorism: Suicide Strikes." *Ha'aretz*, April 20.

Bauman, Zygmunt. 2006. *Liquid Fear.* Cambridge: Polity.

————. 2007. *Liquid Times: Living in an Age of Uncertainty.* Cambridge: Polity.

Baumgarten, Helga. 2005. "The Three Faces/Phases of Palestinian Nationalism, 1948–2005." *Journal of Palestine Studies* 34, 4: 25–48.

Beatty, Andrew. 2005. "Emotions in the Field: What Are We Talking About?" *Journal of the Royal Anthropological Institute* 11: 17–37.

Beck, Ulrich. 1992. *Risk Society: Towards a New Modernity.* London: Sage.

Beinin, Joel. 2003. "The Israelization of American Middle East Policy Discourse." *Social Text* 21, 2: 125–39.

Ben-Ari, Eyal. 1989. "Masks and Soldiering: The Israeli Army and the Palestinian Uprising." *Cultural Anthropology* 4, 4: 372–89.

Ben-Ari, Eyal, and Yoram Bilu. 1997. *Grasping Land: Space and Place in Contemporary Israeli Discourse and Experience.* SUNY Series in Anthropology and Judaic Studies. Albany: State University of New York Press.

Ben-Ari, Eyal, and Galeet Dardashti. 2001. "Tests of Soldierhood, Trials of

Manhood: Military Service and Male Ideals in Israel." In *War, Politics and Society in Israel: Theoretical and Comparative Perspectives*, ed. Daniel Maman, Zeev Rosenheck, and Eyal Ben-Ari, 239–68. New Brunswick, N.J.: Transaction.

Ben-David, Orit. 1997. "Tiyul (Hike) as an Act of Consecration of Space." In *Grasping Land: Space and Place in Contemporary Israeli Discourse and Experience*, ed. Eyal Ben-Ari and Yoram Bilu. Albany: State University of New York Press.

Ben-Eliezer, Uri. 1998. *The Making of Israeli Militarism*. Bloomington: Indiana University Press.

———. 1997. "Rethinking the Civil-Military Relations Paradigm: The Inverse Relation Between Militarism and Praetorianism Through the Example of Israel." *Comparative Political Studies* 30, 3: 356–74.

Ben-Eliezer, Uri, and Yuval Feinstein. 2007. "'The Battle over Our Homes': Reconstructing/ Deconstructing Sovereign Practices Around Israel's Separation Barrier on the West Bank." *Israel Studies* 12, 1: 171–92.

Benvenisti, Meron. 2000. *Sacred Landscape: The Buried History of the Holy Land Since 1948*. Berkeley: University of California Press.

Berdahl, Daphne. 1999. *Where the World Ended: Re-Unification and Identity in the German Borderland*. Berkeley: University of California Press.

Berger, Sharon. 2000. "IKEA to Open Its Biggest Middle East Store in Netanya." *Jerusalem Post*, December 29.

Berlant, Lauren Gail. 2000. *Intimacy*. Chicago: University of Chicago Press.

Billig, Miriam. 2006. "Is My Home My Castle?: Place Attachment, Risk Perception, and Religious Faith." *Environment and Behavior* 38, 2: 248–65.

Bilu, Yoram, and Eyal Ben-Ari. 1992. "The Making of Modern Saints: Manufactured Charisma and the Abu-Hatseiras of Israel." *American Ethnologist* 19, 4: 672–87.

Binks, Eve. 2000. "Coping with Political Violence in Northern Ireland: A Dissociation Perspective." In *ISPP 31st Annual Scientific Meeting*, Paris.

Bisharat, George. 2007. "Talbiyeh Days: At Villa Harun ar-Rashid." *Jerusalem Quarterly* 30: 88–98.

Bleich, Avraham, Marc Gelkopf, and Zahava Solomon. 2003. "Exposure to Terrorism, Stress-Related Mental Health Symptoms, and Coping Behaviors Among a Nationally Representative Sample in Israel." *JAMA* 290: 612–20.

Blom Hansen, Thomas. 2001. *Wages of Violence: Naming and Identity in Postcolonial Bombay*. Princeton, N.J.: Princeton University Press.

Blom Hansen, Thomas, and Finn Stepputat, eds. 2001. *States of Imagination: Ethnographic Explorations of the Postcolonial State*. Durham, N.C.: Duke University Press.

Bornstein, Avram. 2001. "Ethnography and the Politics of Prisoners in Palestine-Israel." *Journal of Contemporary Ethnography* 30, 5: 546–74.

———. 2002a. "Borders and the Utility of Violence: State Effects on the 'Superexploitation' of West Bank Palestinians." *Critique of Anthropology* 22, 2: 201–20.

———. 2002b. *Crossing the Green Line Between the West Bank and Israel*. Philadelphia: University of Pennsylvania Press.

Boullata, Terry. 2005. "In the Spirit of Activism." In *Against the Wall: Israel's Barrier to Peace*, ed. Michael Sorkin. New York: New Press.

Bourdieu, Pierre. 1977. *Outline of a Theory of Practice*. Cambridge: Cambridge University Press.

Bourke, Joanna. 2005. *Fear: A Cultural History*. Emeryville, Calif.: Shoemaker & Hoard.

Bowman, Glen. 1991. "The Politics of Tour Guiding: Israeli and Palestinian

Guides in Israel and the Occupied Territories." In *Tourism and the Less-Developed Countries*, ed. David Harrison, 121–34. London: Belhaven Press.

————. 2004. "About a Wall." *Social Analysis* 48, 1: 14–20.

Boyd, Stephen W. 2000. "'Heritage' Tourism in Northern Ireland: Opportunity Under Peace." *Current Issues in Tourism* 3, 2: 150–74.

Brown, Wendy. 1995. *States of Injury: Power and Freedom in Late Modernity*. Princeton, N.J.: Princeton University Press.

B'Tselem. 2004a. "Facing the Abyss: The Isolation of Sheikh Sa'ad Village—Before and After the Separation Barrier." February. http://www.btselem.org/Download/200402_Sheikh_Saed_Eng.rtf.

————. 2004b. "Judgment of the High Court of Justice Regarding Beit Sourik." http://www.btselem.org/english/Separation_Barrier/Beit_Surik_Ruling.asp.

————. 2007. "Absolute Prohibition: The Torture and Ill-Treatment of Palestinian Detainees." Joint report with Hamoked, May. http://www.btselem.org/English/Publications/Summaries/200705_Utterly_Forbidden.asp.

Bucaille, Laetitia. 2004. *Growing Up Palestinian: Israeli Occupation and the Intifada Generation*. Princeton, N.J.: Princeton University Press.

Buchli, Victor. 2002. "Introduction." In *The Material Culture Reader*, ed. Victor Buchli. Oxford: Berg.

Butler, Judith. 1993. *Bodies That Matter: On the Discursive Limits of "Sex."* New York: Routledge.

————. 1997. *The Psychic Life of Power: Theories in Subjection*. Stanford, Calif.: Stanford University Press.

Buzan, Barry, Ole Waever, and Jaap De Wilde. 1998. *Security: A New Framework for Analysis*. Boulder, Colo.: Lynne Rienner.

Caldeira, Teresa P. R. 2000. *City of Walls: Crime, Segregation, and Citizenship in São Paulo*. Berkeley: University of California Press.

Campbell, David. 1992. *Writing Security: United States Foreign Policy and the Politics of Identity*. Manchester: Manchester University Press.

Campos, Michelle. 2007. "Remembering Jewish-Arab Contact and Conflict." In *Reapproaching Borders*, ed. Sandy Sufian and Mark Levine. New York: Rowman & Littlefield.

Carsten, Janet, and Stephen Hugh-Jones. 1995. *About the House: Lévi-Strauss and Beyond*. Cambridge: Cambridge University Press.

Certeau, Michel de. 1988. *The Practice of Everyday Life*. Berkeley: University of California Press.

Clarke, Alison J. 2001. "The Aesthetics of Social Aspiration." In *Home Possessions: Material Culture Behind Closed Doors*, ed. Daniel Miller. Oxford: Berg.

Clarke, Richard. 2000. "Self-Presentation in a Contested City." *Anthropology Today* 16, 5: 12–18.

Cohen, Shelly. 2004. "Epilogue: A Moment of Change? Transformations in Israeli Architectural Consciousness Following the 'Israeli Pavilion' Exhibition." In *Constructing a Sense of Place: Architecture and the Zionist Discourse*, ed. Haim Yacobi. Surrey: Ashgate.

Cohen, Stanley. 2001. *States of Denial: Knowing About Atrocities and Suffering*. Cambridge: Polity Press.

Cohen-Hattab, Kobi. 2004. "Zionism, Tourism, and the Battle for Palestine: Tourism as a Political-Propaganda Tool." *Israel Studies* 9, 1: 61–85.

Collier, Stephen J., Andrew Lakoff, and Paul Rabinow. 2004. "Biosecurity: Towards an Anthropology of the Contemporary." *Anthropology Today* 20, 4: 3–7.

Comaroff, Jean, and John L. Comaroff. 2004. "Criminal Obsessions, After

Foucault: Postcoloniality, Policing, and the Metaphysics of Disorder." *Critical Inquiry* 30, 4: 800–824.

Counihan, Carol. 1999. *The Anthropology of Food and Body: Gender, Meaning, and Power.* New York: Routledge.

Crossley, Nick. 2001. *The Social Body: Habit, Identity and Desires.* London: Sage.

Csordas, Thomas. 1999. "Embodiment and Cultural Phenomenology." In *Perspectives on Embodiment: The Intersections of Nature and Culture,* ed. Gail Weiss and Honi Fern Haber. New York: Routledge.

———. 2002. *Body/Meaning/Healing.* New York: Palgrave.

———, ed. 1994. *Embodiment and Experience.* Cambridge: Cambridge University Press.

Dahles, Heidi. 2002. "The Politics of Tour Guiding: Image Management in Indonesia." *Annals of Tourism Research* 29, 3: 783–800.

Das, Veena, Arthur Kleinman, Mamphela Ramphele, and Pamela Reynolds. 2000. *Violence and Subjectivity.* Berkeley: University of California Press.

Das, Veena, and Deborah Poole, eds. 2004. *Anthropology in the Margins of the State,* Advanced Seminar Series. London: James Currey.

Dillon, Michael, and Luis Lobo-Guerrero. 2008. "Biopolitics of Security in the 21st Century: An Introduction." *Review of International Studies* 34: 265–92.

Dinero, Steven. 2004. "New Identity/Identities Formulation in a Post-Nomadic Community: The Case of the Bedouin of the Negev." *National Identities* 6, 3: 261–75.

Dominguez, Virginia R.1989. *People as Subject, People as Object: Selfhood and Peoplehood in Contemporary Israel.* Madison: University of Wisconsin Press.

Douglas, Mary. 1966. *Purity and Danger: An Analysis of Concepts of Pollution and Taboo.* London: Routledge.

Dowty, Alan. 2005. *Israel/Palestine.* Cambridge: Polity Press.

Edkins, Jenny. 2003. *Trauma and the Memory of Politics.* Cambridge: Cambridge University Press.

Ellis, Mark. 2004. "The Mural-Covered Wall: On Separation and the Future of Jews and Palestinians in Israel/Palestine and the Diaspora." *Chicago Journal of International Law* 5, 1: 271–85.

El-Or, Tamar, and Eran Neria. 2004. "The Ultraorthodox Flaneur: Toward the Pleasure Principle. Consuming Time and Space in the Contemporary Haredi Population of Jerusalem." In *Consumption and Market Society in Israel,* ed. Yoram S. Carmeli and Kalman Applbaum. Oxford: Berg.

Ezrahi, Yaron. 1997. *Rubber Bullets: Power and Conscience in Modern Israel.* New York: Farrar, Straus & Giroux.

Faier, Elizabeth. 2004. *Organizations, Gender, and the Culture of Palestinian Activism in Haifa, Israel.* New York: Routledge.

Falah, Ghazi.1989. "Israeli State Policy Toward Bedouin Sedentarization in the Negev." *Journal of Palestine Studies* 18, 2: 71–91.

Feigenbaum, Harvey, Jeffrey Henig, and Chris Hamnett, eds. 1999. *Shrinking the State: The Political Underpinnings of Privatization* Cambridge: Cambridge University Press.

Feldman, Allen. 1994. "From Desert Storm to Rodney King via Ex-Yugoslavia: On Cultural Anaesthesia." In *The Senses Still: Perception and Memory as Material Culture in Modernity,* ed. C. Nadia Seremetakis. Chicago: University of Chicago Press.

———. 2003. "Political Terror and the Technologies of Memory: Excuse, Sacrifice, Commodification, and Actuarial Moralities." *Radical History Review* 85: 58–73.

Feldman, Ilana. 2000. "Home as Refrain: Remembering and Living Displacement in Gaza." *History & Memory* 12, 2: 10–47.

———. 2008. *Governing Gaza: Bureaucracy, Authority, and the Work of Rule, 1917–1967.* Durham, N.C.: Duke University Press.

Feldman, Jackie. 2007. "Constructing a Shared Bible Land: Jewish Israeli Guiding Performances for Protestant Pilgrims." *American Ethnologist* 34, 2: 351–74.

Fenster, Tovi. 1997. "Spaces of Citizenship for the Bedouin in the Israeli Negev." *Progress in Planning* 47, 4: 291–306.

Foley, Malcolm, and John Lennon. 2000. *Dark Tourism: The Attraction of Death and Disaster.* London: Continuum.

Forte, Tania. 2003. "Sifting People, Sorting Papers: Academic Practice and the Notion of State Security in Israel." *Comparative Studies of South Asia, Africa and the Middle East* 23, 1–2: 215–22.

The Forward. 2005. "Bombing Ups Ante in Upcoming Election." December 9.

Foucault, Michel. 1980. "The Eye of Power." In *Power/Knowledge: Selected Interviews and Other Writings, 1972–1977,* ed. Colin Gordon, 146–65. Brighton: Harvester.

———. 1994a. "Security, Territory, and Population." In *Ethics: Essential Works,* ed. Paul Rabinow, 67–71. London: Penguin.

———. 1994b. "Technologies of the Self." In *Ethics: Essential Works,* ed. Paul Rabinow. London: Penguin.

———. 1998. *The History of Sexuality.* Vol. 1, *The Will to Knowledge.* First Vintage ed. London: Penguin.

Frykberg, Mel. 2008. "Large Israeli Military Drills Raise Alerts." *Middle East Times* (Metimes.com), April 8.

Gampel, Yolanda. 2000. "Reflections on the Prevalence of the Uncanny in Social Violence." In *Cultures Under Siege: Collective Violence and Trauma,* ed. Antonius C. G. M. Robben and Marcelo M. Suárez-Orozco, 48–69. Cambridge: Cambridge University Press.

Gell, Alfred. 1985. "How to Read a Map: Remarks on the Practical Logic of Navigation." *Man* n.s. 20: 271–86.

Giacaman, Rita, Abdullatif Husseini, Nahida H. Gordon, and Faisal Awartani. 2004. "Imprints on the Consciousness: The Impact on Palestinian Civilians of the Israeli Army Invasion of West Bank Towns." *European Journal of Public Health* 14, 3: 286–90.

Glassner, Barry. 1999. *The Culture of Fear: Why Americans Are Afraid of the Wrong Things.* New York: Perseus.

Gordon, Neve. 2008. *Israel's Occupation.* Berkeley: University of California Press.

———. 2009. "The Political Economy of Israel's Homeland Security." New Transparency Project, Working Paper III, IRSP IV, http://www.surveillanceproject.org/projects/the-new-transparency.

Green, Linda. 1999. *Fear as a Way of Life: Mayan Widows in Rural Guatemala.* New York: Columbia University Press.

Green, Sarah F. 2005. *Notes from the Balkans: Locating Marginality and Ambiguity on the Greek-Albanian Border.* Princeton, N.J.: Princeton University Press.

Greenberg, Hanan. 2008a. "Military Drill Leaves 100 'Dead'." *Yediot Aharonot,* ynet.com, April 7.

———. 2008b. "Home Front Drill: Sirens Heard Throughout Israel." *Yediot Aharonot,* ynet.com, April 8.

Grossman, David. 1993. *Sleeping on a Wire: Conversations with Palestinians in Israel.* New York: Farrar, Straus, and Giroux.

Gupta, Akhil. 1995. "Blurred Boundaries: The Discourse of Corruption, the Culture of Politics, and the Imagined State." *American Ethnologist* 22, 2: 375–402.

Guy, Simon. 2004. "Shadow Architectures: War, Memories, and Berlin's Futures." In *Cities, War, and Terrorism: Towards an Urban Geopolitics*, ed. Stephen Graham. Oxford: Blackwell.

Gutwein, Daniel. 2006. "Some Comments on the Class Foundations of the Occupation." *News from Within* 12, 4. http://alternativenews.org/index. php?option=com_content&task=view&id=434&Itemid=70#Danny%20Gutwein.

Ha'aretz. 2004. "8 Killed, 72 Hurt in Jerusalem Bus Bombing." February 26.

Hadar, Dea. 2004. "Journey to Inner Space." *Ha'aretz*, June 2.

Hage, Ghassan. 2003. " 'Comes a Time We Are All Enthusiasm': Understanding Palestinian Suicide Bombers in Times of Exighophobia." *Public Culture* 15, 1: 68–89.

Haggerty, Kevin D., and Richard V. Ericson. 2000. "The Surveillant Assemblage." *British Journal of Sociology* 51, 4: 506–622.

Hai, Yival, Yuval Azulai, and Jack Khoury. 2008. "Home Front Commander Says Israelis Are Ready to Meet Any Threat." *Ha'aretz*, April 9.

Hajjar, Lisa. 2005. *Courting Conflict: The Israeli Military Court System in the West Bank and Gaza.* Berkeley: University of California Press.

Halkin, Talya. 2004. "Writing Beyond the Green Line." *Jerusalem Post*, June 9.

Hallward, Maia Carter. 2008. "Negotiating Boundaries, Narrating Checkpoints: The Case of Machsom Watch." *Critical Middle Eastern Studies* 17, 1: 21–40.

Hammami, Rema. 2004. "On the Importance of Thugs: The Moral Economy of a Checkpoint." *Middle East Report* 231: 26–34.

———. 2006. "Human Agency at the Frontiers of Global Inequality: An Ethnography of Hope in Extreme Places." Inaugural address, International Institute of Social Science, April 20.

Hammami, Rema, and Salim Tamari. 2001. "The Second Uprising: End or New Beginning?" *Journal of Palestine Studies* 30, 2: 5–25.

Handelman, Don. 2004. *Nationalism and the Israeli State: Bureaucratic Logic in Public Events.* Oxford: Berg.

Handelman, Don, and Elihu Katz. 1995. "State Ceremonies of Israel: Remembrance Day and Independence Day." In *Israeli Judaism: The Sociology of Religion in Israel*, ed. Shlomo Deshen, Charles Liebman, and Moshe Shokeid, 75–85. New Brunswick, N.J.: Transaction.

Hannah, Kim. 2001. "Oslo-Bashing Is Now 'In'." *Ha'aretz*, October 30.

Harel, Amos, and Avi Issacharoff. 2009. *34 Days: Israel, Hezbollah, and the War in Lebanon.* Trans. Ora Cummings and Moshe Tlamim. New York: Palgrave Macmillan.

Hartman, Tod. 2007. "On the Ikeaization of France." *Public Culture* 19, 3: 483–98.

Helman, Sarah. 1997. "Militarism and the Construction of Community." *Journal of Political and Military Sociology* 25: 305–32.

———. 1999. "From Soldiering and Motherhood to Citizenship: A Study of Four Israeli Peace Protest Movements." *Social Politics: International Studies in Gender, State & Society* 6, 3: 292–313.

Hobfoll, Stevan E., Daphna Canetti-Nisim, and Robert J. Johnson. 2006. "Exposure to Terrorism, Stress-Related Mental Health Symptoms, and Defensive Coping Among Jews and Arabs in Israel." *Journal of Consulting and Clinical Psychology* 74, 2: 207–18.

Horowitz, Dan, and Moshe Lissak. 1989. *Trouble in Utopia: The Overburdened Polity of Israel*. Albany: State University of New York Press.

Hovsepian, Nubar, ed. 2008. *The War on Lebanon: A Reader*. Northampton, Mass.: Olive Branch Press.

Humphrey, Caroline. 2001. "Contested Landscapes in Inner Mongolia: Walls and Cairns." In *Contested Landscapes: Movement, Exile and Place*, ed. Barbara Bender and Margot Winer, 56–68. Oxford: Berg.

———. 2005. "Ideology in Infrastructure: Architecture and Soviet Imagination." *Journal of the Royal Anthropological Institute* 11: 39–58.

Huysmans, Jef, Andrew Dobson, and Raia Prokhovnik, eds. 2006. *The Politics of Protection: Sites of Insecurity and Political Agency*. London: Routledge.

International Court of Justice. 2004. *Legal Consequences of the Construction of a Wall in the Occupied Palestinian Territory, Summary of the Advisory Opinion of 9 July 2004*. http://www.icj-cij.org.

Israel Central Bureau of Statistics. 2007. "Supply of Selected Goods to the Domestic Market." December. http://www1.cbs.gov.il/www/yarhon/p3_e.htm.

———. 2009a. "Persons Aged 20 and Over, by Religiosity and by Selected Characteristics." http://www1.cbs.gov.il/reader/shnaton/templ_shnaton_e.html?num_tab=st07_04x&CYear=2009

———. 2009b. "Sales Values Indices of Chain Stores by Commodity Groups, 2000–2009." http://www1.cbs.gov.il/www/yarhon/p2_e.htm.

Israel Ministry of Defense. 2003. "Mercav Ha'tefer" (Security Fence). http://www.securityfence.mod.gov.il/.

Jackson, Richard. 2005. *Writing the War on Terrorism: Language, Politics and Counter-Terrorism*. Manchester: Manchester University Press.

Jacoby, Tami Amanda. 2007. *Bridging the Barrier: Israeli Unilateral Disengagement*. Hampshire: Ashgate.

Jamjoum, Lama. 2002. "The Effects of Israeli Violations During the Second Uprising 'Intifada' on Palestinian Health Conditions." *Social Justice* 29, 3: 53–72.

Jean-Klein, Iris. 2001. "Nationalism and Resistance: The Two Faces of Everyday Action in Palestine During the Intifada." *Cultural Anthropology* 16, 1: 83–126.

———. 2002. "Palestinian Martyrdom Revisited: Critical Reflections on Topical Cultures of Explanation." In *Cornell Law School East Asian Law and Culture Conference Series*. Ithaca, N.Y.: Cornell Law School, Berkeley Electronic Press.

Jerusalem Post. 2008. "Syrian Official: We're Prepared for War." April 8.

Kahn, Susan Martha. 2000. *Reproducing Jews: A Cultural Account of Assisted Conception in Israel*. Durham, N.C.: Duke University Press.

Kallus, Rachel. 2004. "The Political Role of the Everyday." *City* 8, 3: 349–69.

Kanaaneh, Rhoda Ann. 2002. *Birthing the Nation: Strategies of Palestinian Women in Israel*. Berkeley: University of California Press.

Kaplan, Amy. 2003. "Homeland Insecurities: Transformations of Language and Space." In *September 11 in History: A Watershed Moment?*, ed. Mary L. Dudziak, 55–69. Durham, N.C.: Duke University Press.

Kaplan, E. Ann. 2005. *Trauma Culture: The Politics of Terror and Loss in Media and Literature*. New Brunswick, N.J.: Rutgers University Press.

Karsh, Efraim. 2003. "Revisiting Israel's 'Original Sin': The Strange Case of Benny Morris." *Commentary* 116, 2: 46–50.

Katriel, Tamar. 1995. "Touring the Land: Trips and Hiking as Secular Pilgrimages in Israeli Culture." *Jewish Folklore & Ethnology Review* 17, 1–2: 6–13.

Katz, Yaacov, and Yaacov Lappin. 2008. "PM Declares 'Emergency' in Drill." *Jerusalem Post*, April 6.

Kelly, Tobias. 2004. "Returning Home?: Law, Violence, and Displacement among West Bank Palestinians." *PoLAR: Political and Legal Anthropology Review* 27, 2: 95–112.

———. 2006a. "Documented Lives: Citizenship, Fear and the Uncertainties of Law During the Second Palestinian Intifada." *Journal of the Royal Anthropological Institute* 12, 1: 89–106.

———. 2006b. *Law, Violence and Sovereignty Among West Bank Palestinians.* Cambridge: Cambridge University Press.

Kershner, Isabel. 2005. *Barrier: The Seam of the Israeli-Palestinian Conflict.* New York: Palgrave Macmillan.

Khalidi, Rashid. 2006. *The Iron Cage: The Story of the Palestinian Struggle for Statehood.* Boston: Beacon Press.

Khalidi, Walid, and Sharif S. Elmusa. 1992. *All That Remains: The Palestinian Villages Occupied and Depopulated by Israel in 1948.* Washington, D.C.: Institute for Palestine Studies.

Kimmerling, Baruch. 1978. "The Israeli Civil Guard." In *Supplementary Military Forces: Reserves, Militias, Auxiliaries,* ed. Louis Zurcher and Gwyn Harries-Jenkins, 107–25. New York: Sage.

———. 1985. *The Interrupted System: Israeli Civilians in War and Routine Times.* New Brunswick, N.J.: Transaction Books.

———. 1993. "Patterns of Militarism in Israel." *European Journal of Sociology* 2: 1–28.

———. 2001. *The Invention and Decline of Israeliness: State, Society, and the Military.* Berkeley: University of California Press.

Klare, Michael. 2001. "Redefining Security: The New Global Schisms." In *Approaches to Peace,* ed. David Barash. New York: Oxford University Press.

Kol Ha-Ir. 2004. "Azza Ze Po" [Gaza Is Here]. January 30.

Kol Ha-Zman. 2004. "Shomer Akhi Anohi" [My Brother's Keeper]. February 6.

Korn, Alina. 2004. "Reporting Palestinian Casualties in the Israeli Press: The Case of *Ha'aretz* and the Intifada." *Journalism Studies* 5, 2: 247–62.

Koury, Stephanie. 2005. "Why This Wall?" In *Against the Wall: Israel's Barrier to Peace,* ed. Michael Sorkin. New York: New Press.

Kuchler, Susanne. 2005. "Materiality and Cognition: The Changing Face of Things." In *Materiality,* ed. Daniel Miller. Durham, N.C.: Duke University Press.

Kurz, Anat N. 2005. *Fatah and the Politics of Violence.* East Sussex: Sussex Academic Press.

Lagerquist, Peter. 2002. "Private Security, Colonial Wars." www.eurozine.com, October 23.

———. 2004. "Fencing the Last Sky: Excavating Palestine after Israel's 'Separation Wall'." *Journal of Palestine Studies* 2: 5–35.

Lagerquist, Peter, and Jonathan Steele. 2002. "Group 4 Security Firm Pulls Guards out of West Bank." *The Guardian,* October 9.

Lansky, Na'amah. 2004. "You Thought You've Gotten Used to Security Checks Everywhere? Wait Until You Experience the Checks at the Lev-Talpiyyot Mall." *Kol Ha-Ir,* January 2.

Latour, Bruno. 2005. *Reassembling the Social: An Introduction to Actor-Network-Theory.* New York: Oxford University Press.

Lawrence, Patricia. 1997. "Violence, Suffering, Amman: The Work of Oracles in Sri Lanka's Eastern War Zone." In *Violence and Subjectivity,* ed. Veena Das, Arthur Kleinman, Mamphela Ramphele, and Pamela Reynolds. Berkeley: University of California Press.

Leach, Edmund. 1977. *Custom, Law, and Terrorist Violence.* Edinburgh: Edinburgh University Press.

Leavitt, John. 1996. "Meaning and Feeling in the Anthropology of Emotions." *American Ethnologist* 23, 3: 514–39.

Lefkowitz, Daniel. 2004. *Words and Stones: The Politics of Language and Identity in Israel.* Oxford: Oxford University Press.

Lentin, Ronit. 2000. *Israel and the Daughters of the Shoah: Reoccupying the Territories of Silence.* Oxford: Berghahn.

———. 2002. "Postmemory, Received History and the Return of the Auschwitz Code." www.eurozine.com. September 6.

Lichtman, Sarah A. 2006. "Do-It-Yourself Security: Safety, Gender, and the Home Fallout Shelter in Cold War America." *Journal of Design History* 19, 1: 39–55.

Light, Duncan. 2000. "Gazing on Communism: Heritage Tourism and Post-Communist Identities in Germany, Hungary and Romania." *Tourism Geographies* 2 (2): 157–76.

Linn, Ruth. 2002. "Soldiers with Conscience Never Die—They Are Just Ignored by Their Society. Moral Disobedience in the Israel Defense Forces." *Journal of Military Ethics* 12: 57–76.

Lis, Jonathan. 2004. "Queen of the Jerusalem Night." *Ha'aretz,* January 23.

Lisle, Debbie. 2006. "Defending Voyeurism: Dark Tourism and the Problem of Global Security." In *Tourism and Politics: Local Frameworks and Global Realities,* ed. Pete Burns and Marina Novelli. London: Pergamon.

———. 2007. "Encounters with Partition: Tourism and Reconciliation in Cyprus." In *Contested Spaces: Sites, Representations and Histories of Conflict,* ed. Louise Purbrick, Graham Dawson, and Jim Aulich, 94–117. London: Palgrave Macmillan.

Loader, Ian. 1999. "Consumer Culture and the Commodification of Policing and Security." *Sociology* 33, 2: 373–92.

Lochery, Neill. 2005. *The View from the Fence: The Arab-Israeli Conflict from the Present to Its Roots.* London: Continuum.

Lockman, Zachary. 1996. *Comrades and Enemies: Arab and Jewish Workers in Palestine, 1906–1948.* Berkeley: University of California Press.

———, ed. 1989. *Intifada (Hb): The Palestinian Uprising Against Israeli Occupation.* Cambridge, Mass.: South End Press.

Lomsky-Feder, Edna. 1995. "The Meaning of War Through Veterans' Eyes: A Phenomenological Analysis of Life Stories." *International Sociology* 10, 4: 463–82.

Lomsky-Feder, Edna, and Eyal Ben-Ari. 2000. *The Military and Militarism in Israeli Society,* SUNY Series in Israeli Studies. Albany: State University of New York Press.

———. 2010. "The Discourse of 'Psychology' and the 'Normalization' of War in Contemporary Israel." In *Militarism and Israeli Society,* ed. Gabriel Scheffer and Oren Barak. Bloomington: Indiana University Press.

Lori, Aviva. 2002. "The Age of Anxiety." *Ha'aretz,* May 15.

Low, Setha M. 2003a. *Behind the Gates: Life, Security, and the Pursuit of Happiness in Fortress America.* New York: Routledge.

———. 2003b. "The Edge and the Center: Gated Communities and the Discourse of Urban Fear." In *The Anthropology of Space and Place,* ed. Setha M. Low and Denise Lawrence-Zuniga, 387–408. Oxford: Blackwell.

Lutz, Catherine. 1988. *Unnatural Emotions: Everyday Sentiment on a Micronesian Atoll and Their Challenge to Western Theory.* Chicago: University of Chicago Press.

Lynk, Michael. 2005. "Down by Law: The High Court of Israel, International Law, and the Separation Wall." *Journal of Palestine Studies* 35, 1: 6–24.

Lyon, David. 2003. *Surveillance after September 11*. Cambridge: Polity.
———. 2005. "The Border Is Everywhere." In *Global Surveillance and Policing: Borders, Security, Identity*, ed. Elia Zureik and Mark B. Salter, 66–82. Cullompton, Devon: Willan Publishing.
Lyon, Margot. 1995. "Missing Emotion: The Limitations of Cultural Constructionism in the Study of Emotion." *Cultural Anthropology* 10, 2: 244–63.
Ma'ariv. 2004. "9 Dead in Bus Bombing." *Ma'ariv International*, January 30.
Mahmood, Saba. 2001. "Feminist Theory, Embodiment, and the Docile Agent: Some Reflections on the Egyptian Islamic Revival." *Cultural Anthropology* 16, 2: 202–36.
Makdisi, Saree. 2008. *Palestine Inside Out: An Everyday Occupation*. New York: Norton.
Malinowski, Bronisław. 1948. *Magic, Science and Religion, and Other Essays*. Boston: Beacon Press.
Maman, Daniel, Eyal Ben-Ari, and Zeev Rosenhek, eds. 2001. *Military, State, and Society in Israel*. New Brunswick, N.J.: Transaction.
Mansour, Camille. 2002. "The Impact of 11 September on the Israeli-Palestinian Conflict." *Journal of Palestine Studies* 32, 2: 5–18.
Marris, Peter. 1996. *The Politics of Uncertainty: Attachment in Private and Public Life*. New York: Routledge.
Masalha, Nur. 1991. "A Critique of Benny Morris." *Journal of Palestine Studies* 21, 1: 90–97.
Massad, Joseph. 1996. "Zionism's Internal Others: Israel and the Oriental Jews." *Journal of Palestine Studies* 25, 4: 53–68.
Mehta, Anna, and Liz Bondi. 1999. "Embodied Discourse: On Gender and Fear of Violence." *Gender, Place and Culture* 6, 1: 67–84.
Mehta, Deepak, and Roma Chatterji. 2001. "Boundaries, Names, Alterities: A Case Study of a 'Communal Riot' in Dharavi, Bombay." In *Remaking a World*, ed. Veena Das, Arthur Kleinman, Margaret Lock, Mamphela Ramphele, and Pamela Reynolds. Berkeley: University of California Press.
Merleau-Ponty, Maurice. 2005 [1962]. *Phenomenology of Perception*. London: Routledge.
Mertz, Elizabeth. 2002. "The Perfidity of Gaze and the Pain of Uncertainty: Anthropological Theory and the Search for Closure." In *Ethnography in Unstable Places: Everyday Lives in Contexts of Dramatic Political Change*, ed. Carol J. Greenhouse, Elizabeth Mertz, and Kay B. Warren. Durham, N.C.: Duke University Press.
Michael, Kobi. 2007. "Military Knowledge and Weak Civilian Control in the Reality of Low Intensity Conflict—the Israeli Case." *Israel Studies* 12, 1: 28–52.
Migdal, Joel S. 2004. "Mental Maps and Virtual Checkpoints: Struggles to Construct and Maintain State and Social Boundaries." In *Boundaries and Belonging: States and Societies in the Struggle to Shape Identities and Local Practices*, ed. Joel S. Migdal. Cambridge: Cambridge University Press.
Milesa, William F. S. 2002. "Auschwitz: Museum Interpretation and Darker Tourism." *Annals of Tourism Research* 29, 4: 1175–78.
Miller, Daniel. 2001. *Home Possessions: Material Culture Behind Closed Doors*. Oxford: Berg.
———. 2005. *Materiality*. Durham, N.C.: Duke University Press.
Miller, Steven. 2001. "International Security at Twenty-Five: From One World to Another." *International Security* 26, 1: 5–39.
Mitchell, Timothy. 1991. "The Limits of the State: Beyond Statist Approaches and Their Critics." *American Political Science Review* 85, 1: 77–96.

Moghadam, Assaf. 2003. "Palestinian Suicide Terrorism in the Second Intifada: Motivations and Organizational Aspects." *Studies in Conflict & Terrorism* 26: 65–92.

Mol, Annemarie. 2002. *The Body Multiple: Ontology in Medical Practice.* Durham, N.C.: Duke University Press.

Mol, Annemarie, and John Law. 2002. "Complexities: An Introduction." In *Complexities: Social Studies of Knowledge Practices*, ed. Annemarie Mol and John Law. Durham, N.C.: Duke University Press.

Monk, Daniel Bertrand. 2002. *An Aesthetic Occupation: The Immediacy of Architecture and the Palestine Conflict.* Durham, N.C.: Duke University Press.

Montel, Jessica. 2004. "Don't Hijack the Security Fence." *Jerusalem Post.* February 10.

Morris, Benny. 1987. *The Birth of the Palestinian Refugee Problem, 1947–1949.* Cambridge: Cambridge University Press.

———. 2004. "Israel Did What It Had to Do in 1948." *Jerusalem Post*, February 10.

Naaman, Dorit. 2006. "The Silenced Outcry: A Feminist Perspective from the Israeli Checkpoints in Palestine." *NWSA Journal* 18, 3: 168–80.

Nahmia, Roee. 2008. "Syria to Hold Emergency Drill." *Yediot Aharonot*, ynet.com, April 9.

Navaro-Yashin, Yael. 2002. *Faces of the State: Secularism and Public Life in Turkey.* Princeton, N.J.: Princeton University Press.

———. 2005. "Confinement and the Imagination: Sovereignty and Subjectivity in a Quasi-State." In *Sovereign Bodies: Citizens, Migrants, and States in the Postcolonial World*, ed. Thomas Blom Hansen and Finn Stepputat, 103–19. Princeton, N.J.: Princeton University Press.

Neocleous, Mark. 2007. "Security, Commodity, Fetishism." *Critique* 35, 3: 339–55.

Neuman, Tamara. 2004. "Maternal Anti-Politics in the Formation of Hebron's Jewish Enclave." *Journal of Palestine Studies* 33, 2: 51–70.

Neuman, Yair, and Mor Levi. 2003. "Blood and Chocolate: A Rhetorical Approach to Fear Appeal." *Journal of Language and Social Psychology* 22, 1: 29–46.

Newburn, Tim. 2001. "The Commodification of Policing: Security Networks in the Late Modern City." *Urban Studies* 38, 5–6: 829–48.

Newman, Saul, and Michael P. Levine. 2006. "War, Politics and Race: Reflections on Violence in the 'War on Terror'." *Theoria* 56, 110: 23–49.

News24.com. 2004. "Israel Wants Barrier Tourism." *News24.com*, July 16.

Nordstrom, Carolyn. 1997. *A Different Kind of War Story.* Philadelphia: University of Pennsylvania Press.

Nowotny, Helga. 2003. "Dilemma of Expertise: Democratizing Expertise and Socially Robust Knowledge." *Science and Public Policy* 30, 3: 151–56.

O'Sullivan, Arieh. 2003. "Dichter: We've Failed to Protect Our Citizens." *Jerusalem Post*, December 16.

———. 2004. "Counterterror Adviser: Israelis Too Complacent." *Jerusalem Post*, April 8.

Ochs, Juliana. 2006. "The Politics of Victimhood and Its Internal Exegetes: Terror Victims in Israel." *History and Anthropology* 17, 4: 355–68.

Paperman, Patricia. 2003. "Surveillance Underground: The Uniform as an Interaction Device." *Ethnography* 4, 3: 397–419.

Pappe, Ilan. 2004. *A History of Modern Palestine: One Land, Two Peoples.* Cambridge: Cambridge University Press.

———. 2006. "What Does Israel Want?" July 14. http://electronicintifada.net/v2/article5003.shtml.

———. 2007. *The Ethnic Cleansing of Palestine.* Oxford: Oneworld Publications.

Peled, Yoav. 1998. "Mizrahi Jews and Palestinian Arabs: Exclusionist Attitudes in Development Towns." In *Ethnic Frontiers and Peripheries: Landscapes of Development and Inequality in Israel,* ed. Oren Yiftachel and Avinoam Meir. Boulder, Colo.: Westview.

Penslar, Derek Jonathan. 2001. "Zionism, Colonialism and Post-Colonialism." *Journal of Israeli History* 20, 2–3: 84–98.

Peteet, Julie. 1994. "Male Gender and Rituals of Resistance in the Palestinian Intifada: A Cultural Politics of Violence." *American Ethnologist* 21, 1: 31–49.

———. 1997. "Icons and Militants: Mothering in the Danger Zone." *Signs: Journal of Women in Culture and Society* 23, 1: 103–29.

———. 2005. "Words as Interventions: Naming in the Palestine-Israel Conflict." *Third World Quarterly* 26, 1: 153–72.

Pettigrew, Joyce. 2000. "Parents and Their Children in Situations of Terror: Disappearances and Special Police Activity in Punjab." In *Death Squad,* ed. Jeffrey A. Sluka. Philadelphia: University of Pennsylvania Press.

Rabab, Abdulhadi. 2003. "Where Is Home? Fragmented Lives, Border Crossings, and the Politics of Exile." *Radical History Review* 86: 89–101.

Rabinowitz, Dan. 1997. *Overlooking Nazareth: The Ethnography of Exclusion in Galilee.* Cambridge: Cambridge University Press.

———. 2003. "Borders and Their Discontents: Israel's Green Line, Arabness and Unilateral Separation." *European Studies* 19: 1–15.

———. 2004. "Building a Fence, Constructing an Identity: Unilateral Separation and the Israeli Mainstream." *Annals of Japan Association for Middle East Studies* 19, 2: 3–13.

Rabinowitz, Dan, and Abu Baker Khawla. 2005. *Coffins on Our Shoulders: The Experience of the Palestinian Citizens of Israel.* Berkeley: University of California Press.

Ram, Uri. 2004. "The State of the Nation: Contemporary Challenges to Zionism in Israel." In *Israelis in Conflict: Hegemonies, Identities and Challenges,* ed. Adriana Kemp, Uri Ram, David Newman, and Oren Yiftachel, 305–21. East Sussex: Sussex Academic Press.

———. 2008. *The Globalization of Israel: McWorld in Tel Aviv, Jihad in Jerusalem.* London: Routledge.

Rana, Junaid, and Gilberto Rosas. 2006. "Managing Crisis." *Cultural Dynamics* 18, 3: 219–34.

Rao, Vyjayanthi. 2007. "How to Read a Bomb: Scenes from Bombay's Black Friday." *Public Culture* 19, 3: 567–92.

Reddy, William. 1997. "Against Constructionism: The Historical Ethnography of Emotions." *Cultural Anthropology* 38, 3: 327–51.

Reed, Adam. 1999. "Anticipating Individuals: Modes of Vision and Their Social Consequences in a Papua New Guinean Prison." *Journal of the Royal Anthropological Institute* 5: 43–56.

———. 2002. "City of Details: Interpreting the Personality of London." *Journal of the Royal Anthropological Institute* 8, 1: 132.

Riles, Annelise. 2000. *The Network Inside Out.* Ann Arbor: University of Michigan Press.

Robin, Corey. 2004. *Fear: The History of a Political Idea.* Oxford: Oxford University Press.

Romann, Michael, and Alex Weingrod. 1991. *Living Together Separately: Arabs and Jews in Contemporary Jerusalem.* Princeton, N.J.: Princeton University Press.

Rosaldo, Michelle Z. 1980. *Knowledge and Passion: Ilongot Notions of Self and Social Life.* Cambridge: Cambridge University Press.

———. 1984. "Toward an Anthropology of Self and Feeling." In *Culture Theory: Essays on Mind, Self, and Emotion,* ed. Richard A. Sweder and Robert A. LeVine. Cambridge: Cambridge University Press.

Rosenfeld, Maya. 2004. *Confronting the Occupation: Work, Education, and Political Activism of Palestinian Families in a Refugee Camp.* Stanford, Calif.: Stanford University Press.

Rosner, Shmuel. 2000. "Has Crisis Changed Hillary Clinton?" *Ha'aretz,* February 25.

Rotbard, Sharon. 2003. "Homa Umigdal." In *A Civilian Occupation: The Politics of Israeli Architecture,* ed. Rafi Segal, David Tartakover, and Eyal Weizman. London: Verso.

Rousso, Nira. 2003. "Kitchen Secrets: They Can Take the Heat." *Ha'aretz,* September 12.

Royhman, Yinon. 2006. "War That Wasn't: 'Night of the Ducks.'" *Yediot Aharonot.* ynet.com, November 19.

Rudge, David. 2004. "Survey: Public Moral Firm Despite Terrorism." *Jerusalem Post.* May 26.

Sa'di, Ahmad H. 2002. "Catastrophe, Memory and Identity: Al-Nakbah as a Component of Palestinian Identity." *Israel Studies* 7, 2: 175–98.

Said, Edward. 1978. *Orientalism.* London: Penguin.

Sandler, Joseph. 1960. "The Background of Safety." *International Journal of Psychoanalysis* 41: 352–56.

Sasson-Levy, Orna. 2003. "Military, Masculinity, and Citizenship: Tensions and Contradictions in the Experience of Blue-Collar Soldiers." *Identities: Global Studies in Power and Culture* 10, 3: 319–45.

Saunders, Nicholas J. 2001. "Matter and Memory in the Landscapes of Conflict: The Western Front 1914–1999." In *Contested Landscapes: Movement, Exile and Place,* ed. Barbara Bender and Margot Winer. Oxford: Berg.

Savitch, H. G., and Yaacov Garb. 2006. "Terror, Barriers, and the Changing Topography of Jerusalem." *Journal of Planning Education and Research* 26, 2: 152–73

Scheper-Hughes, Nancy, and Philippe Bourgois. 2004. "Introduction: Making Sense of Violence." In *Violence in War and Peace,* ed. Nancy Scheper-Hughes and Philippe Bourgouis. Oxford: Blackwell.

Schiff, Ze'ev. 1985. *A History of the Israeli Army: 1874 to the Present.* New York: Macmillan.

Segal, Rafi and Eyal Weizman, eds. 2003. *A Civilian Occupation: The Politics of Israeli Architecture.* London: Verso.

Segev, Tom. 1993. *The Seventh Million: The Israelis and the Holocaust.* New York: Hill and Wang.

———. 1999. *One Palestine, Complete: Jews and Arabs under the British Mandate.* New York: Holt.

———. 2002. *Elvis in Jerusalem: Post-Zionism and the Americanization of Israel.* Trans. Haim Watzman. New York: Metropolitan Books.

———. 2005. "The Paradox of Jerusalem." *Ha'aretz,* June 6.

———. 2007. *1967: Israel, the War, and the Year That Transformed the Middle East.* New York: Metropolitan.

Sela, Avraham. 2007. "Civil Society, the Military, and National Security: The Case of Israel's Security Zone in South Lebanon." *Israel Studies* 12, 1: 53–78.

Selwyn, Tom. 2001. "Landscapes of Separation: Reflections on the Symbolism of By-Pass Roads in Palestine." In *Contested Landscapes: Movement, Exile and Place,* ed. Barbara Bender and Margot Winer. Oxford: Berg.

Sered, Susan. 1992. *Woman as Ritual Experts: The Religious Lives of Elderly Jewish Women in Jerusalem.* New York: Oxford University Press.

———. 1993. "Religious Rituals and Secular Rituals: Interpenetrating Models of Childbirth in a Modern, Israeli Context." *Sociology of Religion* 54, 1: 101–14.

Seremetakis, Nadia. 1994. *The Senses Still: Perception and Memory as Material Culture in Modernity.* Chicago: University of Chicago Press.

Shafir, Gershon, and Yoav Peled. *Being Israeli: The Dynamics of Multiple Citizenship.* Cambridge: Cambridge University Press.

Shalev, Arieh Y., Rivka Tuval, Sarah Frenkiel-Fishman, Hilit Hadar, and Spencer Eth. 2006. "Psychological Responses to Continuous Terror: A Study of Two Communities in Israel." *American Journal of Psychiatry* 163 (4): 667–73.

Shalit, Erel. 1994. "The Relationship Between Aggression and Fear of Annihilation in Israel." *Political Psychology* 15, 3: 415–34.

Shapira, Anita. 1992. *Land and Power: The Zionist Resort to Force, 1881–1948.* Oxford: Oxford University Press.

Sharon, Ariel. 2002. "PM Sharon's Address to the Knesset." April 8. http://www.mfa.gov.il.

Sharoni, Simona. 1994a. *Gender and the Israeli-Palestinian Conflict: The Politics of Women's Resistance.* Syracuse, N.Y.: Syracuse University Press.

———. 1994b. "Homefront as Battlefield: Gender, Military Occupation and Violence Against Women." In *Women and the Israeli Occupation: The Politics of Change,* ed. Tamar Mayer, 107–22. London: Routledge.

Shavit, Ari. 2003. "Elective Affinities." *Ha'aretz,* January 7.

———. 2004. "A Jewish Soul." *Ha'aretz,* February 13.

———. 2005. "Dividing the Land: What Comes Next?" *Ha'aretz,* June 24.

Shehori, Dalia. 2004. "Post Zionism Is Dead or in a Deep Freeze." *Ha'aretz,* April 21.

Shelach, Oz. 2003. *Picnic Grounds.* San Francisco: City Lights.

Shiffer, Zalman F. 2007. "The Debate over the Defense Budget in Israel." *Israel Studies* 12, 1: 193–214.

Shilo, Shani. 2005. "Being in the Know: The Latest Trends in Home Design." *Ha'aretz,* December 5.

Shlaim, Avi. 2000. *The Iron Wall: Israel and the Arab World.* London: Allen Lane.

Showers, Carolin. 1992. "Compartmentalization of Positive and Negative Self-Knowledge: Keeping Bad Apples Out of the Bunch." *Journal of Personality and Social Psychology* 62, 6: 1036–49.

S'idov, Yossi. 2003. "Hillel Kovea Uvda ba-Shetaḥ [Hillel Establishes Facts on the Ground]." *Kol Ha-Ir,* October 24.

Silverstein, Michael, and Greg Urban, eds. 1996. *Natural Histories of Discourse.* Chicago: University of Chicago Press.

Sinai, Ruth. 2005. "Sharp Rise in Number of Women Killed by Men Carrying Licensed Guns." *Ha'aretz,* November 27.

Singer, Roni. 2004. "Police Lower Alert in Tel Aviv." *Ha'aretz,* March 2.

Slyomovics, Susan. 1998. *The Object of Memory: Arab and Jew Narrate the Palestinian Village.* Philadelphia: University of Pennsylvania Press.

Smith, Steve. 2005. "The Contested Concept of Security." In *Critical Security Studies and World Politics,* ed. Ken Booth. Boulder, Colo.: Lynne Rienner.

Solomon, Zahava, and Rony Berger. 2005. "Coping with the Aftermath of Terror: Resilience of Zaka Body Handlers." *Journal of Aggression, Maltreatment & Trauma* 10, 1: 593–604.

Somer, Eli, Eli Buchbinder, Maya Peled-Avram, and Yael Ben-Yizhack. 2004. "The

Stress and Coping of Israeli Emergency Room Social Workers Following Terrorist Attacks." *Qualitative Health Research* 14, 8: 1077–93.

Sorkin, Michael. 2004. "Urban Warfare: A Tour of the Battlefield." In *Cities, War, and Terrorism: Towards an Urban Geopolitics,* ed. Stephen Graham. Oxford: Blackwell.

Sorkin, Michael, ed. 2005. *Against the Wall: Israel's Barrier to Peace.* New York: New Press.

Spitzer, Carsten, Sven Barnow, Harald J. Freyberger, and Hans Joergen Grabe. 2006. "Recent Developments in the Theory of Dissociation." *World Psychiatry* 5, 2: 82–86.

Stadler, Nurit, Eyal Ben-Ari, and Einat Mesterman. 2005. "Terror, Aid and Organization: The Haredi Disaster Victim Identification Teams (Zaka) in Israel." *Anthropological Quarterly* 78, 3: 619–51.

Stearns, Peter N. 2006. *American Fear: The Causes and Consequences of High Anxiety.* New York: Routledge.

Stein, Rebecca L. 2002. "Israeli Leisure, 'Palestinian Terror,' and the Question of Palestine (Again)." *Theory & Event* 6, 3.

Stein, Rebecca L., and Ted Swedenberg, eds. 2005. *Palestine, Israel, and the Politics of Popular Culture.* Durham, N.C.: Duke University Press.

Steinberg, Jerusalem. 2003. "Book 'Em, Dan-O." *Jerusalem Post,* September 19.

Stoler, Ann Laura. 2008. *Along the Archival Grain: Epistemic Anxieties and Colonial Common Sense.* Princeton, N.J.: Princeton University Press.

Stoler-Liss, Sachlav. 2003. "'Mothers Birth the Nation': The Social Construction of Zionist Motherhood in Wartime in Israeli Parents' Manuals." *Nashim: A Journal of Jewish Women's Studies & Gender Issues* 6: 104–18.

Strangea, Carolyn, and Michael Kempab. 2003. "Shades of Dark Tourism: Alcatraz and Robben Island." *Annals of Tourism Research* 30, 2: 386–405.

Strasler, Nehemia. 2003. "The Danger of Peace." *Ha'aretz,* October 17.

Suleiman, Yasir. 2004. *A War of Words: Language and Conflict in the Middle East.* Cambridge: Cambridge University Press.

Taussig, Michael. 2004. "Terror as Usual: Walter Benjamin's Theory of History as State of Siege." In *Violence in War and Peace,* ed. Nancy Scheper-Hughes and Phillipe I. Bourgois, 269–71. Oxford: Blackwell.

Tilley, Christopher. 1994. *A Phenomenology of Landscape: Places, Paths, and Monuments.* Oxford: Berg.

Troen, S. Ilan. 2003. *Imagining Zion: Dreams, Designs, and Realities in a Century of Jewish Settlement.* New Haven, Conn.: Yale University Press.

Trottier, Julie. 2007. "A Wall, Water and Power: The Israeli 'Separation Fence.'" *Review of International Studies* 33: 105–27.

Tuval-Mashiach, Rivka, Sara Freedman, et al. 2004. "Coping with Trauma: Narrative and Cognitive Perspectives." *Psychiatry* 67, 3: 280–93.

Usher, Graham. 2005. "Unmaking Palestine: On Israel, the Palestinians, and the Wall." *Journal of Palestine Studies* 137: 25–43.

Volkov, Vadim. 2000. "Between Economy and the State: Private Security and Rule Enforcement in Russia." *Politics and Society* 28 (December): 483–501.

Warren, Kay B. 1998. *Indigenous Movements and Their Critics: Pan-Maya Activism in Guatemala.* Princeton, N.J.: Princeton University Press.

Weber, Max. 1947. *The Theory of Social and Economic Organization.* New York: Oxford University Press.

Weizman, Eyal. 2004. "Strategic Points, Flexible Lines, Tense Surfaces, and Political Volumes: Ariel Sharon and the Geometry of Occupation." In *Cities, War, and Terrorism,* ed. Stephen Graham. Oxford: Blackwell.

————. 2005. "Hollow Land: The Barrier Archipelago and the Impossible Politics of Sharon." In *Against the Wall: Israel's Barrier to Peace*, ed. Michael Sorkin. New York: New Press.

————. 2007. *Hollow Land: Israel's Architecture of Occupation*. London: Verso.

Werman, Robert. 1993. *Notes from a Sealed Room: An Israeli View of the Gulf War*. Carbondale: Southern Illinois University Press.

West, Harry G., and Todd Sanders, eds. 2003. *Transparency and Conspiracy: Ethnographies of Suspicion in the New World Order*. Durham, N.C.: Duke University Press.

Westervelt, Eric. 2007. "Israel Haunted by Nuclear Threat from Iran." NPR.org. August 23.

Winer, Stuart. 2003. "Safe Architecture." *Jerusalem Post*, September 21.

Yamin-Wolvovitz, Tal. 2004. "No Security at Security Barrier Construction Sites." *Ma'ariv International*, March 16.

Yamin-Wolvovitz, Tal, and Meitar Shlaider. 2003. "Alert Relaxed in Tel Aviv After Terror Attack Foiled." *Ma'ariv*, March 3.

Yan, Yungxian. 2003. *Private Life under Socialism: Love, Intimacy and Family Change in a Chinese Village, 1948–1999*. Stanford, Calif.: Stanford University Press.

Yehoshua, A. B. 1980. *Bizchut Ha-Normaliut [In the Name of Normalcy]*. Tel Aviv: Schocken.

Yiftachel, Oren. 1998. "Democracy or Ethnocracy: Territory and Settler Politics in Israel/Palestine." *Middle East Report* 207: 8–13.

————. 2006. *Ethnocracy: Land and Identity Politics in Israel/Palestine*. Philadelphia: University of Pennsylvania Press.

Yiftachel, Oren, and Avinoam Meir. 1996. "Frontiers, Peripheries, and Ethnic Relations in Israel: An Introduction." In *Ethnic Frontiers and Peripheries: Landscapes of Development and Inequality in Israel*, ed. Oren Yiftachel and Avinoam Meir, 1–13. Boulder, Colo.: Westview.

Yoaz, Yuval. 2005. "High Court Halts Fence Construction Around Beit Surik." *Ha'aretz English*.

Young, James E. 1990. *Writing and Rewriting the Holocaust: Narrative and the Consequences of Interpretation*. Bloomington: Indiana University Press.

Zertal, Idith. 2005. *Israel's Holocaust and the Politics of Nationhood*. Cambridge: Cambridge University Press.

Zerubavel, Yael. 1995. *Recovered Roots: Collective Memory and the Making of Israeli National Tradition*. Chicago: University of Chicago Press.

Žižek, Slavoj. 1989. *The Sublime Object of Ideology*. London: Verso.

Zulaika, Joseba. 1995. "The Anthropologist as Terrorist." In *Fieldwork Under Fire: Contemporary Studies of Violence and Survival*, ed. Carolyn Nordstrom and Antonius C. G. M. Robben, 206–23. Berkeley: University of California Press.

————. 2003. "The Self-Fulfilling Prophecies of Counterterrorism." *Radical Historical Review* 85: 191–99.

Zulaika, Joseba, and William A. Douglass. 1996. *Terror and Taboo: The Follies, Fables, and Faces of Terrorism*. New York: Routledge.

Index

Abbas, Mahmoud, 7, 37
abandonment, of the state. *See* failure
Abu Dis, 155–56
Abu El-Haj, Nadia, 52, 55, 149
advertisements, 69, 80–81, 129, 143
aesthetics, 16, 45–52, 123–24, 128, 130–31, 170n7
airport. *See* Ben Gurion Airport
alertness, 12, 16; and parenting, 29–30; and fear, 77; for suspicion, 79–98; and travel, 99–113
Almog, Oz, 22, 83
America. *See* United States
anxiety. *See* fear
Arafat, Yasser, 7, 25, 37
architecture, 16, 21, 49–51, 62, 133–34, 149; discourses of, 47–50, 170n4
Aretxaga, Begoña, 56, 85, 167n13
army. *See* Israeli Defense Forces; military
artifacts, 12, 39, 42, 44, 59, 64, 77, 120, 124–27, 135, 170n5. *See also* materiality

Bar-Tal, Daniel, 26, 171n9, 172n11
Barak, Ehud, 140, 163, 175n4
Barak, Oren, 24, 112
barrier. *See* separation wall
Bedouin, 29, 33, 83–84, 86–89
Beit Jala, 138–39, 146
Ben Gurion Airport, 24, 163
Ben-Gurion, David, 22, 23, 27, 68, 70
Berlant, Lauren, 4, 135
Blom Hansen, Thomas, 37, 55, 173n2
body. *See* embodiment
bomb shelter, 17, 122, 124, 163–64, 174n8

bombing. *See* suicide bombing
Bornstein, Avram, 61, 67, 176n18
Bourdieu, Pierre, 14, 102
buffer zones, 25, 175n3
buses: alertness on, 92–93, 94–95; calculations for, 107–11; fear of, 2, 12, 99–100, 114; guards on, 11. *See also* travel
bypass roads, 24, 66, 146, 147 Fig 12, 171n4
bystanders, 35–36, 43

Café Hillel: manager of, 47–48; patrons of, 45–46, 51–52; rebuilding of, 16, 41–50, 53–56; security at, 40, 42–43, 56–63, 164–65; and state, 38, 52–56, 61–62; suicide bombing at, 35–37
cafés: architecture for, 50–52; avoided, 119, 128; and checkpoints, 56–58; as fortresses, 11, 48–49; as national symbol, 40–41, 45; seating in, 46, 51–52; security at, 57–58; takeout from, 129. *See also* Café Hillel
Caldeira, Teresa, 49, 134
cell phones, 30, 39, 40 Fig 3, 164
checkpoints, 26, 56–58, 87–89; Palestinian experiences of, 56, 65, 120, 173nn12, 5, 175n8
Civil Guard (Ha-Mishmar ha-Ezrahi), 29, 79–80, 84, 169n18; in Arad, 86–89; and suspicion, 84–89; training for, 84–85
comfort, 4, 17, 18, 143, 151, 159, 165–66; at home, 121–22, 130, 131–37; uncanny, 17, 124–27
commutes. *See* travel
compartmentalization, 109–10, 117

Acknowledgments

This book is the product of many layers of guidance and support.

For their intellectual and practical wisdom, I thank Yael Navaro-Yashin, Alan Macfarlane, and Dan Rabinowitz. Madeleine Reeves, Yaacob Dweck, and Vanessa Ochs were keen, close, and very valued readers of this manuscript as it neared completion. I am so grateful to those who read parts and wholes of the manuscript at different stages and offered their insight: Allan Arkush, Glenn Bowman, Carl Bialik, Avram Bornstein, Matthew Carey, Irrit Dweck, Harri Englund, Paola Fillipucci, Caroline Humphrey, Amy Kaplan, Toby Kelly, Ashley Lebner, Victoria Moul, Peter Ochs, Maja Petrovic-Šteger, Sveta Roberman, and Marilyn Strathern. I received engaging feedback from the members of the Cambridge University Department of Social Anthropology writing seminar. Three readers for the University of Pennsylvania Press provided good counsel.

For their assistance with translation, transliteration, transcription, and citations, I thank Judith Loebenstein-Witztum, Rona Atlas, Merav Berkeley, and Julie Schiff. I also thank the librarians at the Jewish National and University Library in Jerusalem, Sari Shrager in the Arad Municipal Archives, and the archivists at the Ben-Gurion University Archives of the Negev. At the University of Pennsylvania Press, I thank Peter Agree for his generous encouragement and Alison Anderson, Julia Rose Roberts, Chris Bell, Sandra Haviland, and Kathy McQueen for ensuring a smooth publication process.

My fieldwork was enriched by the hospitality, warmth, and perception of four Israeli families, and my thanks goes to Yair, Ayalah, Tali, Shlomi, Ruthi, Avi, Ricki, and Sharon. My research benefited greatly from conversations with Nira Rousso, Jessica Waller, Miri Lowenberg, Ali Qleibo, Anat Turgeman, Binyamin Blum, Elly Teeman, Renee Levine Melammed, Noam Zion, Eyal Ben-Ari, Shalva Weil, Bella Savran, Amos Oz, Hannah

Maschler, Michael Maschler, Rochelle Furstenberg, Nancy Ordway, Alan Novins, Aluma Rice, Avner Shiffman, Ronit Aloni, Aviv Gal, Aubrey Isaacs, Avital Aharoni, Ayala Avrahami, Bezalel Tabib, Hannah Kaduri, Uri Perry, Bensi Aran, Ivgy Moshe, Rachel Abromson, and Nadia Granitz. I treasure the perspectives of Roberta Bernstein, Yosef Berkovich, Savta Yaffa Bar Giora, and Sabba Ze'ev Shiffman, all of blessed memory.

My research was funded by the Gates Cambridge Trust; St. John's College, Cambridge; the William Wyse Fund of Trinity College, Cambridge; the Council for British Research in the Levant; the London Friends of Hebrew University; and the Samuel and Evelyn Linden Scholarship. A Smithsonian Institution Postdoctoral Fellowship at the National Museum of American History allowed for comparative research and time to write.

I thank my parents, Peter and Vanessa Ochs, who fulfill and also transcend all of these categories of acknowledgment. I thank my sister Elizabeth for her continuously warm support and my children Harry and Emanuella for their indispensible grounding. I dedicate this book to Yaacob Dweck, who enabled this book to be part of doing life together, and whom I thank most of all.